The Pillars of Finance

Also by Guy Fraser-Sampson

MULTI-ASSET CLASS INVESTMENT STRATEGY

PRIVATE EQUITY AS AN ASSET CLASS (2nd ed)

ALTERNATIVE ASSETS: Investments for a Post-Crisis World

NO FEAR FINANCE

THE MESS WE'RE IN: Why Politicians Can't Solve Financial Crises

INTELLIGENT INVESTING: The Practical and Behavioural Aspects of Investment Strategy

The Pillars of Finance

The Misalignment of Finance Theory and Investment Practice

Guy Fraser-Sampson

Cass Business School, London, UK

palgrave
macmillan

First published 2014 by
PALGRAVE MACMILLAN

Palgrave Macmillan in the UK is an imprint of Macmillan Publishers Limited, registered in England, company number 785998, of Houndmills, Basingstoke, Hampshire RG21 6XS.

Palgrave Macmillan in the US is a division of St Martin's Press LLC, 175 Fifth Avenue, New York, NY 10010.

Palgrave Macmillan is the global academic imprint of the above companies and has companies and representatives throughout the world.

Palgrave® and Macmillan® are registered trademarks in the United States, the United Kingdom, Europe and other countries.

ISBN 978-1-137-26405-3

This book is printed on paper suitable for recycling and made from fully managed and sustained forest sources. Logging, pulping and manufacturing processes are expected to conform to the environmental regulations of the country of origin.

A catalogue record for this book is available from the British Library.

A catalog record for this book is available from the Library of Congress.

Typeset by MPS Limited, Chennai, India.

Contents

Acknowledgements

This book is based in part on my PhD studies at Cass Business School into the nature of investment risk, and some of my PhD paper, such as the literature review, is directly quoted. I would like to thank Richard Gillingwater, the former Dean, for encouraging me to undertake this project in the first place, Steve Haberman, his successor, for his support thereafter, and Professor Steve Thomas, my supervisor, for all his patient guidance. Thanks are also due to Tim Price, who introduced me to the works of Ludwig von Mises, which turned out to be a revelation.

Chapter 1

Introduction

Rather a long time ago I found myself sitting in a finance class as I studied for an MBA. For any reader who has studied finance themselves, we had just got to the stage where the lecturer was explaining that the risk premium of any investment was the same as its excess return. I struggled in vain to get my head around this. How could something good and desirable (excess return) constitute 'risk'?

> 'I'm sorry,' I said, 'but I don't understand.'

The lecturer looked at me condescendingly.

> 'The maths really isn't that difficult,' he said, 'but I'll happily take you through it again if you like.'
>
> 'No, I understand the maths,' I replied. 'I just don't understand what you mean by "risk". How are you defining it?'

He stared at me blankly, as a murmur of agreement spread among the non-financial folk in the room. Then his face cleared.

> 'Just learn it this way for the exam, OK?'

I suppose the problem was in large part that I had originally studied law and gone on to qualify as a lawyer. If your mind has been trained to approach any question by working out which rules might apply and then reviewing the facts to see where the best fit might lie, then the meaning of words is key. Legal rules are framed in language (they could hardly be anything else) so it is important to understand what they say as precisely as possible. More cynically, it is also helpful to be able to suggest ways in which their meaning may be manipulated to serve the ends of one's own client, but again this is impossible without a good understanding of language and meaning generally.

When you study law at university you are required to study something called jurisprudence, which is essentially the philosophy of law. Thus, in addition to the dry stuff of statutes and cases you are forced to consider questions such as 'what makes a good law?', 'are we required to obey a bad law?', and even more fundamentally 'what is a law?' While many of my fellow undergraduates were unhappy about this, resenting the lost opportunity of being able to study an additional practical module such as Company Law or Succession, I found it immensely enjoyable. Perhaps this had something to do with the fact that I had already read quite a lot of philosophy myself, and had found it a worthwhile experience despite much of it being written in language so impenetrable that I vowed then and there that should I ever find myself faced with the task of writing a book, then I would endeavour to do so in as open and entertaining a way as possible.

My concern with the meaning of risk stayed with me over the years, at first as no more than a niggle in the background, but as I saw more and more examples of people reaching obviously bad decisions through what felt like a slavish adherence to an obviously artificial concept then it grew steadily stronger. The more I thought about it, the more I wondered not whether Finance had got it wrong (that was obvious to me), but how and why, and why on earth nobody else seemed to think that any of this was of any consequence.

Jurisprudence offered a clue to this last point. If the students of every subject were also forced to study philosophy then perhaps they too would be able to take a wider view, one of which the practical skills and technical knowledge that they were taught formed a part, but not the whole. One in which these wider considerations could be seen as giving context and meaning to the specialist theory. One where, should conflict arise between this overarching intellectual framework and the narrow thinking of the discipline itself, then the latter would be thrown into question and forced to justify itself.

The Italian philosopher Benedetto Croce encapsulated what I had in mind far more eloquently. He said that a heart in the right place, rather than a mind in a high state of training, was the more likely source of truth.[1] It seemed to me that what I was already starting to term Finance World was evolving highly intelligent ways of seeking knowledge, but starting from the wrong place and taking aim at the wrong targets. Instead of seeking to impose order upon apparently random data, they should have been asking themselves basic questions such as 'what is finance?' and 'how does it operate?'

I was subsequently lucky enough to be allowed to study for a PhD on the nature of investment risk under the supervision of Professor Steve Thomas at Cass Business School, and the literature review which appears later in the book is taken directly from my PhD thesis. This was an interesting and comforting process, since as I pursued it I became aware that in fact others too had harboured doubts about the traditional view of risk. The works of others revealed that even the word 'traditional' is misleading here, since the truly traditional view had been that risk was too complex ever to be properly understood, and certainly incapable of mathematical calculation, whether in the way that Finance World proposed or otherwise.

On the contrary, the prevailing view was of fairly recent origin, having been advanced in a single article by Harry Markowitz in 1952. The choice of the word 'advanced' is deliberate since Markowitz never actually said that what he was calculating was the same thing as risk, though it is implicit (he actually used the phrase 'an undesirable thing'). Upon these rather shaky foundations Finance World then piled a mass of mathematical techniques, many of which form part of what has become known as Modern Portfolio Theory.

I was also lucky enough to be guided towards the works of various eminent research scientists, books which I would

---

[1] As interpreted by Clive James in *Cultural Amnesia*, Picador, London 2007.

not normally have tackled despite being a compulsive reader. Understanding how scientists pursued their quest for knowledge raised yet more questions about how and why Finance World operated as it did and, as will become apparent, I read the likes of Popper to get a clearer grasp of just what a 'science' might be in the first place.

Over the years I slowly moved towards a very different view of risk. I also started to try to sketch out a framework for gaining a better understanding of the whole broad sweep of finance in the same way that scientists had done in fields such as physics. To this end, it was not enough to look at risk in isolation, at least not until one could fix its own meaning and place in the overall scheme of things. It was this that gave me the idea for the pillars of finance which, with the appropriate addition of upper case letters, duly became the title of this book.

The purpose of the pillars of finance is to frame and advance our own quest for knowledge, in the same way that time, space, and causation do for physicists. This is particularly necessary in the case of finance, since nobody seems ever to have asked, let alone attempted to answer, the most fundamental question of all, namely 'what is finance?' A sneaky look at the closing paragraphs of the book will reveal that I advance the suggestion that finance is some sort of function of return, risk, and value operating in the presence of time and human behaviour. This may or may not be a proposal that will stand the test of time (indeed, I hope not, since only by a hypothesis being discarded and a new and potentially better one being adopted can progress be made), but it does at least offer a decent starting point.

What was required, then, was a study of all these pillars, not just risk, and that is what this book attempts to do. It is important to recognise from the outset that this is not an easy task, as may be guessed from the facts that this book has been ten years in gestation, and has taken me well over a year to write.

One problem is that nobody appears ever to have considered most of these questions before, and the works of those who have, such as Ludwig von Mises, appear to have been ignored to an extent which in the hands of a conspiracy theorist might well produce accusations of them having been deliberately suppressed. Perhaps this has something to do with the Markowitz-type view having hardened into something approaching religious dogma. Whatever the case, there is little guidance to be found from anything written after the Second World War, at least not within the realm of finance.

Another problem is that it is impossible to look at any of the pillars in isolation. I have where possible sought to push and pull them into dedicated chapters of their own, but such an approach requires some repetition of both material and argument. After much consideration I took the view that this was an acceptable price to pay for the benefit of at least partial compartmentalisation of topics, and I would ask the reader's indulgence in this regard. For example, much of the discussion about return mirrors what we need to say about time, there are equally obvious cross-overs between return and risk, while issues such as subjectivity, perception, behaviour, emotion, and even the nature of knowledge itself are threads which run through everything we need to consider.

Mention of these matters raises another obvious requirement: it is not possible to seek any understanding of finance without considering other academic disciplines such as psychology and philosophy. In addition we will look at examples drawn from art, literature, and various other areas.

Bringing these two factors together, some chapters offer vignettes drawn from real life which invite the reader to adopt a different perspective on various aspects of finance, hopefully prompting some new insights in the process. I have learned over the years, in both teaching and speaking assignments, that people tend to respond to images and stories much more readily than they do to dry facts, so please accept these in the spirit in which they are intended (which is at least partly as fun).

Incidentally, I believe that it was in the application of disciplines such as philosophy to finance that I began to make real progress. As we will see, a school of philosophy called Logical Positivism undoubtedly played a key role, largely unrecognised today, in enticing finance down a wrong turning from which it has yet to return. Similarly, it was when I considered the difference between a subjective, as opposed to an objective, perspective that my ideas on the nature of risk started to fall into place.

I soon realised that once you approach finance in a spirit of honest enquiry, rather than noting and accepting what Finance World would have you believe, it not only becomes quickly apparent that we hardly understand anything at all, but also that the existing framework has been sloppily constructed. Nobody has ever bothered properly to define the terms or set the parameters. Instead, finance has simply been assumed to be whatever makes it most convenient for academics to pursue their own particular fields of enquiry, and whatever causes the least friction with an investor's chosen methodology.

To make this rather naïve construction seem less silly, Finance World has set finance within the imposing field of science, thus legitimising the purely mathematical techniques which they have chosen to employ. Yet ironically as soon as one subjects finance to any rigorous analysis it can be seen that not only is it not a science, but also that even those who are most vociferous in their declarations of its scientific nature actually treat it in a most unscientific way. We will be considering this with the assistance of Karl Popper, who, as noted already, wrote extensively on what qualifies as a 'science' and what does not. We will see that, far from being a science, finance as it has been practised more closely resembles the development of religion as described by Frazer in *The Golden Bough*,[2] with belief elevated to the status of sacred dogma, and high priests initiating adepts into its mysteries. In such an atmosphere, honest enquiry tends to be seen as dissent, or even heresy, and treated accordingly, usually accompanied by accusations of lack of understanding.

It was this failure of finance to address the most fundamental questions such as 'what is finance?', let alone 'what is

---

[2] James Frazer *The Golden Bough*, Wordsworth Editions, London 1993 but originally published in 1890.

risk?', that got me thinking what a pity it was that, unlike law studies, finance did not include any comparable subject to jurisprudence, especially when I found out that scientists (real scientists, that is) were encouraged to study the philosophy of science.

While it lies beyond the scope of this book, this almost certainly explains why, until very recently, finance was seen as operating in a sterile vacuum of numbers and mathematical processes, entirely divorced from either behavioural factors or ethical considerations. In the current environment, of course, ethical issues have forced their way to the foreground and finance is struggling to adapt and evolve with this new development. In part this is because, since it has no equivalent of jurisprudence, it has no conceptual frame of reference with which to consider these soft, qualitative questions that require value judgement rather than mathematical calculation.

In part, though, it is because to accept the need to do so upsets the cosy existing view of risk. Once you accept that ethical considerations are relevant you must accept that investors and financiers will at least consider and seek to avoid being exposed to the opprobrium of the press and the public, to say nothing of their peers. Indeed, anybody who is today engaged in any way in the taking of investment decisions, whether as principal or adviser, will know that this 'headline risk' or 'reputational risk' can be the most important factor in deciding whether or not to adopt a particular course of action. Yet to admit that there is material risk attaching to an investment which is not capable of mathematical calculation flies in the face of the present approach.

It is this tendency of science to ignore anything that cannot be calculated which forced a narrow, mathematical approach on finance. In such an environment it is irrelevant to consider people's behavioural impulses, or what impact they may have upon others, society, or the financial system as a whole. In fact finance expressly abjures any such enquiry, requiring us to believe that all investors are rational.

The practical consequences of this failure by finance properly to enquire into the nature of its cogs and levers can be seen all too clearly as part of the origins of the crisis which began in 2007. Because risk had been misunderstood, it was mis-described and mis-priced. At the same time, things which were undoubtedly 'risk' were ignored because they did not fit the accepted definition. Arguably, all these factors remain in place today.

Meanwhile the awkward squad has been growing larger and more vociferous. Just within the last two weeks of the writing of this book, I twice heard the validity of Modern Portfolio Theory being openly challenged: once at a family office investment conference, and once on a radio programme. The cracks between financial theory and investment reality have widened into a yawning gap and people are starting to notice, though as yet they have questions but no answers. This book is designed, if not to supply them, at least to suggest where to look.

As to that, I promised some vignettes and different perspectives so let us dive straight into the wonderful world of Douglas Adams.

Chapter 2

The ultimate question

In Douglas Adams's *Hitchhiker's Guide to the Galaxy* series of novels (described by its creator as a trilogy in five parts), a race of super-intelligent beings build a massively powerful computer called Deep Thought to find the answer to the Ultimate Question: Life the Universe, and Everything. After seven and a half million years of consideration, it gravely announces that the answer is 42.

There is a direct analogy here with the world of traditional finance, in that whenever you ask a broad, conceptual question you are guaranteed to receive a narrow, calculated answer which may or may not be correct. In fact, it is almost guaranteed *not* to be correct, but we will come back to that. What is much more important is to understand why this might be.

A closer examination of *Hitchhiker's Guide to the Galaxy* (a work to which we will return) reveals an important clue. When Deep Thought eventually spews out its solution to the Ultimate Question (chosen, said Adams, because 42 was by far the most amusing of all the two digit numbers), his baffled minders finally think to ask the great machine what the question was. Deep Thought confesses that it does not know. His creators realise to their horror and embarrassment that they have wasted seven and a half million years trying to find the answer to a question, without first defining which was the correct question to ask.

A further clue is that computers, no matter how powerful they may be, are of course incapable of conceptual thought, and must therefore always turn towards a calculated answer to any question, or, perhaps more precisely, one that is capable of calculation. It is a method of response which also seems to afflict many who labour in the field of finance.

Ask a question such as 'what is the risk of this investment?' and we will receive a '42' type response – probably something like '14.3 per cent', without even specifying 14.3 per cent of what. We are implicitly challenged to take issue with the answer, and the challenge usually goes unanswered. Even if we did challenge it, we would be curtly assured that the answer was correct, and indeed it would be – in the sense of having been correctly calculated.

The inventor of the world's first programmable computer was of course the brilliant mathematician Alan Turing, who built it in conditions of great secrecy during the Second World War with self-educated post office electrical engineer Tommy Flowers. Sadly, because of the highly secret nature of their work (the British had it in mind to use the machine and its successors to crack Soviet codes in the same way as it had helped to crack the German codes originated by the Enigma machine) both were denied true recognition for their achievement for many years. Turing was awarded a relatively lowly civilian decoration (the OBE) where surely a Nobel Prize would have been more appropriate had people known the full story, while Flowers received the even more humble MBE and was sent back to work repairing telephone exchanges. Turing was to die of cyanide poisoning in mysterious circumstances in 1954, by which time he was seen as a security risk by British Intelligence following a conviction for homosexuality, which would not be de-criminalised in the UK until as late as 1967.

Turing wrote a classic paper on computers in 1950, although it was based on work which he did during the war, to which he could of course allude only obliquely, though it does contain confirmation that binary digital computers had already been developed and, by clear implication, that he had played a major part in the process. Its dry academic title was *Computing Machinery and Intelligence* but, as Turing made clear in the very first sentence, it set out to consider the question 'can machines think?'

There then follows a very important little passage, the significance of which is usually overlooked. Turing says that in order to consider this question it is first necessary to arrive at definitions of 'machine' and 'think' respectively. This may seem an obvious thing to say, and thus trivial to remark upon, but it is actually very significant indeed with regard to the world of traditional finance. As we will see, finance does not set out by defining its terms. It simply accepts whatever definitions have already been arrived at and, again as we will see, these have been put in place originally in a very artificial and irrational way by limiting the sort of questions which might be asked during that discussion, and thus restricting both the number and nature of possible answers.

It is in such apparently simple and obvious steps that true genius can perhaps most readily be discerned. For this is not an approach which Turing adopts simply for the purposes of this paper. On the contrary, an obituary published by the Royal Society in 1955 makes it clear that this:

> strong preference for working everything out from first principles instead of borrowing from others – a habit which gave freshness and independence to his work

was a lifelong practice, and indeed that even while at school he had been the despair of his science teachers by constantly challenging anything which they advanced as a proven fact. Clearly Turing was one of life's awkward squad; we will be meeting more members of this exclusive club in later chapters.

Turing defines the sort of machine which he has in mind as a digital computer, and gives an analogy of a human computer. This human is required to function according to set rules from which he is not allowed to deviate. He may perform any number of calculations, whether addition, subtraction, division, or multiplication. He also has an infinite supply of paper upon which to perform and store these calculations, and a desktop calculator to assist him.

He has more problems when it comes to 'thinking', since he readily admits that there are alternative views of this. He is quite clear, though, that it is more than simply making calculations and following rules, another acute observation which has sadly been lost upon the practitioners of traditional finance:

> The popular view that scientists proceed inexorably from well-established fact to well-established fact, never being influenced by any improved conjecture, is quite mistaken. Provided it is made clear which are proved facts and which are conjectures, no harm can result. Conjectures are of great importance since they suggest useful lines of research.

Turing believes that, as so defined, no computer then available was capable of 'thinking', but that by about 2000 this would have changed. Scientific opinion is still divided upon the extent to which this prediction may or may not have been proved correct, but Turing's paper remains a classic and is still discussed today on a daily basis.

It is perhaps best known for its postulation of what Turing called 'The Imitation Game' in which a man (A) and a woman (B) sit in different rooms, being asked questions by an observer (C) in a third room and answering them by teleprinter. C's task is to determine which of A and B is a man. A's task is to confuse and mislead C. B's task is to help him. Turing's idea was that you would run the game a large number of times, and then repeat the experiment with a computer taking the part of A. Would there be a difference in C's success rate?

Of course, as Turing himself admits, this is not the same thing as determining whether a machine can 'think', but whether it can be developed in such a way that can fool C into thinking that it is a man. (Note that C's objective is not, as many observers have wrongly stated, to decide which of the players is human but (effectively) to decide which is a woman. It is unclear why Turing stated the problem in this way.) It may be that what he has in mind is for a powerful enough computer to be capable of being programmed with the best way of responding to any possible question, though whether this would satisfy his own proffered definition of 'thinking' is open to question. Whatever the case, Turing admitted that such a thing was not possible (though he believed it would be in the future), but he suggested at various times that a computer might be more capable of human-like thought, or of seeming to be capable of it, if some totally random element, such as a random number generator, was built into its processes.

So, by Turing's definition, a computer is capable of calculation and of following processes that can be expressed by 'is/is not' logic, and can in fact do so much more quickly and efficiently than any human. He might have added, though it is probably implied by his provision of an infinite supply of paper, that a computer is capable of finding 'best fit' solutions to problems by means of iteration (running the same calculation many times with just one input varying each time, in order to confine answers within a constantly narrowing range of uncertainty). It can appear to think intuitively, but only by effectively rolling a die or spinning a roulette wheel as part of its workings.

Even Turing, though, despite his high expectations of the development in artificial intelligence, drew back from suggesting that a computer would ever be capable of conceptual thought. If you present a computer with a blank sheet of paper then it will remain a blank sheet of paper unless and until you program the computer to do something. It is incapable of writing down, as a human might if he or she was recording his or her thoughts, something such as the following:

> What shall I think about today?
> What are the topics I have been considering lately?
> Which of these shall I choose to consider today?
> What exactly is it that I wish to resolve?
> How shall I frame the relevant question?
> How shall I define the terms which I use to frame my question?
> ... and so on.

This is exactly the mistake made by the inventors of Deep Thought. They believed that if they produced a computer with sufficient capacity, it would be able to choose exactly how to express the question to which they wished to know the answer, and to define precisely each term used in that question.

They might also have spotted that 'Life, The Universe and Everything' is not actually a question in the first place, but that is another matter.

They were wrong of course. No matter how powerful and sophisticated the computer, these tasks are beyond it and probably always will be. You can program a computer how to respond to an infinite number of individual questions. You can even give it fuzzy logic so that it appears to be able to 'learn' from past experience (although all it is really doing is noting a particular combination of circumstances and assuming that whenever they recur in the future, so will the same outcome), but you cannot grant it the power to take a blank sheet of paper, gaze out of the window, and come up with a conceptual question which it wishes to debate with itself. You cannot get it, in Turing's words, to 'conjecture'.

Conversely, even human beings, who *are* capable of conceptual thought, cannot calculate an answer to a question whose terms are ambiguous ('what is the risk of this investment?') or which is simply incapable of a calculated solution ('do you think Janet would make a good wife for John?').

In the first example, it all depends what you mean by risk, and, even if you define this clearly, it still depends on whether you have chosen something that can be measured in the first place, and whether you have the available data and formulae with which to do so. It also assumes that there are no other variable factors which you need to take into account, such as the circumstances of different investors, or changing economic conditions.

In the second example, there is no recognised way of calculating an answer based on any accepted, objective, quantitative scale. In any case, it would depend upon what John was looking for in a wife, whether he was correct in his views, and how well I know Janet. It might also depend on how well Janet might be able to conceal her true nature from me, and on the circumstances in which I thought it was likely Janet and John might find themselves during their married life together.

Important points, surely, and yet points which are simply ignored by traditional finance. Not so much ignored, in fact, as simply airbrushed out of existence. Remember Joseph Heller's *Catch-22*, a made-up phrase which has passed into everyday usage. The original Catch-22 related to airmen trying to get relieved from combat flying on the grounds of insanity (echoes of Klinger in *MASH*). The regulations provide that in order to be relieved you must be insane, but they also provide that the act of making an application to be relieved from combat flying is the act of a sane man. Thus, no application can ever succeed.

As we will see in later chapters, Finance World uses a similar device. Though it is never expressly stated in this way, it is as follows:

> *Principle A: it is possible to calculate the answer to any question*
> *Principle B: you may not ask any question to which it is not possible to calculate the answer.*

Obviously if you restrict the number and type of questions which it is possible to ask, then you also restrict the scope of debate. What you are effectively doing is to rule certain matters as being unsuitable for discussion. For conceptual enquiry, Turing's conjecturing, requires language which is rich in subtle shades of meaning, and yet clear and precise. The English language, by the way, is ideally suited for this task since it is an amalgam drawn from at least three different linguistic sources, and has a much larger and richer vocabulary than, say, French where one French word often has to do service for three or four English words, all of which have slightly different connotations; a difference which it is often difficult to express properly in French translation.

Suppose however that you were deliberately to restrict the number of words available for use, perhaps even to restrict the number very severely? This is exactly the situation which George Orwell imagines in *1984*. He envisages a dictatorial regime simply expunging from the language any terms which refer to things they do not wish to have discussed. In place of standard English they create Newspeak, 'the only language in the world whose vocabulary gets smaller every year'.

In addition, the words they retain relate only to their antonym, that is, a word with precisely the opposite meaning. Thus, in describing conduct there may be 'good' and 'bad', but no 'tolerable', 'reasonable', 'excusable', or any of the other many words which could be used to describe shades of meaning in between. In such circumstances, conceptual discussion of course becomes impossible – exactly what the regime wants; you cannot discuss or think about something which you cannot describe or define.

Let us go back to the question 'what is the risk of this investment?'

Suppose that the investment in question were some shares in a Russian oil company, then an intelligent response might be to begin by listing all the various different types of risk to which such an investment might be subject: oil price risk, currency risk, Russian political risk, stock market risk, terrorist risk, and so on. An even more intelligent response might be 'well, it all depends'.

Perhaps it all depends on what you mean by 'risk', or on the particular circumstances of each individual investor, or on what the available alternative investments might be, or even on why you want to know the answer to the question in the first place. Traditional finance however will not even pause to consider these wider ramifications but will simply spew out an answer like 42. It is content that the answer is the correct answer to *a* question. It is not concerned as to whether it is the correct answer to *the* question which you wish to pose. It can produce a correct answer (but only, as we will see, to certain types of question), but it cannot determine what is the correct question to be asking in the first place.

Why is it that finance, like Deep Thought, is incapable of resolving any situation except by churning out numbers which may or may not make sense? Well, the two most important clues to this mystery have already been disclosed. Finance (1) never stops to consider 'what is the right question to ask?', and (2) is incapable of answering any question except by means of mathematical calculation.

How is it able to get away with this? Effectively by use of Newspeak. Finance has evolved a language of its own, which it forces us to use, and in so doing effectively strangles any possibility of conceptual thought. Suppose, for example, that you did indeed begin your consideration of the question by saying 'well, it all depends what you mean by risk'. Roget's *Thesaurus* lists well over twenty words which are synonymous with the adjective 'risky' yet each of which has its own subtle shade of meaning. Finance Newspeak however recognises only one. It then compounds this problem by using the word in a sense which has no bearing at all on how it is used in everyday speech. So, not only are we denied an opportunity to go back to first principles for ourselves, as advocated by Turing, but we are actively misled, since everybody outside the world of finance (and even quite a few within it) will never realise that what is being described is not even 'risk' in the generally accepted sense of the word at all.

Traditional finance, then, may validly be compared to a totalitarian dictatorship which actively suppresses conceptual debate because it cannot handle its possible consequences, and which feeds false information to the population into the bargain.

For once you allow people to debate, for example, 'is this government better or worse than its predecessors?' you prompt discussion not only of what 'better' or 'worse' might signify in these circumstances, and to what extent even these terms may be incapable of general agreement, but also what constitutes a 'government'. From here it is but a short step to asking what forms of government may be appropriate, and how and why a government might need to prove its validity, for instance by due democratic process. Much easier simply to stop people from being able to ask 'what is government?' in the first place.

Traditional finance has its own chosen means of stopping this discussion dead in its tracks. First, it would rule the question unacceptable because it is not capable of a mathematically calculated answer. Second, no discussion would in any event be possible because the word 'government' would either no longer form part of the language, or would have been ascribed a set definition from which you would be unable to depart through fear of having electrodes attached to your genitals.

As we will see in a later chapter, when we consider the concept of knowledge itself, sciences such as physics rest upon firm foundations. A physicist would probably state that physics rests upon three interlocking things: space, time, and causation, and would be able to define exactly what was meant by each. A traditional finance tyro would, if pressed, probably venture that the three pillars of finance are risk, reward (or return), and value. Yet follow-up questions such as 'what is risk?', 'what is return?', and 'what is value?' would be met either by a blank stare, or an attempted explanation of how they might be calculated in particular circumstances.

For traditional finance is incapable of conducting conceptual debate. Like Deep Thought, it is capable of spitting out a neat calculated solution to any problem which may be stated as a mathematical formula or a logic proposition, but it is incapable of framing the question in the first place, or of testing whether the right question is being asked, or even of ascertaining whether it is appropriate to be stating it as a formula or proposition.

The fact that we need to to ask these very necessary questions about the nature and validity of the pillars of finance but are unable to do so, masks an even greater need which lies unfulfilled. Before we can even embark upon this process, we need to find the answer to our own Ultimate Question: what is finance?

What is finance? How do we define it and describe it? Have we actually understood even the basic points of what it is and how it operates? Should we not at least consider the possibility that what we know as 'finance' is actually an impostor, who has kidnapped the true finance and locked it away in a cellar somewhere while it carries on a massive deception on the world at large, having stolen the prisoner's clothes and identity?

As we will see, the answer to this last question is actually 'yes'. What the world knows as finance is really the biggest intellectual confidence trick ever to be perpetrated, one that has seduced the finest minds in the finest universities and investment banks, a lie upon which a whole industry and sub-industries have been built, and a deception, moreover, which has enjoyed such total and prestigious support that none has felt able to question it.

Like the builders and operators of Deep Thought, we have been blinded by its supposed intelligence, and have thus felt unable to question its thought process. To have suggested at any time that it didn't actually know what it was doing would have required great moral courage, and possibly suicidal leanings. Like the subjects of the Emperor walking through the streets naked, we have felt compelled to admire the fine fabric and workmanship of his imaginary clothes. It takes an innocent child to shout out the truth: that His Majesty doesn't have any clothes on.

We need to understand why this totally false view of finance has been able to hold sway for so long, but in order to do so we must consider how this state of affairs came to pass in the first place.

This is an important point which is lost not only on those who practice finance, but on all those who labour in just about any field of study today. As the base of human knowledge has expanded rapidly, so we have each been forced to study a smaller and smaller area in greater and greater detail. As our knowledge has deepened, it has inevitably grown narrower. It is like pushing a cloth down through a hole in a table with your finger. The deeper it goes, the less of the surface of the table will it cover. If we are truly to understand finance, we need to try to put this process into reverse, since its mysteries cannot be grasped in isolation.

The great cricket writer and commentator John Arlott put this as well as anyone when he said 'what do they know of cricket, who only cricket know?' Substitute 'finance', or indeed anything else for 'cricket', and there you have it. In order to understand something you have to know not only what it is and how it operates, but how it came about and what beliefs and other influences operated upon it in the process. Arlott himself, incidentally, put his beliefs into practice. As well as being a renowned authority on cricket, he was an acknowledged international expert on the red wines of Bordeaux, a soccer journalist, an active human rights campaigner who was an early and vociferous opponent of apartheid, a police officer, and for many years the BBC's poetry correspondent, credited with discovering the young Dylan Thomas.

So, in our quest for the answer to our own Ultimate Question we will be dealing not with formulae and calculations but with images and illustrations drawn from history, psychology, literature, philosophy, and science. Why? Because they have all operated upon finance in the past, influencing its development, and continue to do so today. In the process we will hopefully establish what sort of an animal finance is, or at least what sort it is not. This is important, since it will influence the way in which we approach it. If a forensic scientist is examining a myxomatosis virus and is asked whether it constitutes a threat to the patient's health, he or she will need to know whether the specimen has been taken from a human or from a rabbit before a sensible answer can be given.

In this way we will hopefully come to know the right questions to ask to unlock the prisoner in the cellar, and bring him blinking and uncertain into the daylight. We also need to be able to recognise how much damage the impostor has inflicted on the world of investment in the meantime, and why, and how.

There are some in the world of traditional finance who may see this exercise as irrelevant or, still worse, a threat. It is neither of these things. For it is only by asking the right questions, from a secure base of understanding how things came to be as they are, that we might go about trying to get things right in the future – and that surely is in everyone's interests. After all, we need to choose some new clothes for the prisoner to wear on his release.

That is what this book is about ... and our quest for an explanation will begin in Kansas City in 1931.

Chapter 3

A game of chance

It is a well-known axiom in bridge playing circles that it is generally a mistake to partner your spouse.

No matter how distraught you might become as a relative stranger forgets to draw trumps, or fails to lead back your suit for the third time in succession, there is always a last veneer of politeness which prevents you from saying 'what do you think you're doing, you bloody idiot?' If the person in question is one with whom you go to bed every night, and wake to the sound of all those personal little noises which they make in the bathroom in the morning, then somehow that last veneer of civilised behaviour fails to kick in.

Not for nothing are husband and wife combinations dreaded at bridge clubs around the world. Even those who possess that priceless quality of being able to take infinite comfort from the misfortunes of others finally get rather tired of comments such as 'you stupid cow!' being bandied back and forth across the table between their opponents. The following true story may perhaps demonstrate what I have in mind.

One evening in 1931 Mr and Mrs Bennett, residents of Kansas City, invited their friends and neighbours Mr and Mrs Hoffman round for a friendly game of bridge. It was however to prove rather less 'friendly' than the invitation might have suggested. For Mr and Mrs Bennett were going through one of those little spats which make up such an indispensable part of marital bliss. Perhaps Mr Bennett had come home late the night before and fallen over the milk bottles on the doorstep? Perhaps Mrs Bennett had burnt the toast at breakfast? We will never know what domestic incidents might have led up to the events of this particular evening. Of the events themselves however we are very well informed, for reasons which will shortly become clear.

As the game progressed, Mrs Bennett began, regrettably, to make caustic remarks about Mr Bennett's bidding and play. Mr Bennett's male pride forced him to respond in kind. Eventually what was to prove the last hand of the evening was dealt, on which Mr Bennett opened One Spade, his left hand opponent overcalled Two Diamonds, and Mrs Bennett resolutely responded Four Spades, which was passed out and thus became the contract in which Mr Bennett had to play the hand.

Unfortunately, Mr Bennett failed to make his contract, going one off. Perhaps he got greedy and tried for an over-trick, a tactic that can frequently result in losing two tricks instead of gaining one. Who knows? Who cares?

Well, actually Mrs Bennett cared very much. So much, in fact, that as the hand drew to a close, and the final score became evident, she started screaming uncontrollably at her husband.

Going one off in Four Spades had been Mr Bennett's first mistake. He now made his second. Believing his wife to have become hysterical, he leaned across the table and slapped her vigorously across the face. When this failed to have the desired effect, he decided to do it a couple more times. Perhaps to his surprise, this only seemed to make matters worse. Mrs Bennett rose from her chair and ran out of the room, gibbering incoherently with rage.

Mr Bennett had probably just embarked on an apology for his wife's strange behaviour, and the Hoffmans were undoubtedly glancing significantly at each other and saying that they really must be going now, when Mrs Bennett abruptly re-entered the room holding, as the report records, 'the family automatic weapon'.

Readers will doubtless be familiar with such concepts as 'the family beach umbrella', or 'the family cocker spaniel', but 'the family automatic weapon' may prove a somewhat surprising image with which to grapple. It may help to remember that Kansas City is in the United States of America, a country in which, for example, it is legal for a psychopath to enter the state of Florida carrying a gun, but illegal for a child to enter the state of Florida carrying an orange.

Mr Bennett now made the understandable decision that discretion might prove the better part of valour and, as any red-blooded male would surely have done in the same circumstances, ran off to hide in the downstairs toilet. As he locked the door behind him, he doubtless reflected with a smirk of satisfaction that any man could feel totally safe when shut securely in his own guest bathroom. If so, this would prove to be his third and last mistake.

For Mrs Bennett was not a woman to be so easily cheated of her prey. Having grimly pursued her husband, gun in hand, she now coolly and efficiently fired two shots through the door. Unfortunately, the guest bathroom being very small, Mr Bennett was directly behind the door and both bullets entered his body, killing him more or less instantly. As he slumped to the floor mortally wounded, perhaps his last fleeting moments were spent berating himself for not having bought a house with a larger guest bathroom.

Unsurprisingly, Mrs Bennett was tried for her husband's murder. Surprisingly, she was acquitted, though convicted of the lesser crime of manslaughter. It was rumoured that the judge who presided at her trial was himself a keen bridge player, and had considerable sympathy for her situation. This sympathy may in turn have been encouraged by an analysis of the fateful hand by Eli Culbertson, the world's greatest bridge expert, which gave it as Culbertson's considered opinion that Mr Bennett could actually have made Four Spades had he played the cards differently.

Mrs Bennett subsequently became something of a celebrity, since ladies of good family from all over America wanted to meet and greet the woman who had shot her husband dead in front of witnesses and got away with it. Perhaps they came enquiring after tips as to how they might repeat her feat themselves. However history does not record how easy or difficult Mrs Bennett might have found it from this point onwards to persuade people to partner her at bridge …

... but I digress. There are actually a number of features of this story which may serve as a useful introduction to the world of finance.

Let us first consider what actually happens when you play bridge. As we have seen, there is an auction, at the end of which a member of the partnership which has made the highest bid gets to play the hand, and has to try to make at least as many tricks as they bid. So, when you actually come to play the hand you have an agreed target which you are trying to achieve.

This raises a number of questions. Exactly what are you trying to achieve? How do you measure it for the purpose of seeing if you have been successful? If you have been successful, exactly what have you gained? What can go wrong? What might you be able to do to lessen the chances of something going wrong? A lot of questions, all of which we will explore in much more detail later in the book, but let us see if we can at least think about the basic concepts behind them.

First a question which we did not ask, perhaps because it seems ridiculous. Do you *know* what it is that you are trying to achieve?

'Of course,' Mr Bennett will huffily reply. 'I am trying to make Four Spades.' (For those readers who are not bridge players, this means making ten tricks out of the available thirteen with spades as the trump suit.)

Yet, whisper who dares, bridge players do sometimes forget which contract they are playing in. It is not unknown for a declarer (the person playing the hand) to look very surprised when one of their apparent winners is trumped by the opponents and exclaim 'oh, I thought we were playing in No Trumps!'. The opposite can also be the case. One player might triumphantly 'trump' once he has run out of a suit and start to lead to the next trick, only to be asked caustically (by Mrs Bennett perhaps) 'what on earth are you doing? We're playing in No Trumps.'

So, in those situations at least, it can be quite possible not to know exactly what you are trying to achieve. Not to know because you have forgotten, or misunderstood in the first place.

What about another situation? What about a dream or nightmare in which you are playing a hand of bridge but without any idea of what the contract is, perhaps because you have suddenly found yourself sitting at a bridge table with three total strangers and no recollection of how you got there?

> 'Ah, yes,' you will say, 'but that couldn't happen in real life.'
> 'Oh, couldn't it?' I reply. 'Just look around you.'

For, crazy though it may sound, a great many of the world's investors, including some of the biggest, do not actually know exactly what it is that they are trying to achieve. This may be because they have never actually got around to discussing and agreeing their objectives. More worryingly, it can because they have misunderstood them. They think they are playing in Four Spades when actually they are playing in Three No Trumps, or vice versa.

In fact, the situation might be even more nightmarish than that which I have just outlined. Suppose that you were to find yourself suddenly in the middle of a hand, just as before, with no idea of what contract you were playing in, but presume this time you are subject to yet another disadvantage. This time, you don't know the rules of the game, either.

> 'Oh, that's crazy,' you say. 'Nobody would ever try to play bridge if they'd never had a bridge lesson. It would be like trying to take off in a plane if you'd never had a flying lesson.'
>
> 'Oh, really?' I would reply. 'In that case I'd better not tell you about what's happening to your pension money.'

For if you are a member of an employer's pension plan, then the trustees of that plan will almost certainly have never studied investment or finance in their lives, yet they are making hugely important investment decisions every month of the year in respect of other people's money.

So, understanding the basic rules of the game, and what you are fundamentally trying to achieve are in fact important pre-requisites to answering any of the other questions, and we will look at the whole issue of investment strategy in some detail. The good news is that you do not really need to understand finance. You just need to have an enquiring mind and ask the right questions.

Now, how do you measure your achievement? Surely there is no problem here. There must be a means of scoring at bridge, or the game would be a nonsense. Well, yes and no.

First, in bridge there is a concept known as vulnerability, and this changes from one hand to another. Since either partnership can be vulnerable or non-vulnerable this means there are four possible combinations, and these rotate so that each combination occurs once every four hands. Vulnerability changes certain aspects of the scoring. Basically if you are vulnerable then you are rewarded more handsomely for making certain types of contract, but punished more heavily if you fail.

In other words you will find yourself at different times and in different circumstances in anything from a low risk/low reward situation to a high risk/high reward situation. It will probably not surprise you to hear that exactly the same thing happens in finance. The important thing, in bridge as in finance, is to know which of the situations currently applies, and understand the various trade-offs inherent within it.

Second, there is a further level of complexity which we must consider, and again one which directly parallels the world of finance. Even once you have worked out your score, there are different ways of assessing it, only one of which will really be appropriate to your situation.

If you are playing rubber bridge, as the Bennetts and the Hoffmans would have been, then you simply add up your points until you come to one hundred, and the first partnership to reach one hundred wins that game. A rubber consists of the best of three games.

Serious players however very rarely play rubber bridge (though some do so as a form of gambling, at which large amounts of money can change hands). They play duplicate, the form of bridge most widely found in clubs, and almost exclusively in tournaments. Here the scoring is different. What is important is not whether you made your contract or not, and how many points you either made or gave away, but how well you did relative to other people playing the same hand.

Even this is not the end of the matter however. Different forms of scoring apply if you are playing 'teams', in which case you are normally only comparing your results with one other pair (your opponents who have been playing the same cards in a different room), than if you are playing 'pairs', in which case you might be comparing your performance with several hundred or even thousand others, who might be playing in the same convention centre, or even independently all around the world and scoring using the internet.

In the world of finance, we find a directly comparable situation. There are at least three ways of calculating returns, and even variations of methodology within these. Just as in bridge, you have to know which is the appropriate one to use, and why. Just as in bridge, the way of scoring can affect your objective, and your tactics. In rubber bridge, for example, your main objective is to make your contract, and you may well deliberately give up a trick in order to increase your chances of making it (this is called a safety play). In pairs duplicate however if you give up the trick but nobody else does then you will have a dramatically bad score, despite having achieved your apparent objective. As we will see, this same decision is made on a regular basis by investors around the world. What can go wrong?

It is here that things can get really complex. A good bridge player will have an instinctive understanding of what might go wrong and will, so far as possible, seek either to take steps to the lessen the chances of adverse consequences, or to delay a key decision until the last possible moment in the hope that fresh information will become available which will narrow the range of possible alternatives. Sadly, most investors are very bad at this indeed.

Here we get into the complex world of risk, or rather what the traditional world of finance thinks of as 'risk' which, as we will see, is not at all how you or I would understand the term. This area has long been dreaded by anyone studying finance as being incredibly difficult, and impossible to understand by anyone who does not have a PhD in applied mathematics. There is a reason for this. The subject of 'risk' is normally taught by people who have a PhD in applied mathematics, and who present it as being incredibly difficult. In this way they can convincingly demonstrate that they are much cleverer than everybody else in the room, and hopefully impress the pants off the girl in the third row wearing a tight sweater.

The good news is that the subject of risk is not really difficult at all, and can be expressed and discussed quite adequately without the need for even a single mathematical formula, let alone a whole blackboard of them. Risk is complex, but not complicated. As we will see, understanding it comes down to asking the right sort of questions, rather than limiting ourselves to only asking questions which we have checked in advance can be answered by arithmetic.

For example, let us take a look at what might go wrong for Mr Bennett as he plays his hand. Incidentally, you will not have noticed it, but we have just made a huge assumption in the course of the last sentence. We have assumed that in looking at risk, we are concerned with what might go wrong. Traditional finance does not do this. When it looks at risk it is concerned with something else entirely, as we will see in due course … but back to Mr Bennett.

Let us make the equally huge assumptions, by the standards of traditional finance and everyday investor practice, that Mr Bennett both understands the rules of the game and knows what he is trying to achieve. He will now be looking at the hand and considering what might go wrong.

First, there is the skill of his opponents, since through their defence they have the power to affect the outcome. He may have some notion of this if they are opponents against whom he plays regularly. On the other hand, if he has just sat down to play against them in a tournament he will almost certainly never have come across them before. So, he may or may not

have any real idea about this. In other words, this is a risk element the extent of which is unknown or uncertain.

Note too that, even if the extent of it was known, it would not be something that could be mathematically calculated. Even if there was some sort of numeric ranking system, this would be approximate rather than precise, and would not be able to cater for the fact that one of the pair might suddenly have a flash of uncharacteristic brilliance, be badly hung-over from the night before, have just had an argument with their spouse, and so on.

Nor is it a risk element over which Mr Bennett has any control. There may be things which he could do to try to throw them off their game, such as 'false carding' or he may, if he knows in advance that they are highly skilled, try to avoid being drawn to play against them in the first place, but their skill level itself is something outside his control. It is intrinsic to his opponents. For Mr Bennett, it is in the nature of an uncontrollable environmental issue, such as whether it is raining outside or not.

Second, there is the lie of the cards. This is also outside his control. However, unlike the skill of his opponents, this risk factor is capable of mathematical calculation, and good bridge players routinely do so, the really good ones almost unconsciously. Each player can see two hands (their own and the dummy, which is face up on the table) and the statistical odds of how the remaining cards are distributed in the other two hands can thus be assessed. For example, if you can see nine cards out of the thirteen in a suit, then there are only three splits possible for the remaining four. They can be distributed between the other two hands four–zero, three–one, or two–two, and the odds of these occurring are (roughly) 10 per cent, 50 per cent, or 40 per cent respectively.

However there is another very important point here which is understood by bridge players but not in general by investors. Any statistical calculation can only ever serve as a guideline, not a firm principle or rule, and must give way to any observations which suggest inconsistency. For example, if there are six cards outstanding then there is only 1.5 per cent probability, or three chances in two hundred, that all six of them will lie in one particular unseen hand. Yet if one of the other players has made a pre-emptive bid in that suit during the auction, then it is effectively 100 per cent certain that they *do* all lie in that one hand, since you cannot usually make a pre-emptive bid without a minimum of six cards in the suit.

Also unlike the skill of his opponents, there are things that Mr Bennett can do about this, for example, by what are called safety plays. If he is faced with five missing cards but cannot stand a four–one or five–zero split, he might decide to gamble on them splitting three–two. The odds that he will be successful are reasonable: about 68 per cent. However if he can afford to give up a trick in the suit first, then he can increase his chances to 96 per cent. In other words, there are steps he can take to reduce his risk, or 'de-risk' the situation, albeit at the expense of giving up some potential extra reward.

Third, there is the risk that Mr Bennett may just not play the hand very well, as seems actually to have happened. As Eli Culbertson pointed out, there was a better way of playing the cards. There is yet another obvious parallel here with the world of finance. Bridge, like finance, cannot function in a vacuum, but requires human actions as an engine. In studying bridge, like studying finance, we are essentially studying human behaviour. Some days Mr Bennett will play well and some days he will play badly. Some days he will make good decisions and some days he will make bad decisions. Sometimes he may be angry that a previous hand has gone badly, and allow this to affect his concentration. Sometimes he may know that he currently has a very bad score and play more recklessly in order to try to improve it, even at the expense of possibly doing even worse.

Traditional finance deals with this risk by simply ignoring it. We will see later why this is so. It assumes that all players have equal knowledge about the hand (whereas Mr Bennett may, for example, have forgotten that somebody played the ace of spades at trick two) and will always make the logically correct decision when faced with a choice of different alternatives (whereas in reality this is almost always a judgement call, and heavily intuitive and subjective). Traditional finance simply cannot handle the fact that investors are human beings, whereas as we have already seen it is sadly only too evident that bridge players are.

Fourth, we have also touched upon an element of risk which Mr Bennett might deliberately introduce himself. He might decide, as 'pairs' players frequently do, that the contract in which he is playing was so much the obvious one at which to arrive that every pair in the room are likely to be playing in it, and are almost certain to make it. In that case, he might decide that making an overtrick is likely to give him a very good score indeed, since although the difference will be small in absolute terms (perhaps 650 points compared to 620), in *relative* terms, which is how duplicate bridge is scored, it could be enormous – perhaps the difference between 50 per cent and 100 per cent.

So he may decide not to content himself with making the ten tricks he requires, but try to win an extra one as well to give him that elusive difference over what is likely to happen at every other table playing the same board. The problem with this is, as mentioned already, that the attempt to make an overtrick can, should it fail, actually give away an extra trick (or, in No Trumps, sometimes three or four) so that, far from making an overtrick for a 'top', Mr Bennett could actually fail to make his contract and score a 'bottom' relative to everyone else who went for the safe approach and made sure of their contract. Again, we will see that there is a direct parallel to this situation in the world of finance.

Finally, there is the risk of Mr Bennett getting shot. This in turn might be broken down into the risk of him getting shot during the hand, which would prevent him from making his contract, and the risk of him getting shot after the hand has ended, in which case it would have no affect on the outcome. The first type of risk is material, whereas the second is not. An alternative view might be to say that the latter type of risk is material to the investor but not to the investment, whereas the former is material to both.

The risk of Mr Bennett getting shot is of course extremely small. He remains to this day the only recorded bridge homicide victim. Again, traditional finance would deal with this risk by ignoring it. Not just finance, in fact, but also the world of actuarial science, which specialises in the study of how and when people are likely to die, and is thus of some relevance to our story. The same would hold true, though, for any other area of study which is obsessed with statistical calculations.

Actuaries, so the saying goes, are people who would find life as an audit accountant too exciting. One of the problems which we encounter regularly in the world of finance, incidentally, is that the actuaries have emerged from studying fifty year old railway timetables in their spare bedroom, and have ventured into the area of giving investment advice.

If any risk is statistically insignificant, an actuary would argue, then you can safely assume that it will never actually occur. Yet Mr Bennett, as he cowers in his guest bathroom one night in 1931, might view things rather differently. As we will see, it is in the blithe assumption that we can safely ignore the chance of certain events occurring, even if they might have an extreme consequence if they *do* occur, that many of the problems with traditional finance can be found.

This also illustrates an important point which we will be considering and yet which Finance World, that lofty metropolis constructed over the decades on the alluvial silt of an uninterrupted flood of finance PhD theses and academic articles, completely ignores. It all depends from whose point of view you are considering things. Finance World would look at the gun, perhaps considering what type of weapon it is and how many bullets it holds, whereas Mr Bennett would have been considering, had he been asked, how likely it was that his wife would fire it, and what the chances were of some of those bullets finding a new home in soft and vital parts of his cowering body.

Let us consider what helpful advice we might be able to offer Mr Bennett. This might be different according to our point of view, and which one we choose might be highly revealing of our attitude to finance. There are three broad possibilities.

An investment strategist might advise Mr Bennett that he should forget about going for the overtrick, and be content to make his contract. As we will see, a huge debate currently rages in the world of investment as to which of these strategies might be preferable.

A behaviourist might advise Mr Bennett to try to defuse the situation should he fail to make his contract by nodding sagely and saying something like 'ah, of course it would have played very differently on a diamond lead, partner.' This is usually a sound policy, since before your partner has a chance to analyse this statement and recognise if for the piece of arrant nonsense that it is, it is already time to play the next hand.

An actuary, on the other hand, would take a different approach altogether. He or she would advise Mr Bennett that he should always get someone to shoot him at the beginning of each game of bridge. After all, they would reason, if the odds against getting shot while playing bridge are a million to one, then the odds against getting shot *twice* while playing bridge must be a trillion to one.

Chapter 4

And yet it moves

For a young man growing up in northern Italy in the latter half of the sixteenth century, life must have been full of exciting career choices. That great cultural movement known to history as the Renaissance had already been underway among the Italian city states for over 200 years, and had spawned some of the greatest painters and sculptors who ever lived, as well as three of the greatest poets: Dante, Petrarch, and Boccaccio. Of the humanities, only music had been relatively neglected, but our young man's family were doing their best to remedy that omission; his father was a famous lute player, much in demand in the princely courts of Europe, and one of his brothers would go on to become an even more famous musician, as well as a composer.

Children who grow up in musical households routinely go on to become musicians themselves. Both Mozart and Beethoven, for example, were child prodigies who were first taught and then proudly shown off by their musician fathers. Not always however, and this particular young man, born in Pisa in 1564, was to prove a startling exception to the rule. Not only did he eschew the study of music, but he chose not to labour in any artistic field at all. He was more interested in what he felt was a scientific revolution beginning to erupt around him. So successful would his endeavours prove that no less an authority than Stephen Hawking would later say that he, more than any other individual, was surely responsible for the birth of modern science. His name was Galileo Galilei.

Galileo was not just a great theoretical scientist, but a practical man too. A natural engineer, he would perhaps today have been the archetypal inventor beavering away in his garage workshop. One field of particular interest was telescopes. Remarkably, with no practical training and only written sources from which to learn, he succeeded in a few short years in producing an instrument which was no less than ten times more powerful than that of any competitor. With his wonderful new telescope, he turned to examining the heavens and analysing what he saw.

This of course was where his problems began, and the reason why he is a household name to this day. What Galileo saw through his telescope disturbed him greatly. It seemed to him that his observations and calculations were simply inconsistent with the accepted view of the day that the earth was the centre of the universe, and that all the other heavenly bodies moved around it. He deduced, correctly, that the sun was at the centre of our solar system and that the earth was simply one of a number of bodies which moved around it. This was to become known as the Copernican system, since the theory had already been suggested by the Polish intellectual Copernicus, for whom astronomy was a hobby, his day job being as an expert in public finance.

The problem arose since the church clung instead to the Ptolemaic theory, named after the Greek mathematician Ptolemy, who lived in the second century AD and did much of his great work in the fabled library at Alexandria, one of the wonders of the Ancient World. Ptolemy's view, that the sun and all other heavenly bodies went around the earth, felt right to the church authorities.

After all, the bible said that God had created man in his own image and had created the earth for him to inhabit, and the sun and the stars too. It also said specifically that the earth could not be moved. Surely, then, the earth was at the centre of His grand design?

Actually, Ptolemy's system was a much more complex construction than the simplistic geocentric statement which we usually hear used today. He knew that physical observations did not always seem to fit with exactly what should be happening if the earth was at the centre of the universe, but he explained away these inconsistencies with complicated sets of rules and sub-rules which showed that while the sun did indeed revolve around the earth, it and various other bodies also performed little circular movements of their own while they did so, and that these independent waltzes through time and space explained the apparent irregularities in their orbits.

This led in time to the invention of something called an astrolabe. A sort of astronomical slide rule, it was widely used both by astrologers to cast horoscopes, and by mariners to help them navigate by the stars. In time, with the development of the clock-maker's skills, mechanical ones driven by clockwork began to appear around the fourteenth century, but would by Galileo's time have become very sophisticated indeed.

Remember that Ptolmey's universe involved some very convoluted cycles and epicycles. For these to be faithfully reproduced in an astrolabe, or astronomical clock as the clockwork versions came to be known, requires some bodies to revolve on rings of their own while simultaneously revolving around something else (the earth). That is why the finest examples, which may today be found in museums, are truly a triumph of human artistry and ingenuity.

Beautiful and breathtakingly clever, but phoney of course. Skill, knowledge, and craftsmanship all painstakingly and perfectly deployed, but to a false end. One can have the best gun in the world, but it is of little use if aimed at the wrong target.

All of this was plain to Galileo, but this knowledge placed him in direct and dangerous opposition to the church, which had stated it as dogma that the earth was the centre of the universe. 'Direct' because dogma was something which all Christians were required to believe without question. 'Dangerous' because the Inquisition was at the height of its powers and could, and did, burn people at the stake who dared to take issue with the teachings of the holy church. Copernicus, incidentally, had been acutely aware of this danger, and had allowed his work to be published only when he was dying (it is said that the first copy of it was brought to him on his deathbed), and even then cannily dedicated it to the Pope.

Copernicus was at different times a public official and government adviser, and, like all who move in political circles, had learned to trim his sails so as to avoid any open controversy.

Galileo, on the other hand, was one of the awkward squad, who felt an overpowering desire to spread the truth which he had discovered. Perhaps, naively, he even thought that, if presented with conclusive evidence of its error, the church might change its mind.

However, as Dorothy Parker once cannily observed, you can't teach an old dogma new tricks.

Galileo really should have known this, for he had already had a shot fired across his bows. Denounced to the Inquisition in 1615, he had managed to fudge his position sufficiently for them to find the case not proven, but they affirmed publicly that to believe in Copernicus's theory was contrary to the Bible, and therefore heresy, and Galileo was warned not to pursue the matter further.

So when he finally published his book in 1632 he must have known what to expect. Seen in this light, his decision to publish must rank as one of the bravest acts ever committed in pursuit of intellectual honesty, and is perhaps one of the many reasons for the adulation of Galileo by modern scientists. Predictably, he was arrested by the Inquisition and put on trial for his life before a Papal court in 1633.

Perhaps some old friend visited him in the cells with a message from the Vatican, but however it was done it seems highly likely that in some way a deal was struck, rather like a plea bargain in modern day American trials. Galileo's life was spared, though he was to spend the remaining ten years of his life under house arrest, but only after he had publicly recanted. Humiliatingly, he was forced to stand before the Inquisition and declare on oath that he no longer believed in what he had written, and that the church (and Ptolemy) had been right all along. His book was sentenced to be burnt publicly in place of its author, and the sentence of the court was despatched around Europe to be read aloud in every university to warn students of the dangers of pursuing such irreligious studies.

There is one last piece of the story still to be told however, since it is said that as he was led away to the cells he rebelliously muttered 'eppur si muove' (literally 'and yet it moves').

Just as with the deadly game of bridge played out that night in 1931, there are direct parallels between the world of finance and what happened that day in Rome in 1633.

In traditional finance, certain theories have hardened into dogma. Belief in them is compulsory, on pain not of death, but of ridicule and possible professional exclusion. Rather like the seventeenth-century Inquisition, those who teach and practice traditional finance are very happy, thank you very much, with their comfortable belief system and are frightened of anything or anyone that may challenge it.

Chief among these is the principle that the risk of any investment can be measured by the volatility of its historic returns. You will see that we will rub up against this basic belief at every step of the way; indeed, it will run through this whole book like a leitmotiv. The whole of traditional finance theory is based upon it. Every financial model which has ever been developed, and every investment portfolio which has ever been created, has rested on the assumption that risk and volatility are one and the same. Disagree at your peril, for if it were not true then the whole edifice would come crashing down.

As Dorothy Parker doubtless realised, people believe in dogma as much because they want to as because they have to. Most people are truly happy only when operating within a clearly defined belief system. A perfect current example of this is the continuing rejection by a large part of the world's population of Darwin's theory of evolution, despite overwhelming scientific evidence for its validity. Incidentally, Darwin, like Galileo, initially tried very hard to square his theories with what it said in the bible, for he was a deeply religious man who originally contemplated becoming a priest.

Why should this be? Well, as much as anything it has to do with the nature of dogma itself, and how it comes to be created. Dogma comes into being because a particular source of religious authority declares it to be the truth. As authority defends it more and more vigorously over time, it becomes impossible to abandon the belied without diminishing the stature of whichever religion decreed it to be the truth in the first place. This is as much an issue for the supporters of the religion, who have a deep need to believe what they have been told, as it is for the religion itself. Thus, even today in the supposedly scientific and secular twenty-first century, there are a number of religions around the world which refuse to accept it. There is even a creationist 'museum' in the United States, which portrays a model of Noah's Ark and the animals entering it.

The world of finance is much the same. E.M. Forster, in *Howard's End*, suggested that the reason why people find some of Beethoven's music so disturbing is that it hints at 'chaos and emptiness'. If so, the prospect of the fall of dogma, of a religious belief being comprehensively discredited, must strike a similar chord. The theories which one is taught collectively as traditional finance form a psychological comfort blanket. Deprived of their warm, cosy embrace then people are left having to think for themselves. Surprisingly, many do not seem to like this; on the contrary, they much prefer having a well-defined belief system drummed into them within which they can operate.

As we will see, the chief culprit here is the idea that the volatility of an asset's historical returns (the extent to which they have gone up and down over time or, more precisely, the extent to which they have varied either above or below the average) is the same thing as the risk of holding that investment. We will look in more detail at how this belief came about in Chapter 5, but for the moment let us stick to the idea of finance theory as dogma.

Let us assume for the sake of argument for the moment that this is not so (don't worry, we will see exactly *why* it is not so in due course). We have seen what the disproving of the geocentric universe threatened to do for organised religion – pretty much what the theory of evolution has threatened to do in more recent times. Well, the disproving of the 'volatility as risk' idea threatens to do much the same for traditional finance. That is exactly why the theory is defended even more robustly the more it is questioned, just as the church did with poor old Ptolemy's outdated views.

This is of course unfortunate. In an ideal world, where free speech and a spirit of academic enquiry were encouraged, then ideas could be discarded as they were discredited, and everyone could move on. In the world of science, of which many believe finance to form part, that is of course exactly what is supposed to happen, although as we will see this has been little more than a pious hope in the case of finance. Once belief hardens into dogma then one is stuck with it, but it only becomes dogma in the first place because people choose to make it so.

In the case of Ptolemy, the church authorities decreed what people were required to believe. The situation here is more complex, as indicated already. There is a sense in which, rather than being rigidly imposed by an authoritarian regime, this is something to which many people willingly submit because it is less psychologically stressful to do so than to have to face up to the possible alternatives. In much the same way there are many who choose to reject evolution, since if the religious authorities are shown to have lied about God, then perhaps this somehow diminishes the power of faith or even casts doubt on the very existence of God.

'Much the same', but not entirely the same however. There are some very practical human considerations at work here too. A glance at the shelves in any financial bookshop will reveal that there is a huge body of work, created over the years, devoted to examining and developing traditional finance theory, just as there had been centuries of writing devoted to discussing a geocentric universe. What if all this learning was to be rendered obsolete at a stroke? What if you were someone who had devoted a lifetime to studying traditional finance, and perhaps had laboured mightily to produce some weighty tome chock full of mathematical formulae? Would you really want the whole thing exploded as a myth? What of your life's work then?

Let us look at what has actually happened, and again you will see that there are uncanny parallels with Ptolemy and Galileo.

Based upon Ptolemy's basic principles, highly intelligent people built a body of knowledge which found its ultimate expression in astrolabes. Based on the 'volatility as risk' idea, highly intelligent people built a body of knowledge which found its ultimate expression in – astrolabes.

A succession of weighty stone tablets were laid down by labourers in the field of finance. Chief among them would probably be numbered the Capital Asset Pricing Model, the Miller Modigliani Model, and the Black Scholes Model. It is not important that you know what these are, still less that you know how they work. It is sufficient that you know simply that they exist. Perhaps one more thing too: no matter how mathematically complex they may be, they all depend on the belief that volatility and risk are the same thing. Kick that prop away, and they all come crashing to the ground.

It may surprise you to learn that none of these models can actually operate in the real world. It is as if they have been designed to work in a sealed cabinet in the laboratory, a cabinet which is both totally sterile and a vacuum. Break the seal and allow pesky germs and air to flood in, and the delicate mechanism falls apart.

Those who constructed astrolabes handled the embarrassing fact that things did not always work as they were supposed to by constructing epicycles and sub-rules to show that actually some bodies were performing intricate little manoeuvres of their own at the same time as orbiting the earth. It was not that they were not obeying the rules, they argued, but simply that they *appeared* not to be obeying them.

In the same way, the manufacturers of financial astrolabes handle the embarrassing fact that things do not always work as they should by building in all sorts of sanitising assumptions. It is not that the model will not work in the real world that should concern us, they argue, but rather that the real world should be arranged differently so that the models might work as (clearly) they should.

So, should you feel so inclined, if you look up any of these wonderful constructions you will find a long list of assumptions which you are required to make, since without the support of these assumptions the models simply do not work. What sort of assumptions? Well, to name but a few which you may encounter: that nobody pays tax, that everyone can borrow money at the same rate of interest, and that all investors have exactly the same level of information about each and every investment. I will leave it to you to decide just how realistic you think these might be.

There is actually a well-known psychological phenomenon at work here. Humans attempt to make sense of the world around them. This is, in fact, a very complex process, since on the one hand they can perceive the world only through their senses, and thus are not necessarily perceiving what is 'real' at all, while on the other hand they carry expectations of what reality ought to be which will be a hugely subtle synthesis of their belief systems and their accumulated emotional experiences. Any inconsistency between different perceptions of the world, or between the world as they perceive it to be and the world as they expect it to be, is called cognitive dissonance, and is a source of potentially serious inner conflict.

Research seems to suggest that we are somehow programmed to reduce that conflict by altering our perception of reality to bring it into line with what we expect it to be, since this is less stressful than being forced to change our beliefs. So, in effect, we delude ourselves. This appears to be not a conscious but a sub-conscious process. We really do believe that the altered images we are receiving are correct. It is only when the gap becomes too big a gulf to bridge in this way that we are finally forced to change our beliefs. In extreme cases, sadly, this does not occur and serious mental illness can result.

This was well understood by Douglas Adams, the creator of *The Hitchhiker's Guide to the Galaxy*, a work to which we have already referred. At one point he introduces us to a planet called Kriket, whose inhabitants believe as a matter of religious dogma that they are the only life forms in the universe. One fateful day they are given incontrovertible proof that this is not so, when an alien spaceship crash lands on their planet. Rather than amend their beliefs in line with reality however they set out to bring reality into line with their beliefs. They despatch a race of killer robots into space to eliminate every other life form in the universe.

Traditional finance does exactly the same. Faced with the fact that a model does not work as it is supposed to in the real world, you or I might say 'that's a pity, but let's work on developing one that *does* work.'

Instead they say:

> you don't understand. The problem is not with the model but with reality. If you simply adopt a different view of reality, then the model will work fine. All you have to do is pretend that lots of things which exist, don't really exist after all. See? Simple, isn't it?

There is a well-known adage to the effect that the world of journalism never lets the facts get in the way of a good story. If so, then the world of finance never lets the facts get in the way of a good assumption. Or, as a French diplomat once said to Madeleine Albright, 'ah yes, it may work in practice, but will it work in theory?'

Life would be very much simpler, and so very much more enjoyable, if we could simply assume that anything which troubles or upsets us did not exist. Imagine watching a television interview with a politician who has always particularly irritated you, and simply by saying 'you do not exist' watching him vanish from the screen, leaving the interviewer staring in bafflement and mounting panic at an empty chair. Well, this is exactly what traditional finance does.

There probably is no other way of doing things once it becomes obvious that dogma is at variance with reality. In some countries you can still imprison, torture, or even kill your citizens for daring to hold non-conformist views, but for most of the world that is no longer an option. So your only remaining options are either (1) to abandon the dogma and admit that it really is not true after all, or (2) to set out to bring reality into line with the dogma, which is where the killer robots of Kriket come into play. The killer robots of traditional finance are the sanitising assumptions which it erects around its theories like an intellectual barbed wire fence to keep nasty reality from intruding.

Whisper it who dares, but the whole of traditional finance is actually a huge confidence trick, based upon a fundamental piece of misinformation. It is tantamount to telling children that Father Christmas will creep into their room and leave presents for them, with the difference being that this is a fairly benign deception, and children can anyway be relied upon to grow up and learn the truth about Father Christmas for themselves. With finance, things are infinitely more serious. We are talking about a massive intellectual fraud on the world at large. As we will see in a later chapter, this has led to us being fundamentally mistaken as to the very nature of finance itself. We think it is one thing, but it is not; it is really something very different. This is, to say the least, troubling.

One of the most troubling aspects of all this is that there is no shadowy organisation of international villains at work here. It is not as though all the finance academics and practitioners have got together in a massive conspiracy to impose certain beliefs upon the world (unlike, one suspects, the seventeenth-century church). On the contrary, what has happened here is that highly intelligent and highly principled people have been conditioned through studying finance into thinking in a particular way. So, the worst of which the world of finance can be accused is blinkered thought processes; there is certainly no malicious intent to deceive.

We here tread upon rather controversial territory; this may have something to do with the sort of people who are attracted to a career in finance. It does seem to be the case that many of those who work in finance, and particularly in what might be called 'hard core' finance, share a certain personality type. This is now euphemistically and diplomatically referred to in the United States as a 'Type A' personality.

Type A personalities are usually very intelligent people who have felt themselves drawn to some sort of analytical study. There is a reason for this; Type A personalities crave certainty and find any degree of uncertainty disturbing. They crave control, both over their own situation and that of others; anyone who has ever encountered an obsessive micro-manager in the work environment has been dealing with a Type A personality.

They crave order and abhor any kind of sloppiness; their desktop will usually be empty apart from a neatly squared pad and a freshly sharpened pencil.

The involvement of Type A personalities brings with it a certain accepted view of finance, which we need to consider and dispel. One problem is that Type A personalities tend to believe that there is always one right answer to any question, and that this can be calculated if only one can find the right formula with which to do so. This has probably been the most pernicious of all the threads of confusion and misinformation which have run through the development of financial theory.

Another problem, which is more pertinent to our present consideration of financial theory as dogma, is that Type A personalities are very reluctant indeed to query anything. They need to have a clearly defined task. They need to work within solid, definite parameters. As an American might say, 'they don't do doubt'. They worry – Type A personalities are great worriers, and often about surprisingly trivial things, like travel arrangements – but they do not doubt. They do not question. They are history's bean counters, not history's philosophers or inventors.

Incidentally, they are also not very good at working with non-Type A personalities. If someone should ever say 'have you ever thought about whether we are actually considering the right sort of (insert whatever it may be) ...?' they would find this a dangerous and unnecessary line of enquiry. They simply would not understand the need for it, and would do their best to get rid of this disruptive influence as soon as possible. Thus, sooner or later the whole department tends to fill up with Type A personalities, who happily sit around all day sharpening their pencils and arranging their office furniture with a set-square.

You will see that this has almost certainly been a determining factor in how and why traditional finance theory has gone unchallenged for so long, and how such an immense and outwardly impressive body of learning and literature has been constructed. In an earlier book, I used the image of an Atheist Cathedral to illustrate this.

Suppose you are an atheist standing in a magnificent cathedral somewhere in Europe. All around you is beauty and grandeur. You know that some masons gave up the whole of their working lives to do nothing else but work on this building, and that they did so largely for the love of God and because, in a more superstitious age, they believed that they were greatly increasing their chances of salvation after they died. You can appreciate the artistry, the craftsmanship, the dedication.

Yet the purpose of the building, its divine purpose, its religious significance, will leave you cold. Perhaps your overwhelming feeling will be one of pity for the workmen involved, that they should have given up so much for something that really did not exist, even though they genuinely believed that it did.

This is a potent image, and an apt one. Like those cathedral masons, there are people around the world who have spent their whole careers to date working, diligently and honestly, on a mistaken premise. What they believed to be real was actually only illusory. What they believed to be their life's work to enter the kingdom of heaven was actually just hard labour to produce a huge sterile edifice.

So, our first glimpses of the world of traditional finance have been rather negative ones. We have seen that its basic concepts are not well understood, that terms are often employed misleadingly, that theory has hardened into dogma, and that the whole thing may actually be based upon a massive confidence trick. As we progress, we will be redressing the balance by pointing out where the traditional approach actually works very well, but equally it is important to understand the many situations where it does not, and what we might put in its place.

Chapter 5

Finance and its supporting pillars

Business school students around the world study a subject called generically 'finance', though specific finance modules often bear a variety of different names. Investors, most of whom have previously been business school students, spend their working lives putting 'finance' into operation. The results of their efforts, whether good or bad, then become financial data, are reported and analysed in the financial press, and become in turn the basis of study for the next generation of finance students …

So, finance surrounds us whether we practice it ourselves or not. Even if we do not, much of it will still affect us as it flows through government policy regarding spending, borrowing, and taxation. Yet more governs our personal lives, for all of us will hold at least one of a range of financial products such as insurance, a mortgage, a savings account, or a pension plan.

So much finance, yet do we really understand it? Do we even really understand what finance actually *is*? Is it a science? Is it a branch of applied mathematics (for surely it's about numbers)? How does it work? What makes it work? Do we in fact know very much about it at all?

It would be reasonable to assume that, at the very least, those who teach and practice finance must understand it, must have the answers to these sorts of questions, and yes they do. Finance, they will tell you, is indeed a science. Further, since it is a quantitative discipline based on numerical data then yes, it is indeed also safe to assume that it is a branch of applied mathematics. Literally so, since what these adepts do in practice is to apply mathematical processes to that numerical data in order to calculate the answer to any question they are posed.

To give but three examples, finance theory allows one to calculate the risk of any given investment, to calculate the present value of a stream of future cashflows, and to calculate the risk-adjusted return of any asset. Note the word 'calculate', for it is of fundamental importance. We are talking about mathematics, so it must follow that provided we have the right data, and know the correct technique to apply to it, then we can arrive at the right output; we can calculate the one right answer.

This is of course all wildly exciting (or, at least, wildly exciting to those who are capable of finding mathematics wildly exciting). Using finance theory we can impose order upon apparent chaos. We can measure and tame risk. We can render the prospect of catastrophic loss so unlikely that we can safely disregard it. Most exciting of all, finance theory allows us to predict future outcomes; it is not only a perfect and gigantic computer, it is also a crystal ball.

We will explore in due course how all this works. More importantly, we will be examining, which the world of finance itself does not, what *makes* it work, and how, and why. For we shall be seeking not the unthinking assumptions which make the teaching and practice of finance almost a matter of religious faith, but the cold, unyielding reality of the world as it really is.

It will be our mission to seek out the true nature of finance, and decide which of its teachings we can accept and which we must reject. This may seem an unusual approach to be adopting, but just how unusual you may not fully appreciate. So far as the writer is aware this is the *only* book *ever* to have addressed all these fundamental issues.

During our journey towards a full understanding of the true nature of finance we will be asking some searching questions, such as the ones set out here. Questions which may seem simplistic and yet which, as we will see, are in reality so difficult that finance academics have shied away even from asking them, let alone trying to answer them. Sadly for those who believe in academic ideals, this theme of intellectual cowardice in refusing to face up to difficult questions will run through this book like a whiff of brimstone as we examine so-called modern financial theory. Even more sadly, rather than being exposed and banished from the world's universities and business schools, such conduct has been rewarded with some of the most glittering prizes and appointments that our world has to offer.

Strong words? Perhaps, but if you will suspend judgement until the end of our journey then I am confident that you will no longer take issue with them.

What do we know about finance?

Let us start from the most fundamental level possible. Before we can answer the question 'what do we know about finance?' we first have to define what we mean by 'know'. To do this we have to look at a branch of philosophy called epistemology, which broadly put is the study of knowledge. It deals with issues such as the nature of knowledge and how it can be acquired. It therefore has relevance to every branch of human study.

Since discussion of the nature of knowledge began with the ancient Greeks it is difficult to know where to find a manageable starting point, but since we will be relying on his ideas in a slightly different context shortly, it may be convenient to begin with Kant.

In his major work, *Critique of Pure Reason*,[1] originally published in 1781, he confronts the problem of knowledge head on. For Kant, real things, be they events or objects, belong in the real world, what he calls the noumenal world, the world of 'things in (or as) themselves'.[2] However we ourselves inhabit not the noumenal world but the phenomenal world. We experience not things (noumena) but our perception of them (phenomena), as filtered by our senses and emotions. Since we can never be sure that a phenomenon is an accurate representation

---

[1] Emmanuel Kant *Critique of Pure Reason*, Penguin Classics, London 2007.

[2] 'ding an sich' since Kant wrote in German.

of a noumenon then we can never really 'know' the noumenon, which means we can never really 'know' anything.

Schopenhauer would develop this idea slightly in a rather important way. Kant's view had been essentially objective, considering knowledge of objects as they might be similarly perceived by everyone. It was this sort of 'knowledge' which he felt to be unattainable because of the distorting lens of perception. For him, a noumenon caused a phenomenon to occur.

Schopenhauer saw it rather differently.[3] For him, a phenomenon was not the causative effect of a noumenon, but rather the result of perception generated from within the self. In other words, his approach was subjective, looking outwards from the individual. A phenomenon is thus a result of the relationship between a noumenon and an individual person.

So for Kant, the fact that a perception cannot be guaranteed accurately to convey the reality of a noumenon renders the quest for knowledge futile. For Schopenhauer, this is a starting point not a blind alley. If we can experience only what the phenomenon conveys to us as individuals, then let us use that relationship between the phenomenon and the individual who experiences it as the avenue to broadening our understanding.

This distinction between an objective and a subjective view may at first sight appear trivial, or even idle semantics, but it is not; it is fundamental. As we will see when we come to consider certain key financial topics such as risk, they change completely when viewed from the point of view of the individual (investor) rather than that of the object or noumenon (investment).

Some future thinkers would go on to assert that it was only within the self that any true meaning could be found, but such matters lie beyond the scope of this book. We are concerned with the extent to which it may be possible to 'know' about real objects or events, how such knowledge may be obtained, and upon what it may validly be based.

---

[3] See his doctoral thesis *On the Fourfold Root of the Principle of Sufficient Reason, etc.*, Cambridge University Press, Cambridge 2012. Originally published in 1813. Revised and republished in 1847.

The pillars of physics

As we have seen, at first sight the situation does not appear promising. However both Kant and Schopenhauer agreed that even though we might never be certain about the exact nature of any individual thing, it was reasonable to assume certain broad concepts which might govern things in general. In shorthand, according to Kant, these are: time, space, and causality.

All things, be they objects or events, exist in time and space and are moved (in the case of objects) or made to occur (in the case of events) by causation. If you walk into a room and look at a table, then that table is fixed in both time (the moment in which you observe it) and space (its physical location). If you push the table to a different location not only has it moved onwards in time (since the clock has ticked on a second or two in the meantime) but it has also been displaced to a different physical location. Why? Because you made it move. Your push was the cause which resulted in the effect (the table moving).

These three factors are central to all thought and research in what we would term the natural sciences such as physics and chemistry. We should perhaps try to avoid use of the word 'science' at this point, since its precise meaning is contentious and will form a key subject of debate. However let us call time, space, and causality the pillars of physics, the columns which support its whole lofty edifice.

For the sake of completeness it should be noted that Einstein would later posit that the relationship between time and space may in some circumstances be different to that which earlier physicists, such as Newton, had supposed, but it has never been suggested that there is no relationship, nor that this relationship may not be used to fix an object or event at a certain temporal and spatial location.[4]

Here too, though, new thought again offered a subjective perspective. For, as Einstein pointed out, we need to consider

---

[4] See, for example, H.A. Lorentz *The Einstein Theory of Relativity*, Benediction Classics, London 2012.

not just the location of the event itself in terms of time and space but also that of the observer. If a car travels at a constant speed between two individuals, it will appear to speed up as it approaches the one, but to slow down the further it travels away from the other. So, according to Einstein, even the natural sciences may have to take account of subjectivity.

So we can see that the assumptions made by Kant and Schopenhauer about how the noumenal world is governed have been adopted as the basis of thought and research in the natural sciences and seem to work. Certainly thus far scientists have never made any observations which are inconsistent with such a view (an important qualification, as we will see).

We will return to the question of what can properly be stated as 'known', but it may at this point be useful to consider whether we might be able to think of some equivalent pillars which may prop up the world of finance in the same way that time, space, and causality support the study of physics.

Of course financial events, such as the sale and purchase of a particular stock or the granting and taking of an option, are themselves noumena or 'things in themselves', and they exist in time and space as well as obeying the law of causation, the cause being the coinciding decisions of two individuals to effect the transaction, and the effect being the transaction itself, the event. This is true, but hardly useful, since we are seeking concepts which may help us specifically to understand finance, as opposed to any other branch of human study.

Again in shorthand, it is submitted that four likely candidates might be return, risk, value, and time.

The pillars of finance

We will be considering each of return, risk, value, and time at length later in the book, but let us first note that although we will be dealing with each of them separately in different chapters this is in a sense an artificial (though necessary) approach, since both in theory and reality each operates on the others to such an extent that they are linked, and perhaps even just different components of one much larger and even more complex 'thing'.

To suggest but one example of such complexity, the French philosopher Derrida argued that what gives something its meaning is its opposite or alternative state, for which he used the French word 'différance'.[5] For instance, what gives meaning to an event such as arriving on time at the right location at the end of a journey is the possibility that you might not.

Derrida is far from an easy philosopher to read and understand, ironically since he famously believed that 'there is nothing outside the text'.[6] His remarks on 'différance' are actually made with reference to Hegel. Hegel believed that history consisted of the working out over long periods of powerful trends, each of which generated automatically its own contradictory forces, and that it was how these countervailing trends resolved themselves which represented the progress of history.[7]

Thus the traditional reduction of this dialectic process to 'thesis + antithesis = synthesis' is not strictly accurate since it goes well beyond the idea of a theoretical contradiction, and is more akin to some kind of physical struggle or even negation. However alongside his view of the working of history Hegel suggested that our view of an object encompasses things which are opposed to it so that, even if unconsciously, our sense of its identity is coloured by, or even includes these things. For example, our impression of a leopard may include in part the recognition that it is not a cheetah.

This would suggest that in order to seek to understand the true nature of the thing itself one must first strip away these opposing objects, but no, says Derrida. Far from stripping them away and discarding them we should note their existence and embrace them, for it is this 'différance' which gives meaning to the thing itself.

---

[5] Jacques Derrida *Positions*, Continuum International, London 2004.

[6] 'il n'y a pas d'hors texte'. 'Introduction to the Age of Rousseau' from *Grammatology*, John Hopkins University Press, Baltimore 1998.

[7] Georg Wilhelm Friedrich Hegel *Lectures on the Philosophy of World History*, Cambridge University Press, Cambridge 1980.

Thus in finance what gives meaning to the prospect of selling an investment for a gain is the possibility that one might instead incur a loss. Just as post-Einstein physicists have combined time and space into a single continuum called (somewhat predictably) space-time, so return and risk might be seen as inhabiting the same continuum. Or perhaps they are in effect different sides of the same coin, at least if we view 'risk' as the risk of incurring a loss, a topic to which we will return.

Such a view runs directly counter to the prevailing attitude, which sees return and risk as separate, though related, so that plotted as the *x* and *y* axes of a graph they form a grid system onto which the location of any individual asset can be mapped. Such a universe can be constructed partly because, as we will see, the world of finance attributes a very different meaning to the word 'risk' than the common sense suggestion advanced here.

We can however put definitions and causation to one side at this early stage for it is more useful to start by assessing and recording all that material which is agreed, leaving debate over more contentious matters for later. All would agree, regardless of what meaning they are ascribing to 'risk', that there is some kind of intimate relationship between return and risk.

However as soon as we move to conjecture as to what the nature of that relationship might be, common ground quickly starts to fall away. For example, can return be present on its own, without risk, its evil twin? A knee-jerk response on a common sense basis might be 'no', yet Finance World says 'yes', at least in certain circumstances.

A further problem arises if we want to consider the degree of risk relative to the same level of return in respect of the same asset. Must it remain constant for all investors? Here, by contrast, the answer 'yes' which is advanced by Finance World seems the common sense one, yet this book will argue strongly that the correct answer is almost certainly 'no'.

Even more fundamentally, can the nature of the relationship, whatever it might be, actually be understood at all, or is it simply so complex that it surpasses the power of human comprehension? You may find this a more difficult question to which to volunteer a ready answer. If it helps at this stage, finance academics have for many years believed that not only can it be readily understood, but actually easily calculated.

So really very little is agreed. There is a close relationship between return and risk, and they run together like constant interwoven threads through the whole fabric of finance and investment. Even here we must enter a qualification though, as we have already noted. Finance World's view would require a much longer sentence, ending 'through that part of the whole fabric of finance and investment where both return and risk are present together', for remember that they believe there are some circumstances in which return can exist on its own, unsullied by the presence of risk.

Either way, their status as two of the pillars of finance would surely go unchallenged by all. No matter what lofty construction of finance theory and concepts we wish to erect, return and risk must represent two of our building blocks.

Now what about value? Return comes in two broad shapes: income and capital gain. Neither of these however would have any meaning to us if they did not embody the underlying concept of value. With a capital gain we have quite obviously increased the value of an asset or group of assets from a smaller amount to a larger amount. With income, we are receiving a cashflow or stream of cashflows which likewise must add to our personal store of value, an increase which we can either lock away in the cupboard or go out and spend, possibly reinvesting it in new assets in the process. We even use value as a verb. We 'value' something when it brings us some benefit or advantage, often pecuniary in nature either directly or indirectly.

An alternative use of the verb 'to value' is to assess something's worth, as for example might be done by a professional valuer with a house or a piece of antique furniture, perhaps for tax or inheritance purposes. What the valuer is doing here is putting a number on the value: how much 'value' does the article possess? Whenever a financial transaction takes place, and probably in many more cases when a transaction is considered but does not in fact take place, the parties are each engaged in this sort of exercise, whether formally or instinctively.

So value could be argued to be in fact the prime mover which kicks off all chains of causation in the financial world. Why do we invest? At least partly because we seek to increase our personal store of value. When we move on to consider the effect of time we shall see that investment is probably done in large measure to increase our store of *future* value, to defer expenditure today in favour of expenditure tomorrow, but let us leave such discussion for later.

We have already seen enough of value to accept the principle that if we wish to understand finance, whatever that may be, then we clearly need first to understand value, whatever that may be. Without giving away too much of what is to come, one questionable assumption has already been slipped past the unwary reader as an accepted fact.

In a previous paragraph we talked about assessing how much value a particular asset might possess. Yet, as we will see, it is strongly arguable that an asset does not actually possess any finite amount of value at all, and that its 'value' is simply that which it is perceived to have by any potential individual buyer or seller of it. Thus it is entirely possible for two individuals to value the same asset differently. So, because in doing so they take into account the relationship between its own qualities and their own circumstances, and all of these can and do change, the value of the same asset to the same individual at different times may also vary.

If you were to offer the same glass of water to two men, one of whom was dying of thirst, the latter would value it more, and would therefore be prepared to pay a greater amount of money to acquire it. Yet were you then to offer each a second glass of water for which to bid, the same man would now value that glass of water less highly then he did the first, since he has now slaked his thirst, at least to some extent. We will examine in due course how economic theory deals with these issues.

All of this runs up against various problems, though, not least from accountants and regulators. Accountants have traditionally taken the view[8] that there is such a thing as 'fair value', that it can always be assessed and that, once fixed for a particular asset, it is valid for all the world. Of course, if you consider what it is they do for a living then such a view begins to make sense. If you are trying to decide whether to extend credit to a business, and take a look at its audited accounts to help you make up your mind, you do not want to see an equivocal statement next to, say, 'fixed assets' but a hard, definite amount. We pay accountants to audit accounts, including asset values, and it is difficult to see how this could meaningfully be done without firm valuation principles which result at the very least in consistency of approach.

Where such an approach does become open to question, though, is where an assumption of 'fair value' made for practical purposes gives way to a settled belief that 'fair value' does actually exist as some sort of universal truth. The very word 'fair' should give the game away here. What is a 'fair' value at which an asset might change hands must be a function of the needs and other circumstances of individual investors, and to this we must add the further complexity that each will be trying to buy or sell at a slight perceived surplus or deficit to whatever a 'fair' value might be.

Regulators, egged on by the accountants, take this questionable concept still further by insisting that assets must be 'marked to market', presumably based on an explicit assumption that the value and the price of an asset must be the same, even in abnormal market conditions or where a market is quite clearly not being allowed to operate freely. Again, this may be an understandable and even acceptable fiction to adopt for practical convenience, but seems to have hardened into a belief, a principle. One unfortunate consequence is that any assets which do not have a recognisable public market are often black-listed simply because they are not susceptible to this technique: a wonderful example of trying to bring reality into line

---

[8] Though recently debate within the profession has begun to question whether this is actually the case, at least as a universal truth.

with regulations, rather than drafting regulations which are consistent with reality in the first place.

So value too is problematic, as we will explore in more detail in later chapters. What about time, the one pillar we have not so far considered? Well, here there is at least as much lack of understanding as anywhere.

It is arguable that time is not so much a pillar in itself as a backdrop against which the other pillars may be seen operating. Certainly the natural progression of tomorrow into today and in turn into yesterday requires no explanation. In this sense, individual investments might be seen as small rafts floating along the river of time, with their individual outcomes only becoming clear when they are swept naturally ashore by the current, are somehow manoeuvred into a safe harbour by the crew, or are sunk with all hands by storm or rapids.

Yet time does more than simply offer a dimension within which the others may operate upon each other. For time is a portal to uncertainty. The future is necessarily unknowable, and the further we go into the future then the greater the span of that uncertainty must become. We would probably all be prepared to wager a significant amount of money at even odds that we would still be alive in twenty-four hours time, yet how many of us would be prepared to do the same if twenty-four years were substituted for twenty-four hours?

A doubly appropriate example, perhaps, for uncertainty exercises a powerful emotional pull on human decision making and it is perhaps our underlying sense of the coming of our own death, inevitable as an occurrence yet highly unpredictable as to cause and timing (and hugely undesirable), which acts as some sort of primal angst in which our fear of uncertainty generally is grounded. For we *do* fear uncertainty. Observe investment decision making for even a short time and you will see that there is a disproportionate dread of the future, and a correspondingly irrational premium placed on clinging to the certainty of the present. It is as if time is the slave placed by the Roman Senate in the chariot of a victorious general awarded a triumph, to whisper repeatedly in his ear, as he acknowledges the plaudits of the crowd, 'remember you are mortal'.

So accepting on a (literally) day to day basis something as straightforward as the ticking away of the hours may be simple, but understanding its impact on investment outcomes and how properly to treat it in financial decision making is not. Nor is keeping emotion out of the picture as we do so. In fact, as with all business decisions generally, emotion will frequently not just creep back into the room no matter how hard we try to banish it, but usually end up becoming the dominant factor in determining the outcome.

From those who labour within the field of behavioural finance, we know that we as emotional beings are subject to what are called cognitive biases, which affect the way in which we make decisions, though whether they do so by interfering with our heuristic methods (experience based thought processes) or by distorting our perceptions remains unclear. One of these is hyperbolic discounting, the tendency among even experienced investors when discounting a future value to apply much too high a discount factor, thus putting much too low a current monetary value on some cashflow which we are likely to receive in the future. There can only be one possible driver for such irrational behaviour: a disproportionate fear of future uncertainty.

Certainty and doubt

This emotional craving for certainty, and fear of uncertainty, plays straight into the hands of something else which is destined to play a large part in our story, namely the strange tendency of the world of finance to elevate intellectual theory to the status of religious dogma. The first, of course, can be challenged, while the latter cannot, at least not without the challenger being dubbed a dangerous heretic. Frequently too any such attempt will attract allegations of stupidity ('he just doesn't understand'), or even downright mental instability ('he's mad').

Of course this is absurd. Intellectual progress can be made *only* by challenging what J.K. Galbraith dubbed 'conventional wisdom'.[9] In fact, for Karl Popper, as we will see, it represented the fundamental basis of all scientific method. For him, progress can be made not by repeatedly proving a hypothesis, but by repeatedly trying to *dis*prove it.

As Stephen Hawking says in *A Brief History of Time*:[10]

> [a scientific theory] is always provisional in the sense that it is only a hypothesis: you can never prove it. No matter how many times the results of experiments agree with some theory, you can never be sure that the next time the results will contradict the theory. On the other hand you can disprove a theory by finding even a single observation that disagrees with the predictions of the theory.

Ignoring this essential principle, the world of finance tends instead to close ranks in defence of a series of fixed 'truths', using assumptions to wipe away any troubling spills of reality onto their neatly polished theories. It is perhaps significant, for example, that it is difficult to find even a single published academic paper over the last sixty years or so which raises fundamental doubts about the 'conventional wisdom' view of risk. It is largely in the pages of books, often written not by mathematicians but by investment practitioners, that such criticism is to be found, not in learned journals, where one might, perhaps naively, expect to come across it.

Perhaps this is due, at least in part, to yet another factor which we will consider later in more detail, namely the tendency to think of finance as being 'about numbers', as operating like mathematics, or perhaps even actually *being* a specialist branch of mathematics. If you think like this then you will believe also that aspects of finance can be 'proved' in the sense of a mathematical proof. Again this will operate as

---

9 J.K. Galbraith *The Affluent Society*, Pelican Books, London 1962.

10 Stephen Hawking *A Brief History of Time: From big bang to black holes*, BCA, London 1998.

a powerful disincentive to introduce any doubt into this cosy little world of mathematical certainty, let alone to entertain so ridiculous a notion that finance may not really be 'about numbers' at all.

So let us be under no illusions, as we embark upon our journey, that our endeavours will be welcomed with open arms. On the contrary, as finance academics around the world sit behind their massive bulwarks of false certainty, gazing suspiciously at the surrounding countryside, our endeavours to undermine their foundations will be seen not as an attempt to set them free, but rather as a subversive chiselling away at their cherished beliefs.

No matter how difficult our task may be, though, it is vital that we should pursue it. At the time of writing, much of the world is locked in a financial crisis and economic recession,[11] which has already lasted longer than the worst previously on record. Partly this is the accumulated result of mistaken policy and bad decisions by government, a theme which I explored fully in *The Mess We're In*,[12] and therefore will not trouble the reader with again. Yet this is also due partly to something which most of Finance World finds so awful a thought that it seeks to suppress it at any cost: is it not possible that we have failed to understand even the basic building blocks of finance, and in consequence have sought to rely upon rules which are themselves fundamentally misconceived?

---

[11] The word is here used in its everyday sense of flat economic growth.

[12] Guy Fraser-Sampson *The Mess We're In: Why politicians can't fix financial crises,* Elliott & Thompson, London 2012.

Chapter 6

Periodic return

In order to watch or play any game it is necessary to understand the rules. Those who take part in financial and investment transactions believe they understand the rules, because they have been taught them. Yet actually they do not understand them at all. They only know them, which is not the same thing.

To 'know' something it is sufficient if we can say what it is. To 'understand' something we have to be aware of what it means, in the light of all surrounding circumstances and issues. It may make the distinction clearer to think for a moment in literary terms. To 'know' a passage of Shakespeare it is adequate if we memorise the text so we can recite it by heart. To 'understand' it we have to be aware of the context as well as any possible subtext. Unless we are, then we may be able to record what the words are but not what meaning they are actually supposed to convey.

The context would include all the social and historical nuances which colour the passage and provide the backdrop against which it should be viewed. In his history plays, for example, Shakespeare expects his audience to be familiar with such things as the key events and players in The Hundred Years' War, as well as the various family branches of what he chose to call the Houses of York and Lancaster. It would also include the particular meaning which words had at the time. Some words, such as 'gay', have changed their meaning even quite recently, while others (including, incidentally, 'risk') had not even come into the English language during Shakespeare's lifetime.

The sub-text is also important. Today we think of this as the hidden or coded meaning which a speaker is meaning to impart such as when a Prime Minister says he or she has every confidence in a subordinate, but this can also include what Jung would have thought of as the symbolic meaning of a word. The sub-text changes with time too; when Shakespeare uses the word 'horns', a contemporary audience would instantly have thought of a cuckold, a traditional figure of theatrical fun.

This distinction is important when applied to finance, but usually overlooked. We send finance graduates out into the world clutching *Brealey & Myers*[1] in one hand and a financial calculator in the other, confident in the expectation that in the proper application of the two of them can be found all the secrets of the universe. Yet this is actually an intellectual fraud, for all that *Brealey & Myers* tells them is what they need to know to pass their finance exams, not what they need to understand properly to practice finance in the real world. It gives them the text, but neither the context nor the sub-text.

It tells them nothing of the day to day practice of investment management against which to set their new-found 'knowledge', or of the organisational and behavioural issues which frequently frustrate its application, or warp its operation. Nor does it make explicit the coded messages inherent in the financial rules they have learned. We shall explore later what these may amount to in the case of risk, but let us concern ourselves for the moment with return.

Any proper consideration of return would start with questions such as 'what is return?', 'how should it be measured?', 'for what purpose do we want to measure it, and would this affect our answer to the last question?', and so forth. Having read even this far, it may come as no surprise to learn that the possible answers to these questions are far more complex than current financial education dares to admit, that in consequence it deals with these questions largely by failing to ask them, and that our understanding of 'return' is deficient as a result.

In order to set the scene let us first note some of the key issues of which we need to be aware, and then discuss them,

---

[1] The standard text on corporate finance: Richard A. Brealey and Stewart C. Myers *Brealey & Myers Principles of Corporate Finance*, McGraw Hill, London, 7th edition published 2013.

so far as possible in isolation; 'so far as possible' because in fact they all impinge upon each other.

What are the possible forms or components of return? To what extent is it meaningful to take account of gains or losses which are as yet unrealised, or even contingent? For what time periods should return be calculated and, having done so, how might we use such periodic data? To what extent should a measure of return take into account the effect of passing time on the purchasing power of money? What can past return tell us about likely future return? How can we use return to estimate, or even calculate, risk?

That we can pose all these questions, and more, at even the most preliminary stage of any enquiry into the nature of return, suggests that we face a daunting challenge. It would be possible to devote a separate chapter to each of these questions and yet perhaps serve only to confuse ourselves, since their answers often seem to indicate different directions in which to travel, and are in any event largely meaningless in the absence of our new-found travelling companion, the context. Even then, the context would change with the different circumstances of individual investors at particular points in space-time.

It is therefore proposed to adopt an approach which is necessarily simplistic, but which will hopefully cut through the fog of linguistic and philosophical enquiry to delineate the broad structure of the debate. Let us first try to answer the question 'what is return?' which is, at least at first glance, the relatively simple part of the task in hand. We will then look at two separate schools of thought on return which are largely mutually exclusive, representing very different avenues of approach, and accounting in large part for the very different answers that can be advanced to the other questions set out here.

What is return?

Return could be thought of as the way of measuring the outcome of any investment. Let us hold off for a moment on the obvious question of 'what is an investment?', which this prompts, though it may surprise some to hear that this question is never addressed in any finance course. That is a necessary question, and one which we will examine later in this chapter, but let us keep our focus for the time being on the nature of return.

If return measures the outcome of an investment, then it must also be the measure of success (or otherwise) of any financial transaction for any party to it. Yet even this deceptively simple statement is immediately open to question.

Even in the case of a straightforward investment decision where we buy some shares from someone else on the stock market, the seller's return is clear, since they have previously bought those shares from someone else and will be able very easily to calculate their gain or loss based on the difference between the two prices. We however will not be able to do the same until we sell the shares in our turn. Thus in many cases the return of one party to a transactions will be clear, actual, and quantifiable, while that of the other will be contingent, prospective, an expectation of return in the future rather than the actuality of return today.

Again there is a deliberate over-simplification here, for return can come in two shapes, namely income and capital gain, and company shares (stocks) are an example of an asset which can produce both, so that all parties would have to take into account not only the eventual difference, when known, between their purchase price and the sale prices, but also the value of any dividends received during their holding period.

We shall examine these issues in much more depth, together with the important practical point of whether the accepted measures of return properly reflect the reality of a real life investment in the hands of a real life investor. However before we do so we should note two equally vital points which Finance World simply ignores because they cannot conveniently be fitted into its neat but blinkered view of the universe.

First, there are some investments which are not really 'investments' at all if we define an investment as something which is entered into with a view to achieving a meaningful return, and 'meaningful' as something that will tend to increase, rather than diminish, the purchasing power of our capital.

An example of this may be found in prime government bonds, at least at the time of writing. Suppose a government bond offers a yield to maturity[2] of 1.5 per cent and we buy it intending to hold it to maturity. Yet suppose also that inflation is currently running at 3 per cent: can we be said to have bought that bond in the expectation of financial return? Clearly not, since even if we are a non-taxpayer we are guaranteed to *lose* 1.5 per cent a year in real terms (in purchasing power after the affects of inflation). Why then did we buy the bond?

There are actually two possible answers, both of which give the lie to the cosy Finance World view of rational investors making investment decisions based on arithmetic calculations. After all, anyone can see that 1.5 per cent is less than 3 per cent.

One alternative is that the investor may be forced (by regulation or direct political oversight) into making that decision. Sadly this is the case with many governments and investment institutions around the world today, and I explained in *The Mess We're In*[3] why this is so.

The second is that the purchaser may not be viewing the asset as an 'investment' at all but simply as a cash substitute. For example, investors such as non-life insurance companies and corporate treasury departments may experience sudden and unpredictable demand for cash. Even long-term investors such as pension funds would be wise to keep at least some small part of their portfolio in assets which are both as liquid (capable of being turned quickly into cash) and non-volatile (unlikely to go up or down steeply in price) as possible. While neither of these issues is as cut and dried as some may believe, prime bonds undoubtedly offer the best of both these barren worlds.

---

[2] A return projected over the life of the bond including both income (interest or 'coupon') and capital repayment ('redemption' or 'maturity').

[3] Guy Fraser-Sampson *The Mess We're In: Why politicians can't fix financial crises* Elliott & Thompson, London 2012.

This clearly has huge implications for investment activity generally. If bond markets are heavily populated by forced buyers (and incidentally by central banks re-purchasing their own securities), then whatever bond buyers may be seeking, it cannot be any meaningful financial return, and therefore arguably their purchases are not 'investments' at all. Yet this hugely important distinction between investments and other transactions, which may look similar but are in fact profoundly different, is nowhere understood or even noted in the world of finance. For this reason we will, as already promised, look more deeply in due course at the question 'what is an investment?'

In addition to this important but neglected point that some supposed investment markets are used for non-investment purposes, there is a second consideration.

The financial return on an investment may not be capable of being measured. It may in fact not even be thought of or intended to be 'financial' at all, at least not in the sense of being numerical. It may be emotional. It may even be qualified, whether separately or jointly, by that even more nebulous adjective: ethical.

Two examples may assist. The first will be familiar to anyone who attends entrepreneurial events. Twenty years ago they were populated by people with ideas which they believed could address a meaningful business need and make their founder a lot of money in the process. Today a significant proportion of these people describe themselves as 'social entrepreneurs' and seek only a living wage for themselves but also the opportunity to deliver some defined social benefit. The helping of the jobless back into employment or facilitating foster care for the children of troubled families will never make those who perform these acts rich, but they do have the potential to deliver a very real emotional buzz in the form of knowing that, in no matter how small a way, you have made the world a better place.

Similarly, much investment around the world is carried out on what is usually referred to as a development agenda, particularly by bodies such as the International Finance Corporation. Here, while investment in a potential business or project is still expected to justify itself on a commercial basis, the overriding motive behind the investment will be developing the infrastructure of a country or region, and/or boosting its economic capacity. Clearly there must be some element of 'return' here which is in excess of the fairly modest financial gain that is expected to be forthcoming. The investor must receive something more, something which by definition is not capable of being expressed numerically, at least directly.

The second might take the form of an investor having to choose between the shares of two companies: A and B. A is expected to deliver a higher financial return, yet it is involved in the arms trade, or cigarettes, while B is not. If the investor chooses B on this basis, then clearly motives other then maximising financial return are at work.

The first is an example of a non-financial return, or at least a return which cannot be wholly measured in financial terms. Emotional gratification can be as important to an investor as financial gain. So, without wishing to view the activities of development investors in a cynical manner, might be political success, status enhancement, and growth in power and influence.

The second more properly belongs in our consideration of risk, since it demonstrates that there are certain types of risk, such as reputational and headline risk, which do not operate upon financial returns and thus are not themselves capable of mathematical analysis.

We have now seen various reasons why the traditional view of return is deficient. Return is actually a much more multifaceted concept than finance courses allow. It can be either actual or contingent, concepts we will shortly examine in more detail as we see how return is customarily measured. Yet in practice this important distinction is frequently just ignored.

It can consist of elements which are non-financial in nature; can we simply disregard these because they are incapable of mathematical calculation? Can it still be a valid subject for study when divorced from investment? Or is it only its capacity to measure the outcome of investment transactions and decisions which gives it meaning? For those who practice investment on a daily basis it would probably seem a bizarre notion to view it as anything other than an operator upon investments, yet this pre-supposes some universal agreement on what an 'investment' might be.

So, there are various difficulties, largely unaddressed by finance faculties around the world, in even discussing 'return' since the necessary reference points for any meaningful conversation have never been explored or fixed.

However it may at this point be helpful to begin looking at how return is traditionally viewed, for it will be seen that even within the commonly accepted methodology itself there are numerous problem areas. To do this let us look firstly at the components of return, the different forms which it may take, and then move on to how it may be measured. This will necessarily involve some limited repetition of some matters which have already been touched upon more lightly.

Return: gain and income

Simply put, return comes in one or both of two forms: capital gain and income. An example of the former would include selling a property at a higher price than you paid for it. An example of the latter would be receiving rental income from a tenant of the property. Ideally, when buying the property in the first place you may well have the hope and expectation that you will benefit from both.

Indeed property, or real estate, is a good illustration of the ability of some asset types to produce both capital gain and income. Some, such as gold, can produce capital gain but no income while others, such as annuities, can produce income but no capital gain (at least, not directly). The astute reader will already have spotted a potential problem here. If different types of assets produce different types of return, how can we find a measure of return which is equally fair to all, which is valid across all asset types? We will consider this point later, but for the moment let us simply note it and move on.

Return: realised and unrealised

Accountants and bankers are familiar with the concept of a contingent liability. This is something which might result in an obligation to pay out money to a third party, but equally which may not. We simply cannot be sure about the possible outcome for the time being. It might be dependent on whether someone such as a dismissed employee actually sues us or just goes away quietly and ignores any possible legal claim which they may have. It might be dependent on whether a particular project comes in on time and/or on budget. It might be dependent upon the proper application of a particular tax statute which is currently being disputed by the tax authorities. It might be dependent upon the judgement handed down in a court case awaiting trial.

In short, it is a loss which is subject to uncertainty of outcome, both as to whether it occurs at all and, if it does occur, then to what degree it occurs. In some areas, such as health and safety, the words 'hazard' and 'risk' are used to describe these two considerations. A hazard is something which is undesirable yet which may in fact occur, something which may cause damage. Risk is the extent of damage which may be caused if the hazard actually occurs. A hazard is the possibility that someone working on a tall ladder may fall off it. The risk of this is the degree of injury which they may suffer if they do. We could try to manage the hazard by limiting the height off the ground that a workman may operate without using scaffolding rather than a ladder. We could try to manage the risk by surrounding the ladder with rubber safety matting.

A similar situation arises in respect of gain, the capital element of return, and also in the case of its less welcome negative form, loss. Actually, we will see shortly that we often misunderstand when a gain is really a gain, or when a loss is really a loss, but let us leave that for the moment and focus on uncertainty of outcome.

Suppose that we buy some shares on a stock exchange and that by the end of the year their market price has increased by 5 per cent. Investors and tax authorities alike will claim that a gain of 5 per cent has been 'made' or 'earned', but surely this is not correct. For this is simply the capital gain equivalent of a contingent liability. We *may* have earned a gain of 5 per cent, but the only way we can know that for sure is by selling the shares today, thus crystallising ('realising') the gain by turning the paper value of the shares into cash. We now have what is called a 'cash on cash' return, which we can easily calculate by deducting the cash which we paid for the shares from the cash we realised on their sale.

Suppose however that we choose not to sell the shares today but to defer their disposal to some date in the future. We cannot say in this situation that we have earned a 5 per cent gain, but only that we *might* have done so. Just as a contingent loss is dependent on an externality, so is this gain, with the externality in this case being the market price of the share. It is entirely possible that by the time we decide to sell then the price will be still higher; by the same token, of course, it may have moved in the opposite direction. It may even have dipped below our original purchase price thus turning what we took to be a gain into a loss.

We call a gain of this kind an unrealised gain, to contrast it with the realised gain we would have made had we actually turned the shares into cash. Given what was discussed in Chapter 5 about our human instinct to shy away from uncertainty and cling to what is known, it would seem logical if unrealised gains and losses were ignored, at least as a general rule. Yet in fact the opposite is the case, and this has major implications for things such as accountancy, taxation, pension regulation, and the way in which we measure 'return', none of which are properly understood or even noted. For example, the pension regulation version of this principle, called 'mark to market', can force a pension fund to sell equities when markets plunge, thus crystallising losses, rather than to take advantage of a buying opportunity which may hopefully improve the pension scheme's long-term funding position.

Incidentally, in answer to the obvious question 'why not just sell the shares and then re-invest the cash?', there are in fact a number of reasons why this may not be a good idea. In the case of some assets, such as buildings, there may be considerable transaction costs involved as well as a likely lengthy delay while a fresh asset is found. In the case of some investors, particularly in the United States, there may be adverse tax consequences on sale and purchase. In the case of investment managers they may be wary of being accused of 'churning' (excessive levels of sale and purchase to boost associated dealing fee income).

In order further to demonstrate how we may not fully understand the nature of return, let us turn to the question of how it is customarily measured.

Periodic return

Finance works within the confines of time. When it comes to assessing return, Finance World divides time up into neat little periods and measures the return, whether positive or negative, which has notionally occurred during each such period. 'Notionally' because of course, as we have seen, it may not actually have occurred at all, but as long as its potential to occur is hovering over proceedings then that is deemed good enough.

Since what is being considered is the return which can be ascribed to a particular period of time, these measures are called periodic returns. The period in question can be anything you like: a year, a quarter, a month, even a day. Which is the appropriate length of period to choose should depend largely on what you want to do with the data. For long-term strategic decision making then annual return is customarily used. At the other end of the scale there is a technique called VaR (Value at Risk), which aims to calculate the maximum loss a portfolio is likely to suffer in any one day, and here, naturally enough, daily return is employed. Whether VaR actually tells an investor anything which it is remotely useful for them to know is, sadly, another matter.

Periodic return is the basic building block of Finance World. On its supposedly sure foundations are built a whole array of elaborate models, each gravely proclaiming the truth about some aspect of investment theory, and together reassuringly buttressing the great comforting lie that in financial matters there is always one right answer, and that it can be calculated provided only that you choose the right model to use and have the appropriate inputs to allow it to function.

So ubiquitous is periodic return, in fact, that there is a natural tendency to assume that all return figures with which you are presented are periodic in nature, and annual in particular. As we will see, this gets in the way of a deeper understanding of return because, even when somebody does make the effort to look at return differently and calculate it in a way which arguably more closely approximates to investment reality, most inhabitants of Finance World do not even notice that this has happened. They expect a return figure to be periodic and so they instinctively assume that it is. Even where there may be some dim recognition that something here is different, there is still a residual tendency to assume that even if this is not a periodic return measure, then it must nonetheless behave like a periodic return.

We will deal in due course with what these different lines of approach might be, but we must first look at how Finance World handles return which runs across more than one period.

Let us start by stating a truth which is so obvious that its significance is widely ignored. A periodic return number says nothing at all about what occurred before the period in question began nor what occurred after the period in question came to an end. An annual return for 1955, for example, relates only to what happened in the calendar year 1955 and says nothing about either 1954 or 1956. The importance of this oversight will become clear when we move on to discuss concepts such as compound returns.

Two things flow from this basic principle. The first is that if we are looking at a large number of periods then any one periodic return can have only a marginal impact. For example, if we are looking at annual returns between 1946 and 1995 then we have fifty different annual return figures to consider, and so any one of them will be insignificant in itself in influencing the outcome of whatever it is we are seeking to calculate. The second is that we need to find some way of expressing what happens not just within one single period but across a whole number of consecutive periods. This is where we meet annualised return.

Annualised return

Let us suppose that we are looking at the periodic returns of ten different years, perhaps the performance of a particular share, or market, or portfolio between, say, 1970 and 1979. How might we take these ten annual returns and turn them into some sort of measure of return across the whole ten year period? Well, yes, there is an obvious and easy way of doing this, and yes, Finance World gratefully adopts it. We simply calculate the average return by adding up all ten single year returns and then dividing the resulting number by ten. This average becomes the 'annualised' return. The next time you are reading an advertisement for a particular investment product and there is mention of an annualised return, this is almost certainly what you are seeing.

With the exception only of bonds, this methodology of averaging periodic returns is universally employed by Finance World to measure returns across different periods. There are in fact a number of fundamental conceptual objections to such an approach. It does not reflect the reality of an actual investor holding an actual investment. It takes no account of something called the time value of money. Perhaps most seriously, there are various asset types whose returns cannot validly be measured at all using periodic returns, and therefore this approach does not allow investors properly to assess the relative return of different asset classes. This latter point is of particular importance since, as we will see, Finance World uses periodic returns and annualised returns to measure what it calls 'risk'. Thus such asset types cannot be crammed into the narrow confines of the traditional 'risk model'.

However before we move on to consider these significant practical drawbacks there is one very important mathematical point which we have yet to note.

Arithmetic mean

What has just been described is known to mathematicians as an arithmetic mean. In everyday language that means a simple average, such as we all learn in basic maths classes at school. If we want to know the average height of all the children in the class then we simply measure each one, add up all the individual measurements, and finally divide the total by the number of children in the class.

Mathematicians have no problem with this approach when it is a matter of dealing with numbers which represent discrete values, such as the heights of different individual children. However financial return is a different matter.

Remember that periodic return takes account of contingent as well as actual gain and loss. Thus part of the periodic return, or even all of it in some circumstances, is represented by the extent to which the market price of an asset or group of assets has gone up or down. In other words, the return is measuring not so much the value of an asset but the extent to which that value has increased or decreased since the time it was last measured. It is as if we were trying to measure not the height of each child but the percentage growth in their height since we last carried out this exercise.

So we are here dealing, argue the mathematicians, not with discrete values at all but with increases or decreases in discrete values measured over time and expressed as percentages. Thus if we have made an annual return of 5 per cent what that really means is that we now have 105 per cent of what we had one year ago.

Geometric mean

For such situations a different technique is required, called a geometric mean. Here we do not add the observations (numbers) together, but multiply them. Then, instead of dividing by the number of observations we use that number of roots to effectively revere what we have done by multiplying them, just as with the arithmetic mean we used division to put the additions into reverse. This sounds complicated but really isn't, and non-mathematicians should take comfort from the fact that many calculators and all spreadsheet programs have a geometric mean function, so it really is not necessary actually to understand what the process involves (though it helps!).

Two points fall to be noted before we move on, one of which is extremely important. Let us deal with the relatively trivial one first. If you try to complete a calculation following the aforementioned methodology you will quickly run into trouble if even one of your returns is a negative number. To get around this, we express all the percentages as numbers, with 5 per cent formatted as 1.05, 6.3 per cent as 1.063, and a 5 per cent loss as 0.95. Some people have problems understanding this but don't worry, it only matters if you intend actually to carry out one of these calculations for yourself.

The important point is to understand what this process produces and what it does not, something which is commonly misunderstood by many who should know better. We are shortly to meet something called the time value of money, and many believe that a geometric mean takes this into account. It does not. You will understand this point better once we have looked at the concept of future cashflows. For now, let us just note what a geometric mean produces as its output.

All it does is to answer the question: 'if I was looking for the one multiplier which I could validly apply to each of these annual returns to arrive at the actual result what would it be?' An actual example might be helpful. Suppose that we have five different annual returns and we multiply them in turn to produce a result of 1.225 (which represents a total return of 22.5 per cent across the five periods). We now calculate the fifth root of 1.225 to arrive at 1.0414 which shows us that the geometric mean is 4.14 per cent. Yet what does this actually represent? Simply the one multiplier which, if it represented the return of each individual year, would produce the total return of 22.5 per cent, or 1.225. Let's try it:

$$1.0414 \times 1.0414 \times 1.0414 \times 1.0414 \times 1.0414 = 1.225$$
(after allowing for rounding error).

Again, it does not matter if you do not understand the maths. Understand one thing, though, for it is very important. The calculation of a geometric mean treats the return of every year in exactly the same way, as you can see from this example. Why this is so important will shortly become clear.

Chapter 7

Further reflections of return

It is the primary aim of this book to point out that Finance World has fundamentally and dramatically misunderstood the nature of investment risk. However before this can be done it is necessary to understand how Finance World calculates its own version of 'risk', and before *that* can be done it is necessary properly to understand return, because within the neat mathematical parameters of Finance World one (risk) is seen as a product of the other. Return is used to calculate risk. Remember that word 'calculate', by the way, for it is important.

We started to look in Chapter 6 at how return measures are calculated. We noted that periodic return measures are almost universal (save only for bonds, with which we will deal shortly) and that they suffer from some serious defects. We should now delve into these problem areas a little more deeply, since one of them will lead us naturally to consideration of a totally different way of viewing return.

Periodic return measures do not reflect investment reality

In Chapter 6 it was suggested that periodic return measures do not reflect the reality of a real life investor holding a real life investment. Since the main purpose of finance theory is to guide investors in the decisions that they make, this should be seen as a fundamental flaw. The first limb of this contention, that periodic return does not reflect reality, is in turn composed of two different yet closely related points.

First, periodic return measures force us to take account of contingent gains and losses as well as actual. They treat things which have not happened and may never happen as though in fact they have happened. They take outcomes which are as yet uncertain, and cast them in stone.

Second, they are inconsistent with how an investor views the holding of an asset, or at least how an investor *should* view the holding of an asset. It has been accepted for many years that the value of any corporation, and therefore logically any share in any corporation, is dependent upon the cashflows which the business will generate in the future. These are of necessity uncertain, and require the use of projections based on sensible assumptions, but the principle is not in doubt. Yet periodic return measures prefer notional gains and losses over cashflows.

The first point was deliberately stated very baldly so as not to confuse the issue by having to hedge it about with all sorts of qualifications. It should be conceded at once that there are some situations where little harm is done by using them, or even where we have no effective alternative. What *is* harmful is that people use periodic return measures without stopping to think about the various contingent elements which go into their preparation.

There are two main types of situation where the use of periodic return is fairly unobjectionable. The first is where there is an absolute requirement to plug a number into something as at a particular date. The second is where an investor has a genuinely short-term time horizon.

If you need to prepare the accounts of an investment company, or a pension fund, or measure the performance of an investment manager, then it is all very well being intellectually pure and saying 'but we don't know yet what the final outcome will be; we'll let you know when we sell' because that simply is not an option. There is a need for a figure today, often as a legal or procedural requirement, and the only number that is both available and appropriate is normally a periodic return.

The 'mark to market' provisions of accounting standards and pension regulations would be a case in point. If a public market exists for an asset then it is difficult to see how a photograph of its formal valuation at a particular second in time could be taken except by using the market price. This is both valid and understandable. Where things have gone wrong, particularly in the world of pensions, is not that people have got the 'how' of asset valuation wrong, but rather that they have concentrated on the 'how' and ignored the 'what' and the 'why'. Producing numbers for a statutory audit is one thing. Using them unquestioningly as a basis for planning investment strategy is quite another.

Even here, though, there are a couple of important caveats. Where a number of periods (usually years) are available for review rather than just one, then it is no longer necessarily the case that only periodic figures will be available and appropriate. We shall be looking shortly at a totally different way of calculating return which gives a much more valid guide to performance across multiple time periods.

Also, even where only a single period is under review, caution should be used in applying periodic return as a measure of manager performance. Return may vary widely from one year to another, and what is important is not so much what return has been achieved, but how and why. What decisions did the manager make, what assumptions were these based upon, and in each case were these good or bad based upon what was known (or should have been known) at the time?

Having stated the two elements of the issue separately (contingent return versus cashflows) let us now roll them back into each other and consider the situation more broadly. How does, or should, an investor view the holding of an investment? It is difficult to answer this without touching on the question 'what is an investment?', which is being held back for later, but let us adopt the accepted view that the value of any business is the present value of its future cashflows. In other words, we calculate the value to us of notionally receiving today all the future cashflows stretching out along the timeline into the distance (future).

Yes, of course this is itself a highly artificial exercise. Calculate what we like, the reality is that we are not going to receive those future cashflows today, and anyway any M&A practitioner knows that you can play tunes on the valuation model just by tweaking the discount rate, or changing a few assumptions, or the date on which a terminal value is calculated, or the way in which it is calculated. That is not important to the argument. It is not suggested that any figure for 'value' which is in any sense true, correct or unimpeachable can be identified in this way. It is however contended that the basic principle holds true: in theory, the value of any business, and thus of its shares (equities) is the present value of its future cashflows. Incidentally, this principle is also universally accepted in the case of bonds.

If so, then why should other asset types be any different to equities and bonds? Do investors have a different objective in mind when investing in real estate, for example? There may well be all sorts of considerations such as diversification, inflation hedging, and portfolio diversification, but the basic principle surely remains the same. The investor is hoping that the real estate will generate future cashflows in the form of a lump sum when it is sold, and rental income in the meantime. So with real estate just as much as with equities and bonds the investor is, or should be, viewing the asset which they hold as a stream of future cashflows. The same holds true for all the other main asset types such as private equity, hedge funds, infrastructure, and commodities. Even those, such as gold, which do not generate income still represent a future cashflow which the investor can choose to access at any time by selling the asset.

How sensible is it, then, to use a return measure which takes contingent gains and losses into account rather than just actual cashflows, particularly where we have a choice?

The second limb of the argument that periodic return does not reflect investment reality is that it takes no proper account of time. Remember, we noted in Chapter 6 that by definition an annual periodic return takes no account of anything that happened before or after the year in question. Remember too, we noted that in calculating a geometric mean we effectively assume that each year should be treated in the same way. These are vitally important points, for no periodic return measure, not even 'annualised' returns take account of something called the time value of money.

The time value of money

If given a choice between receiving some cash today and receiving the same sum in, say, a year's time, we would all prefer to receive it today. The reason is partly uncertainty (I may be dead in a year's time), partly inflation (it will buy less of anything in a year's time), and partly that if I have the use of the money for a year I might reasonably expect to be able to increase its value through investment.

In other words, in the case of two identical cashflows, say of $100 each, the value of the present cashflow is greater than the value of the future cashflow. That may sound illogical, so let us clarify things a little. The nominal value of each is the same; each is a $100 bill. So how can one be worth more than the other?

What we are talking about here is the present value in each case, the value today. The value to us in having a $100 bill today is obviously $100, because we can take it straight out to the shops and buy $100 worth of groceries. The value to us today of receiving $100 in a year's time however is less.

There is an easy way to test this. If someone offered you something less than $100 for the bill in your hand today, would you accept it? No. If they offered you something less than $100 now for the right to receive that other bill in a year's time instead of you, would you accept it? In principle yes, depending on whether you thought it was a fair offer.

This is a very fundamental principle of finance theory and is indeed one of the first things that finance students are taught. We can actually calculate the present value of any future cashflow mathematically, by discounting the future value by some percentage rate (the discount rate) though this is not nearly so scientific a process as Finance World would have us believe, since we can choose which discount rate to use, thus introducing a subjective element.

So far, so good. We can discount a single future cashflow back to a present value, the value to us today of receiving that cashflow on its appointed date in the future. We can even do this for cashflows which are due to occur many years into the future. When valuing leasehold reversions, for example, it is sometimes necessary to discount for periods in excess of 100 years.

Where multiple cashflows occur things become a little more complicated, but the basic principle remains the same. We apply exactly the same discount rate to each cashflow and simply run the calculation to arrive at its present value. Then we add up all those individual present values to arrive at the Net Present Value (NPV). This is the value to us today of receiving all those future cashflows on their appointed dates.

Remember that we are assuming that the value of any investment is the present value of its future cashflows. Thus discounting offers us a way of arriving at a valid value for any asset. The only snag is that the cashflows which we receive from an investment during the holding period can be unpredictable. The most extreme example of this is probably a private equity fund, where the cashflows are completely unpredictable both as to their amount and as to their timing. In such a case we can only sensibly calculate anything based upon them in retrospect, at the end of the holding period based on the cashflows which actually occurred.

In other cases, and bonds are a good example of this, the cashflows are perfectly predictable, provided only that no default occurs. A straightforward ('plain vanilla') bond is effectively a loan note, promising to pay the holder a fixed sum on a fixed date ('redemption' or 'maturity') and fixed interest payments ('coupon') in the meantime. The discount rate which we choose to use for our calculations will reflect things like prevailing interest rates and inflation expectations, as well as any perceived default risk. In the case of 'prime' government issuers, such as the United States, the United Kingdom, Germany, and Japan, that default risk is treated as being zero, believe it or not. This is the fabled 'risk free' rate.

So the NPV of a bond will be the same as its market price. The only way this could not be true would be if someone disagreed with the discount rate that was being used, in which case they would perceive the market price as being too low or too high, and would buy or sell the bond in the market as appropriate. Thus a bond is a classic example of the principle that any investment is worth only the present value of its future cashflows, and of the use of discounting in calculating that value (the NPV).

If only there was a way in which we could calculate a return, rather than simply a present value, using discounting of future cashflows. Well, of course there is: the Internal Rate of Return (IRR). An IRR calculates the percentage compound return which an investor will make by receiving a specified stream of cashflows from an asset, treating the initial purchase of the asset as a negative cashflow (since we have to pay money out to buy it). For those who have not studied finance, it uses exactly the same technique and simply finds by a process of iteration the discount rate which, if applied to every cashflow, produces an NPV of zero.

Two important advantages which an IRR has over an annualised return are immediately apparent: first it looks at the actual cashflows of an investment, and second it takes into account the time value of money. There are others which will be mentioned shortly.

There are those who claim that a geometric mean takes into account the time value of money. This is incorrect. It may take into account the fact that the return of each year is based on the outcome of previous years, but it does not take into account the time value of money. Consider for a moment the situation of a cashflow which occurs in year ten of the holding period. If we are discounting by, say, 10 per cent then the present value of that cashflow will only be about 38.5 per cent of its nominal value. Good news for our IRR if it is a negative cashflow, not so good if it is positive. For this reason if you take a series of cashflows and simply change the order in which they occur while keeping their amounts the same, the geometric mean will be largely unchanged, while the IRR will go up and down.

So the IRR reflects the time-adjusted values of the actual cashflows as they actually occur, whereas an annualised periodic return does not. If we believe that the value of any asset to any investor is the present value of its future cashflows, then if we are looking for a meaningful measure of return surely IRR fits like a glove, while periodic return falls by the wayside.

As already pointed out, discounting and cashflows have always been used to calculate both the price of a bond and its yield to redemption, the former being its NPV and the latter the IRR of its remaining cashflows, treating the price of the bond to buy it today as an initial negative cashflow. Yet how many people, even within Finance World, really register that this is the case? Such is the tyranny of periodic return that many believe that the yield of a bond is some sort of annualised return.

The fact that compound returns are in common usage for bonds raises the obvious question of why they have not been adopted for other assets as well, since they seem so closely to reflect investment reality. There is one possible answer to this, which is that, as we will see, Finance World has fixed upon a particular definition of 'risk' which can only be calculated by using periodic returns. No periodic returns, no 'risk'. No 'risk', no Finance World. Oh dear.

Investment time horizon

Time plays a part in another way too. Investors lose sight of the fact that most of them are, or should be, investing for the long term. Investment strategy is about identifying and analysing your liabilities and matching their profile with that of your portfolio. Liabilities are future outflows, while assets are future inflows. The bulk of the world's investors are pension funds, sovereign wealth funds, or life insurance companies. All of these have long term liabilities which are in addition highly predictable, thanks amongst other things to actuarial analysis. Some, such as non-life insurance companies and banks, are not, but the overwhelming majority are.

Not only are they long term, but they usually do not recognise just *how* long term their approach should be. Failure to realise this results in, among other things, under-allocation to long-term assets such as infrastructure, private equity, and real estate. In large part this confusion is driven by unintelligent regulation which tends to focus on liquidity (the ability to turn assets quickly and easily into cash in an emergency) which only really has any relevance to short-term investors, whose liabilities may erupt suddenly and unpredictably. However this failure on the part of investors and regulators alike properly to understand the nature of long-term investors should not obscure the facts. For example, research has shown that Warren Buffett's investment vehicle Berkshire Hathaway has an average holding period of twenty years, and even this figure may be artificially too low as the analysis could be distorted by an unusual number of trades in 2007 as various stocks were sold following the departure of a portfolio manager (in thirteen different years there were no disposals at all).[1]

Thus while there may be some uncertainty about precise numbers, and while regulators act as if this were not in fact the case, it is self-evident that the bulk of the world's large investors are, or should be, long term in their investment outlook, and twenty years may be a representative time horizon for at least some of them.

Given this, is it really meaningful to look at periodic returns, even when 'annualised' over twenty years or more? Given that annual returns can fluctuate widely from year to year, particularly for equities which are most investors' asset class of choice, and given that they include notional gains and losses caused by market movement, is it really meaningful to look at average returns, no matter how calculated, when there is a much better alternative available, namely an IRR? An investor looking to hold an investment for twenty years should be relatively unconcerned about whether its market price goes up or down from year to year. What *should* concern them is the compound return which they will earn from the cashflows generated by that investment over the entire holding period, and a periodic return simply cannot measure this whereas an IRR can and does.

[1] Jacob D. Benedict 'The Warren Buffett Paradox' AMI Investment Management White Paper, 2010. Available online at http://www.amiinvestment.com.

Again, the time value of money should be at the forefront of our thinking. If we are planning to hold an asset for twenty years then whatever happens in eighteen or nineteen years from now, be it good or bad, will be of relatively little consequence today, whereas what happens this year and next will have much more impact on our overall return. The present value of a cashflow due to occur in year nineteen will be very low.

When making decisions, investors recognise the importance of the time value of money. Indeed, as we note elsewhere, they are prey to a cognitive bias called hyperbolic discounting, which causes them to go over the top in this regard because of their fear of uncertainty, so that they not only discount future cashflows, but discount them to a much greater extent than may be justified by logic and financial theory. So how does it make sense for them to use as a yardstick for their ultimate success or failure a measure of return which pays no regard to the time value of money at all?

Invalidity of periodic returns for some asset types

Another shortcoming with periodic return is the difficulty which it encounters in properly expressing the returns made by certain types of assets. The best known example of this would probably be a private equity fund, and the most extreme case within that example would be an early stage venture capital fund, where no clear picture of asset valuation may emerge for eight to ten years, or even longer. Any attempt to calculate an annual return, even if done with best of intentions, might satisfy international accounting standards but would be entirely meaningless from an investment management perspective. Though it lies beyond the scope of this book, there are also almost insurmountable difficulties caused by the way in which private equity funds, and in particular their capital flows, are structured.

Once again, though, IRR rides to the rescue. While it may be a nonsense to try to assess the value of the assets within the fund, it is a simple matter to measure its cashflows. While admittedly some sleight of hand is still required during the life of the fund,[2] by the end a definite and indisputable compound return can be calculated. In other words, IRRs allow us validly to compare the performance, especially the long-term performance, of all different asset classes directly against each other, something which is not possible under the existing system, since asset types such as private equity funds simply cannot be shoehorned into the traditional 'risk model'.

So why use periodic return measures at all?

From what we have seen so far, it is very difficult to justify the use of periodic return as the default measure of investment outcomes. It does not seem fully to reflect the reality of how real life investors approach and view real life investments. It takes into account contingent gains or losses rather than being based solely on actual cashflows. It takes no account of the time value of money. There are certain asset types for which it is widely acknowledged that it is at best a very poor measure.

The only possible excuse for its continued use would seem to be that there is no viable alternative available, yet we know that not to be true. Discounted cashflow measures such as NPV and IRR answer all the problems we've referred to, and moreover are already in use for bonds, instruments which make up a very large part of the world's capital markets.

So why on earth would anyone want to use what seems to be a clearly inferior and unsatisfactory approach when a much better one is freely available? The answer has already been given in passing. Finance World has seized upon a definition of 'risk' that can only be calculated by reference to periodic return. Thus if periodic return were to be abandoned, or even discredited, as a measure of investment outcomes, then the very foundations of Finance World would begin to tremble and collapse.

---

[2] In assuming that remaining assets can be turned into cash at their book value.

It is time now to turn our attention to the concept of risk. However before we do so let us examine exactly how Finance World uses periodic return to calculate risk. In the interests of cogency we will not at this time venture into any of the intellectual background as to the validity of this approach. We do however need to understand how it is done, and what it represents.

Using periodic return to calculate risk

We have seen already in this chapter how a series of periodic annual returns can be 'annualised' by being turned into an average. Let us ignore for our present purposes whether this has been calculated as an arithmetic or geometric mean. All that matters is that it is an average.

At the risk of stating the obvious, an average is a calculated number and will therefore not also appear as one of the observations (the individual annual returns) itself. Suppose we wanted to examine a twenty year period. We would have twenty-one values to look at once we had finished the calculation: the average and the twenty individual annual returns.

Let us assume that we wanted to plot these numbers graphically on a horizontal axis. The lowest, which would almost certainly be a number less than zero (a loss for the year), would be to the far left and the highest would be to the far right. Depending on which period and which asset type we are looking at, the results might be clustered fairly tightly in the middle of the plot, or spread widely. It is this degree of dispersion which Finance World measures and uses for its own purposes as 'risk'.

First you draw a line down the page at the point on the scale where the average occurs. All the remaining numbers will now be to the right of the average (above average) or to the left of the average (below average). By the way, the technical word for an average is a mean (as noted in Chapter 6), and if you ever hear anyone mention 'mean dispersion analysis' or 'dispersion from the mean', then this is what they are talking about.

The way in which the analysis works sounds complicated, but really isn't. You look at each observation and measure its value relative to the average. For example, if the average return is 5.6 per cent then an observation of 7.2 per cent would be recorded as 1.6 per cent, because $5.6 + 1.6 = 7.2$, while an observation of 4.0 per cent would be recorded as -1.6 per cent, a negative number because it sits not above the average but below it. Now we add all these numbers together, just as if we were calculating a simple (arithmetic) mean.

This is where the slightly tricky bit comes in. Because some of the numbers are negative and some are positive they will largely cancel each other out if we simply add them all together, and we will end up with a very small number. We get around this problem by squaring all the numbers before we add them up. This has the effect of making them all positive since if you multiply two numbers which both have the same sign (whether positive or negative) you will always get a result which is a positive number. Having squared them, we then add up all these numbers. The result of this simple addition exercise is something called *variance*, which is a measure of dispersion, the extent to which the observations either cluster around the mean (low dispersion) or spread out widely (high dispersion).

However because we squared all the values to get rid of the minus signs we now have a very large number for variance. To make this easier to handle we take its square root, thus reversing what we did before. The resulting number is the *standard deviation*, and it is as standard deviation that 'risk' is most commonly expressed.

It is not important that you fully understand how this process works, as long as you understand what it is that is being measured. Finance World sees the risk of an investment (other than a bond which we will deal with separately) as being the same thing as its standard deviation, which is a measure of how closely or otherwise its historic periodic returns cluster around the mean (average).

We colloquially call this volatility, which refers to the extent to which the annual return tends to change, or go up and down, from year to year. Hence the expression 'volatility as risk'. If its returns fluctuate within a narrow range the asset will be seen as a low risk investment. If they vary widely from year to year it is seen as high risk.

There are two additional elements to this which should be mentioned for the sake of a fuller understanding. First, there is something called the *Sharpe ratio* which measures the rival attractiveness of different investments by looking at excess return (the return earned in excess of the risk free rate) relative to the standard deviation of that excess return. This is a basic analysis tool for portfolio and asset allocation purposes and is in daily use in investment firms around the world.

Second, it is possible to use the standard deviation to predict the range within which future outcomes will occur. Statistics theory holds that if normal distribution (a nice bell jar shape with most observations clustering around the mean, and becoming more infrequent the further away from the mean one travels) applies, then one can predict with 95 per cent confidence that all future mean outcomes will fall within just under two standard deviations plus or minus the average.

So let us recapitulate what we know about the way in which Finance World approaches the risk of any investment other than a bond. First, it has nothing to do with the chance of losing money, or at least not directly. It is concerned solely with measuring the range of possible outcomes, the extent to which returns might fluctuate. It is common to apply the word 'volatility' to describe this, though it has a more specific scientific meaning.

Second, it is a calculated output derived from a mathematical process. It is the 'one right answer' so beloved of mathematicians. Unless you make a mistake with the calculations then the only way the number can change is if any of the input data change.

Third, it relies on certain assumptions holding true, the most obvious being that normal distribution will always apply to investment returns, and that the past is a good guide to the future. Less obviously, it also relies on the assumption that periodic returns are a valid measure of investment performance.

There is a great deal more that we could discuss about this view of risk, and we will do so in later chapters. It will probably come as no surprise to hear that all three of the statements that have just been made about Finance World's perception of risk are, at the very least, open to serious doubt.

However before we move on to consider risk, let us round up our consideration of return. We have seen that return can be either positive or negative and can be used as a measure of investment outcomes. Seeking out positive return is the main objective of investment activity, though we shall examine this statement more closely in a later chapter. Some return may be non-financial in nature, or at least not capable of precise mathematical calculation.

There is clearly a relationship between return and risk, though at this stage of our discussion it is as yet unclear what this may be. Finance World however is not so reticent. It believes that return, and specifically periodic return, can be used to calculate risk. In practice, this view gives rise to a belief that there is some sort of direct relationship between 'volatility as risk' and return, and that higher levels of return can only be sought out by accepting higher levels of 'risk'.

We have seen that, with the significant exception of bonds, periodic return measures are in universal use, while compound measures such as IRRs are ignored. That this should be so seems curious, given that IRRs reflect real life investor mind-sets, take account of the time value of money, and allow full comparison of all asset types against each other, whereas periodic returns do none of these things.

It seems that we have some understanding of what return is in general, but it is less clear that in practice we understand the precise nature of periodic return, the differences between periodic and compound return, or the reasons for choosing one over the other.

Bonds

As we have seen, bonds are essentially loan notes, paying back an agreed capital sum ('redemption') when the loan period comes to an end ('maturity') and making agreed interest payments ('coupon') in the meantime. Rather curiously, they are viewed by Finance World in a way which is completely different from the treatment which they accord to equities (shares). Even more curiously, this obvious anomaly has never been justified, and is frequently overlooked.

Bonds generate a stream of cashflows: coupon payments and a final redemption payment. Shares offer a stream of cashflows: dividend payments and a final distribution on the winding up of the company either through insolvency or because its business has been discontinued. Of course in practice most investors buy and sell shares disregarding the distribution rights because in practice most public companies do not go bust, and evolve and refine their business models, just as many investors buy and sell bonds in the public market during their lifetime rather than taking them when they are issued brand new, or holding them until maturity. Yet this should not disguise the legal theory which lies beneath these market dealings.

Yes, there are differences. Bond coupon payments must be made or the issuer is placed in default, whereas the directors of a company have a discretion whether to pay a dividend or not and, if so, how much. Bonds are treated as debt on a company's balance sheet whereas money subscribed for shares is treated as capital. A bond has a fixed redemption date whereas a share is open ended. Yet both represent a source of cashflow to an investor.

Even though shares are bought largely with a view to capital gain, there is much research which suggests that it is dividend income, and its reinvestment, which is actually the main driver of long-term equity performance. Some stock exchanges have started to offer 'total return' indices in recognition of this. Capital gain is all very well, but ultimately meaningless unless and until converted into a cashflow by a sale of the shares.

So if both asset types represent a stream of cashflows to an investor, why does it make sense to use compound returns for one (bonds) but not for the other (equities)? Why should one asset type be assessed on actual cashflows and by reference to the time value of money, and not the other? Furthermore, if this is in fact the case, then how can we validly compare their returns against each other?

Once again we are brought back to the same puzzling question. If a demonstrably better alternative exists, why is it not employed instead of periodic return, or at least offered alongside it? Even more puzzling is the question of why nobody is even discussing this. It's as if Finance World, having chosen a defective definition of 'risk', based upon a deficient return measure, is unwilling to allow criticism of the latter since this would inevitably undermine confidence in the former.

Talking of risk, Finance World has also decided to adopt a totally different definition of this to apply to bonds, albeit this time a very sensible one. Since a bond represents the right for the holder to receive coupon and redemption payments from the issuer, then clearly the risk to the holder is that the issuer may default at any time at or before maturity, and it is exactly this 'credit rating' which professional ratings agencies attempt to assess.

However how does it make sense to have these two different views of 'risk' in use at the same time? If we look at bond yields and prices (the two vary directly but inversely against each other) within themselves they have been very volatile in recent decades, so how is it logical to take volatility into account when reviewing equity returns, but not when looking at bond returns? Similarly, if the entitlement of a shareholder is to receive dividend and distribution payments, then how is it logical to ignore the 'risk' that the company may not be willing or able to pay these?

In fact, as we will see in later chapters, both these views of 'risk' are impossible to accept, but that is not the point. According to Finance World finance is a science just as much as physics or mathematics. How can it be scientific to have two different views of risk in use being applied to assets which produce similar benefits, particularly when the two are sometimes used together without any attempt to explain how or why?

There is, for example, something called the equity risk premium which looks at the additional 'risk' involved in investing in equities rather than holding bonds. As you might expect, it does this by using the bond rate, the fabled 'risk free' rate, as a comparator. Yet the 'risk' of an equity is seen as volatility of historical periodic returns, whereas the 'risk' of a bond is seen as the chance of issuer default. How can it possibly be valid to compare these?

Hopefully by this point you will already be troubled by how little we seem to understand key concepts such as return and risk, and by how much we have accepted without question from the sages of Finance World which seems to start falling apart as soon as we subject it to rigorous examination. However it is now time to take a step back.

In his 1959 preface to *The Logic of Scientific Discovery*[3] Karl Popper praises what he calls the 'historical' method as a way of approaching any problem for the first time, namely reading what other people who have approached the same problem in earlier times have had to say about it:

> If we ignore what other people ... have thought in the past, then rational discussion must come to an end, though each of us may go on happily talking to himself ... No doubt God talks to Himself because He has no-one worth talking to. But a philosopher should know that he is no more godlike than any other man.

So in embarking upon our journey in quest of the meaning of risk, let us begin by looking at what distinguished writers from the past have said about risk in the hope that their thoughts may offer us some signposts along the way.

[3] First published as *Logik der Forschung*, Verlag Julius Springer, Vienna 1935.

Chapter 8

Thoughts on risk (pre-War) and the influence of logical positivism

A study of the available literature on the nature of investment risk breaks down very neatly into two historical periods, the first before the Second World War, and the second after it. In fact the crucial breakpoint came, as mentioned earlier, in 1952 with the publication by Harry Markowitz of an article which has not only since achieved cult status within financial circles, but has been elevated by Finance World to the status of religious dogma. It is however apposite to talk of these periods being pre-War and post-War since, in the view of at least one influential writer, it was the experience of the Second World War which created a whole new zeitgeist within which the thinking behind Markowitz's paper would take root and go on to flower. We will review both periods, and see that very different views about the nature of risk were expressed prior to the War from those which gained currency following it.

Briefly, while before the War there was eager discussion as to what risk might be, and whether it was the same thing as uncertainty, there was total agreement that whatever it was it was probably too complex an animal ever to be fully understood and, in particular, that it was incapable of mathematical calculation. After the War this view was simply quietly abandoned and ignored without ever being refuted, or even discussed.

Peter Bernstein, in his book on risk *Against the Gods*,[1] suggests that the reason for this sea-change in attitude had to do

---

[1] Peter L. Bernstein *Against the Gods: The remarkable story of risk* John Wiley & Sons, New York 1996.

with widespread revulsion at the horrific experience of the Second World War, which bred an attitude that international co-operation could and should be organised so as to prevent any recurrence, and so as to improve the human condition in general. This manifested itself partly in the establishment of new international organisations such as the United Nations, the World Health Organization, and the World Bank.

Partly too, though, in an attitude that every aspect of life could and should be scientifically controlled for the greater good; and of course you cannot control something if you cannot understand it, and (so scientists believe) you cannot understand something if you cannot measure it. The novelist Aldous Huxley, himself from a family of distinguished scientists, once said in a letter to his wife's lover (whom he was rather hoping might become his lover as well) that scientists simply ignore anything which they cannot calculate.

To understand something else which strongly influenced such a view, we will also examine a third source of material, which may at first glance seem to have no obvious bearing on the study of finance at all, but which is in fact not only relevant but of great importance. This is the output of a school of philosophical thought known as *logical positivism*.

Pre-War writers

Three writers who actively debated the nature of risk or who (in the case of the third) referred to it authoritatively in passing well before the Second World War were Frank Knight, Ludwig von Mises, and John Maynard Keynes. Frank Knight was an America academic whose views were treated with great respect by von Mises, an intellectual giant who dominated economic discussion (finance was not then taught as a separate discipline) in Vienna both before and after the First World War. He was the spiritual successor of Carl Menger, the founder of the Austrian School, and the mentor in turn of the Nobel Prize-winner Friedrich Hayek whose book *The Road to*

Serfdom,[2] though undeservedly neglected, was surely one of the most important works of the twentieth century.

Keynes was one of modern history's most influential and remarkable people. In addition to his work in economics as academic, writer, and government adviser, he was a successful investor, ran a theatre and a drama festival, and was also just a genuinely warm and kind human being. Sadly he worked himself to death at a relatively young age. In passing, it should be mentioned that he is also one of the most misunderstood or, depending which way you look at it, most abused and manipulated writers who has ever had the misfortune to state their views in print. I showed in an earlier book how his ideas have been twisted by politicians to arrive at a result which is completely contrary to his original intentions.[3]

Knight and von Mises were both writing during the same period. Knight's *Risk, Uncertainty and Profit*[4] ('*Risk*') was originally published in 1921, while von Mises's distinguished publication record began in 1912 and stretched for the next six decades. (Knight himself was actively publishing until the 1960s.) Von Mises references *Risk* in his own works, so it is clear he was aware of Knight's views, though he goes on to develop them in his own way. Keynes in turn references both Knight and von Mises.

In *Risk*, Knight seeks to distinguish between different types of uncertainty, and it has often been said that he distinguishes between 'risk', which is measurable, and 'uncertainty', which is not. In fact, this is an incomplete summary. He actually divides uncertainty into three categories, not two, and classifies them according to how they may (or may not) be assessed.

First, there is uncertainty which he says can be measured by a priori methods. This is a rather strange use of the term 'a priori'. All he seems to mean is empirical observation as to

---

[2] Friedrich Hayek *The Road to Serfdom*, Routledge, London 2001.

[3] Guy Fraser-Sampson *The Mess We're In: Why politicians can't fix financial crises*, Elliott & Thompson, London 2012.

[4] Frank Knight *Risk, Uncertainty and Profit*, University of Chicago Press, Chicago and London 1971.

the occurrence of a number of discrete, defined outcomes, such as rolling a die or tossing a coin. These cases are also sensible of the mathematical calculation of probable outcomes, since the number of outcomes, and their initial probability (one in six, for example), are known. It is this category which he categorises as 'risk', though he does so reluctantly since he recognises that the term contains many ambiguities.[5]

Then there is uncertainty ('true uncertainty') which can be assessed by the use of supposedly representative statistics, such as the chances of a house in a particular area catching fire in any given year. In this case, we could spend years walking the streets taking an 'a priori' approach, noting down the number of burning houses that we observe, but:

> it would be as ridiculous to suggest calculating from a priori principles the number of buildings to be accidentally destroyed by fire ... as it would to take statistics of the throws of dice.[6]

This is an important distinction. The probability of dice throws is capable of mathematical calculation (though, as he points out later, this still does not guarantee the actual outcome), whereas the chance of a house burning down is not. So far as the probability of a house being destroyed by fire is concerned, all we have to go on are statistical inferences drawn from past observation. There then follows a key passage:

> The import of this distinction ... is that the first ... type of probability is practically never met with in business, while the second is extremely common. It is difficult to think of a business 'hazard' with regard to which it is any degree possible to calculate in advance the proportion of distribution among the different possible outcomes. This must be dealt

[5] See page 20 of the 1971 edition, in which he states a preference for the phrase 'measurable uncertainty'.

[6] Frank Knight *Risk, Uncertainty and Profit*, University of Chicago Press, Chicago and London 1971, page 215.

> with, if at all, by tabulating the results of experience. The 'if at all' is an important reservation ...

For, as he goes on:

> the statistical treatment *never* gives closely accurate quantitative results.

The word 'never' (my italics) is an important one, for it is clear from the book as a whole that Knight chose his terms with great care, and was quite deliberately here making a categorical statement. In any situation other than one in which a binomial type distribution with a fairly restricted number of outcomes may be observed and the probability of outcomes calculated, a statistical approach of the mean-variance analysis type can never deliver a 'closely accurate' result. As we will see, both von Mises and Keynes concurred with this view.

Thus the later work of Markowitz and others is clearly divergent from the views of Knight, which would be adopted, though slightly differently stated, by the likes of von Mises and Keynes. This is a point of crucial importance, since the views of the Markowitz school have become not just mainstream but orthodox, while these earlier views are now entirely disregarded. There is an implicit assumption that Knight, von Mises, and Keynes were wrong, but nowhere is this argument made out. We will return to this point later, but let us be very clear from the outset what we are talking about. The pre-Second World War writers (Knight, von Mises, and Keynes) all state categorically that one cannot use a mathematical model to forecast future investment outcomes. The post-Second World War school simply ignore these views, assume without question that such models are possible, and go ahead to construct more and more elaborate versions of them.

Knight's third type of uncertainty, which he calls 'estimates' can be quickly disposed of. This is where even statistical inferences will not help you, and you are left purely with your own subjective judgement. Sometimes, he says, these last two situations may blur together where perhaps you have some statistical data but are then overlaying your own subjective assessment upon it. A good practical example of this might be an experienced investor using subjective judgement to assess in advance the likely range of returns of a twelve year private equity fund.

He also advances the interesting concept[7] that, regardless of whatever sophisticated calculation is proffered based on mean variance, the human perception of risk is essentially binomial, and will regard uncertainty of outcome as whether a particular result occurs in any given number of attempts. He does not advance any empirical evidence for this hypothesis, but it is yet another one which has been disregarded by later writers. A pity since if it could be linked with experimental data it might suggest an argument for invalidating the traditional approach to investment risk altogether.

Let us turn now to the works of von Mises, in particular *Human Action* (1949)[8] and *The Ultimate Foundation of Economic Science* (1962)[9] ('*Foundation*'). In order to understand why the work of von Mises is so important to any proper understanding of risk, it is necessary to go back one step and look at his theories of how markets work. That these should be so little known today is perhaps no more surprising than that the work of the Austrian school in general should apparently have been air-brushed from so many economics books, but they are vitally important, since if they are right, or even partially right, then the whole currently accepted basis of measuring risk comes under fundamental attack.

That this should have been overlooked by so many writers and academics is puzzling but true. Since Keynes refers to the work of both Knight and von Mises in his *General Theory* but that they subsequently disappear from view at some stage after the Second World War suggests the possibility of

[7] See, for example, page 234 of the 1971 edition.

[8] Ludwig von Mises *Human Action: A treatise on economics*, Yale University Press, New York 1949.

[9] Ludwig von Mises *The Ultimate Foundation of Economic Science*, van Nostrand, New York 1962.

a tendency on the part of later writers simply to ignore views which do not agree with their own; very human, but hardly very academic. As mentioned, Bernstein alludes to this in his book, when talking about Markowitz:[10]

> His approach reflects the spirit of the early years after the Second World War, when many social scientists set about reviving the Victorian faith in measurement and the belief that the world's problems could be solved.

By 'solved' he presumably means, or at least implies, 'expressed and calculated mathematically'.

Keynes, let us remind ourselves, published his *General Theory*[11] in 1936, whereas Markowitz's ideas on risk were first published in 1952.[12] Even one year later, Robert Heilbroner's 1953 economics book *The Worldly Philosophers*[13] makes no mention at all of von Mises. Nor does Bernstein's *Against the Gods*,[14] despite being widely touted as a definitive book on the history of risk, Todd Bucholz's *New Ideas From Dead Economists*,[15] nor even Greg Mankiw's *Macroeconomics*.[16] Yet von Mises was widely regarded during his time in Vienna as one of the leading economists in the world, and his academic protégé, Friedrich Hayek, would be reckoned for a while as second only to Keynes until he too blotted his copybook by writing things with which mainstream opinion of the time disagreed.

So just why are von Mises's ideas on how markets operate so subversive? Precisely because they contradict the whole

---

[10] Peter Bernstein *Against the Gods: The remarkable story of risk,* John Wiley & Sons, New York 1996, page 249.

[11] John Maynard Keynes *The General Theory of Employment, Interest, and Money,* Macmillan, London 1936.

[12] Harry Markowitz (1952) 'Portfolio Selection', *Journal of Finance* 7(1).

[13] Robert Heilbroner *The Worldly Philosophers: The lives, times and ideas of the great economic thinkers*, Simon and Schuster, New York 1953.

[14] Peter Bernstein *Against the Gods: The remarkable story of risk,* John Wiley & Sons, New York 1996.

[15] Todd G. Bucholz *New Ideas From Dead Economists,* Penguin, New York 1989.

[16] Gregory Mankiw *Macroeconomics,* Worth, New York 2002.

basic belief system upon which what we now regard (and teach) as traditional financial theory is based.

Traditional theory, as laid down by Adam Smith and developed by the likes of Alfred Marshall (who taught Keynes), held that investors were rational and that market prices were driven up and down by the operation of supply and demand, but largely by demand according to Marshall, who saw supply as generally static in the short term. Demand was in turn driven by marginal utility, under which market participants would seek to satisfy their most pressing needs first, being prepared to forego, as an opportunity cost, something else which they valued less highly. Assuming that a market was able to operate freely, the combined forces of supply and demand would arrive at market equilibrium, a point where supply and demand were balanced, representing a fair price at which most people in the market were willing to transact.

No, says von Mises. Rather than being willing to buy or sell something for an amount of money which they regard as equal in value to the goods being bought or sold, market participants will only exchange something for something else which they regard as being *less* valuable. Both buyer and seller must feel that they are striking an advantageous deal, no matter how slight that advantage may be, otherwise in normal circumstances (in the absence of something like high inflation) they will prefer to keep their money for future spending.

So market activity is dependent upon the value which any individual participant places upon any individual item. By definition these values are dependent upon both feelings and perception. Two different individuals are unlikely to view the same object in the same way at the same time. Nor is the same individual likely to value it in the same way at different times, particularly should their circumstances, including what else they have bought and sold, have changed in the meantime. (This runs directly counter to the assumptions that investors always act rationally, and that risk can and must be calculated objectively, both of which were seized upon as central beliefs in the new religion of Modern Portfolio Theory.)

Since human values are nebulous, variable, and often indefinable, and since market outcomes are the result of human decision making based on such values, then past outcomes cannot predict the future. Von Mises states this very firmly. For example, in the *Foundation*:

> In the sphere of human action there are no constant relations between any factors. There is consequently no measurement and no quantification possible. ... Deluded by the idea that the sciences of human action ape the technique of the natural sciences, hosts of authors are intent upon a quantification of economics ... They try to compute the arithmetical relations among various of these data and thus to determine what they call, by analogy with the natural sciences, correlations and functions. They fail to realize that in the field of human action statistics is always history and that the alleged 'correlations' and 'functions' do not describe anything else than what happened at a definite instant of time ... as the outcome of the actions of a definite number of people. As a method of economic analysis econometrics is a childish play with figures that does not contribute anything to the elucidation of the problems of economic reality.

Elsewhere in the *Foundation* he says:

> Statistics provides numerical information about historical facts, that is, about events that happened at a definite period of time to definite people in a definite area. It deals with the past and not with the future. Like any other past experience, it can occasionally render important services in planning for the future, but it does not say anything that is directly valid for the future.

This is an important thought to which we will return, so let us be quite clear what von Mises is saying here. You can only employ the techniques of the natural sciences such as physics if you can use things like empirical observation extrapolated from scientific experiments, and apply mathematical techniques to analyse the data. Yet financial data is the result not of physical phenomena but of human action, which is in turn caused by human decision making, which is sequentially prompted largely by emotion. So finance is behavioural, not physical. It is at best a social science studying human behaviour, like psychology or sociology, and can never be a physical science such as physics. It is for this reason that neither observation nor mathematical techniques can ever offer any valid universal guide to future outcomes.

For the sake of completeness, von Mises in his approach to uncertainty adopts the same sort of system as Knight, though he uses different terminology. There are, he says in *Human Action*, two different types of uncertainty. First there is Case Probability where you know the possible different outcomes, and the odds of them occurring, but are ignorant as to what the next one will be, such as when rolling a single die.

Second, there is Class Probability, for which he uses the example of a lottery in which five winning tickets will be drawn from ninety that have been sold. Here you know the odds (five out of ninety), but nothing at all about *which* five will be drawn. This is an example of what elsewhere he calls 'gambler's fallacy': just because you may be able to express the odds of a possible outcome mathematically, it does not really add anything to your decision-making skills:

> The treatment of probability has been confused by the mathematicians. From the beginning there was an ambiguity in dealing with the calculus of probability. When the Chevalier de Méré consulted Pascal on the problems involved in the games of dice, the great mathematician should have frankly told his friend the truth, namely, that mathematics cannot be of any use to the gambler in a game of pure chance.
>
> Instead, he wrapped his answer in the symbolic language of mathematics. What could easily be explained in a few sentences of mundane speech was expressed in a terminology which is unfamiliar to the immense majority and therefore

> regarded with reverential awe. People suspected that the puzzling formulas contain some important revelations, hidden to the uninitiated; they got the impression that a scientific method of gambling exists and that the esoteric teachings of mathematics provide a key for winning. The heavenly mystic Pascal unintentionally became the patron saint of gambling. The textbooks of the calculus of probability gratuitously propagandize for the gambling casinos precisely because they are sealed books to the layman.
> (*Human Action*)

If this idea that financial markets are driven by human emotion rather than mathematical factors sounds familiar, it may be because it was advanced by Keynes in no less a book than his *General Theory*:[17]

> a large proportion of our positive activities depend on spontaneous optimism rather than on a mathematical expectation ... our decisions to do something positive ... can only be taken as a result of animal spirits - of a spontaneous urge to action rather than inaction, and not as the outcome of a weighted average of quantitative benefits multiplied by quantitative probabilities.

So here is yet another highly respected economist saying, sixteen years before Markowitz's paper, that it is useless to try to use quantitative methods to predict future market behaviour. All the more puzzling therefore that future finance academics should have simply ignored such views, and tried to do precisely what their predecessors had abjured. To do so moreover without feeling any need even to justify what they were doing, regardless of the fact that it flew in the face of the writings of at least three highly prominent authorities.

---

[17] John Maynard Keynes *The General Theory of Employment, Interest, and Money*, Macmillan, London 1936.

In order to understand why this may be, it is necessary to refer back to the non-financial writers referred to already.

Logical positivism

While the true creators of the school of philosophy known as logical positivism were G.E. Moore and Bertrand Russell, it was Ludwig Wittgenstein from Vienna, for whom lack of ego was never a problem, who claimed to have perfected it with his 1918 work generally called the *Tractatus*[18] and, in so doing, to have solved every problem of philosophy, whereupon he went into extended early retirement as a secondary school teacher in Austria.

The Vienna theme was important. Much hugely influential economic work was being undertaken there and, with various discussion circles operating every evening, including the great Wiener Kreis itself, academic discussion was intense and inter-disciplinary. Russell, visiting from England, would become a regular guest member of the Wiener Kreis. Wittgenstein, though he remained determinedly distant as befitted his lofty intellectual superiority, was its most avidly courted speaker. That the economists paid great attention to what the philosophers were saying is evidenced in the fact that von Mises devoted a significant part of *Foundations* to attacking logical positivism, including 'The Fallacies of Positivism'[19] and 'Positivism and the Crisis of Western Civilization'.[20] It is thus evident both that von Mises considered positivism as having a crucial bearing on economic thought, and that he strongly disapproved; disapproved not of its basic teachings, but the attempts to stretch its application beyond what he saw as its natural borders.

---

[18] Ludwig Wittgenstein *Tractatus Logico-Philosophicus*, Routledge, London 2001.

[19] The last part of chapter 7 (out of 8).

[20] The whole of chapter 8.

Wittgenstein famously reduced his view of 'the totality of truth' to seven very short propositions, which despite being both short and hailed as brilliant, have largely defied any simple explanation by philosophy academics. There is general agreement however that he draws a distinction between what can be 'stated' (*Tractatus* was originally written in German) and what cannot. The last of the seven principles makes it clear that in respect of that which cannot be stated, we must remain silent. In other words, only that which can be 'stated' is a proper subject of philosophy.

What can be stated must be physically observable, or capable of being deduced from physical observation ('the physical world is the totality of truth') and capable of being reduced to a 'proposition', which is in turn a 'truth function'. In other words, to be true, and possessing significance or validity, something must be capable of being reduced to a logic proposition such as 'if A then B, if not A then C'. Hence Wittgenstein's often expressed belief that there are no questions, only puzzles, namely the puzzle of how to frame something in formulaic terms. This was a view with which Karl Popper would famously disagree one cold winter evening in Cambridge, prompting the volatile Wittgenstein to storm out of the room in a rage, having first waved a poker menacingly at his adversary.[21]

Bertrand Russell would himself state the principle of logical positivism more simply: you may not ask a question unless you know in advance that it can be answered. Thus '2+2=?' is a valid subject of enquiry, whereas 'what conduct is ethical?' is not.

Popper, as mentioned, firmly disagreed. He says in *Unended Quest*:[22]

> I have long believed that there are genuine philosophical problems which are not mere puzzles arising out of the use of language.

---

[21] David Edmonds and John Eidinow *Wittgenstein's Poker*, Faber and Faber, London 2001.

[22] Karl Popper *Unended Quest*, Routledge, London 1992.

The evolution of logical positivist thought mirrored a debate which had been raging within what we would today call finance and economics which, as it was waged almost exclusively in the German language, became known as the 'Methodenstreit'. On the one hand the so-called German school argued that only quantitative analysis based on hard data was an acceptable way of advancing understanding. Anything else was idle speculation. This was opposed by the Austrian school (initially represented by Carl Menger, but whose mantle was later assumed by von Mises) who said that data were frequently either not available or unreliable, and that in any event quantitative analysis could only take one so far. They believed that quantitative models could not be used to predict future market outcomes, and that conceptual analysis had a large part to play in advancing knowledge, as did subjective assessment in financial decision making.

Von Mises saw this as a clear case of trying to apply the methods of empirical observation and quantitative analysis of the physical sciences to areas to which they had no application, namely human behaviour and financial uncertainty.

He points out the folly of contending that only that which is measurable may validly be studied. Positivism, he says:[23]

> is not remarkable for that which it contributed, but for that which it wants to see prohibited. Its protagonists are the champions of intolerance and of a narrow-minded dogmatism ... it is the task of epistemology to unmask the fallacies of positivism and to refute them.

Knight, von Mises, and Keynes would all have been acutely aware of the 'Methodenstreit' and of logical positivist thought. They would also have been very aware of the importance of the intellectual stand which they were taking. All of them were arguing strongly against the validity of reducing financial thought to a system of mathematics. Yet somehow, silently and without their arguments ever having been shown

[23] Location 1922 of the Kindle edition.

to be false, positivist thought triumphed completely, to such an extent that after the Second World War writers did not even feel it necessary to acknowledge the existence of the contrary view, much less show how they might refute it.

The influence of the logical positivists is not widely understood today. While the name Wittgenstein would be widely recognised, the nature of his philosophy would not. This is richly ironic, for right at the end of his life Wittgenstein came out of his self-imposed exile to write a book, *Philosophical Investigations*,[24] which was published after his death. In it he effectively contradicts his approach in the *Tractatus*, acknowledging that conceptual analysis and problems of language and definition are indeed valid philosophical approaches. However while everyone has read, or claims to have read, the *Tractatus*, it seems that nobody has read *Philosophical Investigations*, perhaps because it is much longer, but more likely because, unlike the *Tractatus*, it has not been mentioned in trendy films or television programmes.

So here we have a clear and unambiguous concession from Wittgenstein that he was wrong that winter evening in Cambridge when he argued that 'there are no questions, only puzzles', and Popper was right. The search for knowledge is not just about seeking to reduce things to logic propositions and mathematical formulae. It is also, and perhaps more importantly, about questioning the fundamental nature of things, and how they might relate to other things. Concepts and definitions are not irrelevant, they matter. Asking questions to which you cannot necessarily find an answer is not a futile exercise, but a first step in a discussion that may well lead to a deeper, even though not a full, understanding.

Sadly, because just about everyone has missed Wittgenstein's posthumous recantation, the spirit of logical positivism continues to hover over many areas of intellectual endeavour, not least the ivy-covered walls of Finance World. Unless something

---

[24] Ludwig Wittgenstein *Philosophical Investigations*, John Wiley & Sons, New York 2009.

can be reduced to mathematical symbols and calculated, then it is not a valid matter for consideration. If something needs to be defined then one must be sure to define it in such a way that it can be calculated, no matter how artificial or even misleading that definition may be when subjected to linguistic analysis. Well, guess what. Even the great brain of his age, Wittgenstein, finally admitted this approach was wrong, and if Wittgenstein was wrong then Markowitz was wrong. The *Tractatus* was not a guide to a universal system of knowledge after all, but a siren luring the unwary onto the rocks with the prospect of false certainty.

In order to see just how the spirit of the *Tractatus* led the study of finance to so disastrous a shipwreck, we will in Chapter 9 turn to those writers who have dealt with risk since the Second World War, since so far as attitudes to risk were concerned, everything changed at that time, and in 1952 to be exact.

From it being the conventional wisdom that risk was too complex a subject to understand, and incapable of mathematical calculation, suddenly exactly the opposite view came to prevail. Not only could one understand risk but master it, and the tool of that mastery was mathematics. Suddenly understanding risk became nothing more than the performing of a fairly straightforward calculation. It is this view, highly dangerous in itself, that we 'understand' risk which prevails today in finance faculties around the world and forms the implicit basis of the highly complex papers, riddled with algebraic formulae, which are published in academic journals.

It is worth noting that at professional investment conferences, by contrast, speakers and panellists are increasingly starting to question this new conventional wisdom. While few are as yet prepared to reject, or even recognise, the tyranny of periodic returns most discussion is still of a rather puzzled 'but surely volatility can't be all there is to it?' variety. It is however striking that Finance World, which claims to understand, reflect, and express everything that happens in investment markets, should have lost touch with practical reality to quite such an extent.

Why did this happen? The only credible reason that has been expressed so far is that the War bred new attitudes. As Bernstein says, Markowitz's approach:

> reflects the spirit if the early years after the Second World War, when many social scientists set about reviving the Victorian faith in measurement, and the belief that the world's problems could be solved.[25]

This is at best a rather soft, fuzzy explanation, though it undoubtedly has some validity – witness the outbreak during that period of international initiatives, conventions, and organisations all dedicated to achieving lofty humanitarian goals. In fact, though, it could be argued that the most interesting thing about this quotation is that Bernstein incautiously refers to finance as a 'social' science, the significance of which will become clear later.

There is in fact a much better explanation. Better because it is stronger, in the sense that we can prove it through clear empirical observation. Markowitz was simply academically dishonest. 'Dishonest' is a harsh word to use, so let us be quite clear what is meant by it in this context.

An advocate presenting a case has a duty to bring to the court's attention any authorities which are contrary to his argument. Similarly, an academic has a duty to cite all relevant literature, whether it is supportive of his approach or not. As we have already seen, no less an authority than Popper makes it clear that this is a necessary pre-requisite to any genuine advancement of knowledge. Markowitz in his 1952 paper makes no attempt to do this, and it is in this very precise sense that the word 'dishonest' is here employed.

On the contrary, he simply ignores the fact that three intellectual giants had previously argued strongly and cogently that what he was attempting to do – create a mathematical measurement of risk – was both impossible and dangerous. Rather

---

[25] Peter Bernstein *Against the Gods: The remarkable story of risk,* John Wiley & Sons, New York 1996, page 249.

than allowing his readers to hear both sides of the argument and decide for themselves, which would of course involve persuading them that his view should be preferred, he simply silences the opposition and presents his own views alone.

However before we begin to analyse Markowitz's view of risk, let us follow the timeline of comment through to the present day.

Chapter 9

Thoughts on risk (post-War): theory becomes dogma

The stated scope of Markowitz's 1952[1] article is quite clear. He argues that a diversified portfolio must always be preferable to an undiversified one. This is based on the assumption that 'variance of return is an undesirable thing', and a mathematical proof that variance of return may be reduced within an equity portfolio by holding a number of different shares.

Yet because the returns of a large number of individual shares will still be quite highly correlated with each other, it is not possible to eliminate, as opposed to reduce, variance of returns. Nor is it possible for any one portfolio to exhibit both the maximum return and the minimum variance. Once effective diversification has been achieved, then:

> There is a rate at which the investor can gain expected return by taking on variance, or reduce variance by giving up expected return.

Note that Markowitz does not explicitly state that risk and volatility (variance) are the same thing. Yet, as Bernstein would aptly observe, as a result of the article volatility and risk became synonymous and 'Markowitz had put a number on investment risk'.

The reason for this is hidden in plain view right at the beginning of the article:

> The process of selecting a portfolio may be divided into two stages. The first stage starts with observation and

[1] Harry Markowitz (1952) 'Portfolio Selection', *Journal of Finance* 7(1).

> experience and ends with beliefs about the future performances of available securities. The second stage starts with the relevant beliefs about future performances and ends with the choice of portfolio.

Here it seems implicit that Markowitz believes (certainly he is assuming) that by observing past investment outcomes we may predict future ones. It is natural for him to assume that the range within which future outcomes may vary ('variance of return') can be calculated by using observations of past outcomes. Thus it becomes possible to have 'beliefs' about future outcomes, mathematically calculated probabilities rather than mere guidelines derived from experience, judgement, and gut instinct.

It is therefore Markowitz's basic mindset, his assumption that all the material risk of an investment can be calculated as the variance of its historical periodic returns, that has been carried forward and universally adopted, as Bernstein points out, not just his narrow message that diversification could reduce volatility, and was therefore a good thing. The latter would hardly have come as a shattering revelation to anyone who actually worked at investment, as opposed to simply writing about it. The former would harden rapidly into financial dogma.

We have already noted that Markowitz does not attempt to justify his basic belief, nor even to mention the contrary views of Knight, von Mises, and Keynes. He cites only three previous writers, one of them a mathematician on probability, and two writers from just before the Second World War on the nature of value (not risk), one of these writing about value within a firm rather than within a portfolio. Yet despite this striking failure to offer any justification of his concept of volatility as risk, it appears to have been instantly accepted. A search against titles including the phrase 'the nature of investment risk' in a leading academic database[2] for the period from 1952 onwards yields not a single result.

---

[2] Business Source Complete.

Interestingly, another paper which appeared in 1952 took a rather different approach, but seems to have been widely ignored. Roy's 1952 article[3] is essentially a mathematical paper, but it does raise an interesting point. Building on (though not acknowledging) Knight's comment that humans do not equally value a gain or a loss, Roy argues that we do not seek to maximise a gain, but instead seek a measure of gain while still protecting ourselves against a large loss; for example, by the use of a diversified portfolio. He suggests that we should view 'risk' not as volatility per se, but as the risk of not achieving a certain target rate of return, whatever that may be. Interestingly, I advanced a similar view in an earlier book[4] though I had not at that time come across Roy's paper.

Anticipating Robert Jeffery,[5] he also recognises that an individual's view of risk will be conditioned not just by the probability of something occurring but by what that outcome may be. However it seems from the following passage that he is thinking more about the *alternative* outcome:

> Thus, a person may be prepared to revise the level of disaster downwards if the expected return is at the same time raised. For example, he may at one and the same time regard a speculative loss of 10 per cent as a disaster if the expected gain is only 5 per cent, while, if the expected gain is 15 per cent, he will only get excited if his loss exceeds 25 per cent.

Thus his view of 'Safety First'; namely that the theory of investment decisions seeking to maximising the utility of the outcome is unsound, and that probability analysis should

---

[3] A.D. Roy (1952) 'Safety First and the Holding of Assets', *Econometrica* 20(3).

[4] Guy Fraser-Sampson *Multi Asset Class Investing*, John Wiley & Sons, Chichester 2006.

[5] Robert Jeffery (1977) 'Internal Portfolio Growth: the better measure', *Journal of Portfolio Management*, Summer.

instead focus on calculating the optimal way of seeking out a given rate of return.

It is worth pointing out that in more recent years some practitioners have had similar thoughts, particularly in the world of hedge funds,[6] which uses, for example, not just the Sortino ratio (which targets only downside risk) but also the Calmar Ratio, which sets maximum downside against return, and the Omega Ratio, which places maximum downside against maximum upside, exactly the sort of approach on which Roy appears to be musing.

Some writers have gone even further. In 2010 Roszkowski and Davey[7] argued that both risk tolerance and the very perception of risk itself have been misunderstood. Adopting the traditional, rather simplistic, version of Knight's view, with his 'uncertainty' being equated with 'ambiguity', they say:

> in investment contexts the degree of uncertainty can be rather ambiguous and difficult to express in precise mathematical terms. In other words, in the real world [of investment] we typically have to deal more with uncertainty than with risk. People are typically more averse to ambiguity than with risk.

While space does not permit a full discussion of this interesting paper, it is worth noting the implication that one of the reasons behind the widespread refusal to question Markowitz's system may be simply that it induces an emotional state of comfort. Reassurance that what can be calculated can somehow be known, predicted, and planned for. Once seen for what it is, pure uncertainty of outcome, it becomes a source not of reassurance but potentially of fear.

More interesting still is when the authors attempt their own definition of risk, which is both subjective and psychological

---

6 As noted by Cass EMBA Xaio-Xaio Yin in a BMP supervised by the writer in the summer of 2012.

7 M. Roszkowski and G. Davey (2010) 'Risk Perception and Risk Tolerance', *Journal of Financial Service Professionals*, July.

(points to which we will return). Decision making under conditions of investment risk, they say, is (my italics added):

> a function of (1) the *perceived* probabilities of the alternatives, (2) the *perceived* consequences and (3) the psychological propensity of the *individual* to undertake risk.

It may be significant however that this article was published in what many might see as a professional journal for investment practitioners, for from 1952 onwards the academic world of finance appears largely to have given up on the nature of risk. It simply accepts that risk and the volatility of past returns are one and the same thing, and concentrates on applying the principle to more and more advanced statistical techniques to calculate the one right answer to more and more complex questions and datasets. There are occasional heretical voices to be heard, but even these do not really question the fundamental validity of the measure itself, but rather whether there may be some situations where it can be supplemented, or differently applied.

Mostly, those who doubt their faith are troubled by the fact that the 'traditional' (the word ignores the fact that it had only existed since 1952) measure of risk takes no account of time. Smidt[8] questioned the relevance of the model when evaluating the same investment which was held by investors with different time horizons. Trainer et al[9] also pointed to the effect of differing holding periods. Jeffery[10] suggested that many long-term institutional investors might even be regarded as having a holding period of infinity. Levy[11] even goes so far as to say 'what is needed is an appropriate definition of risk'.

---

[8] S. Smidt (1978) 'Investment Horizons and Performance Measurement', *Journal of Portfolio Management*, Winter.

[9] F.H. Trainer, J.B. Yawitz, and W.J. Marshall (1979) 'Holding Period is the Key to Risk Thresholds', *Journal of Portfolio Management*, Winter.

[10] Robert Jeffery (1977) 'Internal Portfolio Growth: The better measure', *Journal of Portfolio Management*, Summer.

[11] R.A. Levy (1978) 'Stocks, Bonds, Bills and Inflation Over 52 Years', *The Journal of Portfolio Management*, Summer.

These sources are all cited by Jeffery in 1984,[12] in a later article which moves beyond issues of time and touches on various other aspects of risk. However even he does not question the sacred model itself, but only the way in which it is used. It focuses, he says, on the probability of a loss occurring rather than the consequence of a loss occurring, a view which would be repeated later by Taleb:

> Volatility per se ... is simply a benign statistical probability factor that tells us nothing about risk until coupled with a consequence. Its measurement is useless until we describe that probability in terms of 'the probability of what'. If the 'what' is of no concern to the given individual or group, then the probability of 'what' occurring is likewise of no concern, and vice versa[13]

Jeffery points out that a portfolio is a collection of assets, some of which, such as bonds, may be 'near to cash', but none of which are actually cash. They are paper assets which may be turned into cash in the future when the investor needs to make payments. These payments, stretching away into the future, can be thought of as the investor's liabilities, and thus the investor's real 'risk' is that at some stage in the future the cash receipts generated by the portfolio will be less than the cash payments required to be made.

This is the approach I advanced in an earlier book,[14] which suggests calculating a target rate of return based on modelling future liabilities and the known starting value of the portfolio, and thinking of risk as failure to achieve that return, so that precisely the outcome envisaged by Jeffery might occur, namely that an investor such as a pension fund might find itself unable to make a future benefit payment.

---

[12] Robert Jeffrey (1984) 'A New Paradigm for Portfolio Risk', *Journal of Portfolio Management* 11(1).

[13] Robert Jeffrey (1984) 'A New Paradigm for Portfolio Risk', *Journal of Portfolio Management* 11(1).

[14] Guy Fraser-Sampson *Multi Asset Class Investment Strategy*, John Wiley & Sons, Chichester 2006.

As that book also points out, Jeffery realises that such an approach must lead to each investor being treated differently, since none will have exactly the same liability profiles. I would express this as risk being a subjective rather than an objective matter, attaching not to an investment itself but to the relationship between that investment and any given investor.

However, Jeffery does not launch a full-scale assault on the traditional model, though he hints gently at it not telling the whole story. Portfolio management, he says, would work much better if:

> a paradigm shift were to occur in the 'rational model' or 'shared belief' that portfolio risk is strictly a function of the volatility of portfolio returns.

It is for each individual investor, he argues, to decide their own ideal exposure to volatility given their own liability profile. He cites Ellis[15] who says:

> the priority objective in investment management is to control risk, not maximise returns.

Jeffery disagrees:

> this risk cannot be determined without knowing a great deal about the future cash requirements of the investor.

An Ellis type approach, he argues, simply results in look-alike portfolios based on some arbitrary split between bonds and equities being held by investors who are not alike at all.

The phrase 'this risk' is revealing because Jeffery sees two different sorts of risk. Portfolio risk, calculated by the traditional measure of the variance of historical returns, and owner's risk. Starting with a dictionary definition of risk (an obvious starting point ignored by Markowitz and those who followed him) as 'the possibility of loss or injury', he argues

---

[15] C.D. Ellis *Investment Manager's Handbook*, Dow Jones – Irwin, Chicago 1980.

that this can only be suffered by the owner of the portfolio, rather than the portfolio itself.

Owner's risk is significantly different in at least two important respects. First, it is not the volatility within the portfolio which is relevant, but the relationship of the possible cash receipts to be generated by the portfolio in the future when overlaid on the stream of future liabilities (if there is an excess of the former over the latter, this risk will be negative). Second, owner's risk encompasses considerations which are outside the portfolio altogether. For example, two corporate pension plans with identical funding positions will not carry the same degree of owner's risk if one sponsor is profitable and asset rich while the other is not. Portfolio risk, he says 'becomes meaningful only when converted to owner's risk'.

However at this point the logical positivists rear their heads and drag him back into the quicksands of mensuration. He is incapable of proceeding any further with owner's risk, he admits ruefully, because he is incapable of quantifying it. It contains various elements, including behavioural factors, which are not capable of mathematical calculation, at least not in a way which would produce the holy one right answer. Because owner's risk cannot be measured ('stated' as Wittgenstein would have said) then it cannot be a proper subject for serious consideration. The *Tractatus*[16] has claimed another victim.

Thus Jeffery's acceptance of the traditional model, precisely because it does allow exact calculation of something (my italics added):

> Because it is axiomatic that there is a direct relationship between risk and reward, it is not surprising that the theoreticians adopted volatility of asset returns as a universal proxy for portfolio risk. They were searching for a *measurable* proxy for risk to explain differences in portfolio returns. Return volatility is a readily available statistic and does indeed work nicely as a measure of portfolio risk.

---

[16] Ludwig Wittgenstein *Tractatus Logico-Philosophicus*, Routledge, London 2001.

It is unfortunate that Jeffery did not have more faith in the power of conceptual analysis and abstract discussion, for he clearly spots some, though by no means all, that is flawed in the traditional view of risk. He accepts without comment, for example, Markowitz's key assumptions that we can use observations of the past to fix beliefs about the future, namely that the future is likely closely to resemble the past, and that normal distribution will always apply to investment outcomes.

One of his key observations has already been noted. Volatility itself is irrelevant as a measure of risk because it tells us nothing about *what* is being risked by the volatility. What is important is not the chance of an outcome falling within a certain range, but what consequences may flow from such an outcome for an individual investor.

Another is equally telling, and widely overlooked or ignored by investors. To accept volatility as a relevant measure you must assume that you may need to turn your entire portfolio into cash almost immediately, yet most investors are at least to some extent long-term investors and thus in respect of at least some part of their portfolio never likely to be forced sellers.

In 1992 Holton[17] spotted another flaw in the traditional risk model, in that it ignored some of the effects of time or, put another way, that it rested on an assumption of randomness, the well-known 'Random Walk' theory. Yet he found that 'over three to five years markets lose much of their randomness'. Put more technically, he discovered that what had appeared to be slight correlations in earlier research of sequential periodic data both persisted and increased over time.

Looking at data for various currencies, he found that some data series were highly volatile in the short term but exhibited low volatility in the long term, while for others the opposite was true. Thus volatility should not be considered in isolation, but relative to likely holding periods. This mirrors

[17] Glyn Holton (1992) 'Time, the Second Dimension of Risk', *Financial Analysts' Journal*, November/December.

some research done by the writer for the purposes of a later book[18] which found that gold exhibited very high volatility as an investment asset in the short term but, certainly if measured in real terms, very low volatility in the very long term. Indeed, in the case of gold, likely length of holding period should almost certainly be the prime factor in deciding whether to hold it within a portfolio at all.

Holton believed that his research had:

> profound implications for risk analysis and, through risk analysis, for the entire asset allocation process. Consider the efficient frontier ... Expected returns are plotted on one axis and volatilities are plotted on the other. The resulting concave curves represent optimal portfolios. It is all very scientific, but what happens if the volatilities are wrong?

Note that at this stage, in 1992, Holton does not challenge the accepted view of risk. On the contrary, he is concerned to see that volatility is more fully understood as a measure of risk, though he does allow himself the smallest of caveats when he says 'for investment professionals, risk and volatility can be *almost* synonymous' (my italics).

Peter Bernstein's 1996 book *Against the Gods: The remarkable story of risk*[19] makes the startling claim that 'Knight and Keynes ... defined risk as it has come to be understood today.'[20] This is so obviously untrue that it may be instructive to examine this statement further, to find out exactly what causes this fundamental misunderstanding, either of what Knight and Keynes said or of what finance writers have said since.

---

[18] Guy Fraser-Sampson *Alternative Assets: Investments for a post-crisis world*, John Wiley & Sons, Chichester 2011.

[19] Peter L. Bernstein *Against the Gods: The remarkable story of risk*, John Wiley & Sons, New York 1996.

[20] Peter L. Bernstein *Against the Gods: The remarkable story of risk*, John Wiley & Sons, New York 1996, page 217.

Some clue to the former may be found in an article which Bernstein wrote in 1999.[21] In this he seems to equate risk with uncertainty, stating that risk and time are inter-connected:

> Risk and time are so intimately related that they are almost the same thing. If life were always now, no risk would exist. The longer we look out into the future, however, the less we know ... There comes a point out there when, as John Maynard Keynes put it so well, we simply do not know. The longer the time horizon, the greater the risk in a decision.

It is difficult to escape the conclusion that Bernstein is directly equating 'risk' with uncertainty of outcome. He does actually quote Knight (twice) on the forward-looking nature of investment outcomes being at the root of the problem of uncertainty. He then seems to take things further, alluding to the risk of an equity investor being the chance of suffering a loss. This idea is in turn based upon some of the views put forward by Jeffrey in his 1984 paper,[22] whose article is cited in his book, though not in his paper.

In the paper, Bernstein sees the key to managing risk as being able to control the company concerned (though it is difficult to see how this might mitigate things such as risk in financial or industrial markets), or being able to 'reverse' the investment decision by using the liquidity of the assets to sell them to someone else. Blithely ignoring the fact that by 1999 many thousands of private equity investors were doing exactly this, he gravely announces that investing in an illiquid company as a minority investor would be 'intolerable'.

It is strange that Bernstein should cite Knight in implying that risk and uncertainty are the same thing, when Knight explicitly says that they are not. Even if he feels that this is

---

[21] Peter L. Bernstein (1999) 'Risk, Time and Reversibility', The International Association for the Study of Insurance Economics, *The Geneva Papers on Risk and Insurance* 24(2).

[22] Frank Ramsey 'Truth and Probability' in *The Foundations of Mathematics and other Logical Essays*, Harcourt Brace, New York 1931.

simply the result of linguistic distinctions, with Knight using the word 'risk' in a particular, eccentric way, then surely he should point this out, if only to avoid confusion. After all, it is the meaning of the word 'risk' which, as much as anything, lies at the heart of the debate.

Stranger still that he should apparently be suggesting (if the original statement is to be held true) that such a view is consistent with how risk is regarded today, in a Modern Portfolio Theory world. Knight and Keynes both said specifically that the uncertainty of investment outcomes is not capable of mathematical measurement. Modern Portfolio Theory says expressly that it is. Markowitz's 1952 paper contains a high level of mathematical content.

Bernstein notes in his book that Markowitz's 1952 paper is concerned specifically with diversification within a portfolio, and that he does not use the word 'risk', talking instead only of the variance of returns as being something undesirable. Yet even he admits in the same paragraph:[23]

> Risk and variance have become synonymous ... Markowitz had put a number on investment risk.

Perhaps the most compelling argument of all is a human one. Markowitz was only twenty-five in 1952. If he had *not* intended to say that the material risk of any investment could be measured by the variance of its historical periodic returns then he had many years afterwards to point this out, but never did so. In the event, as Bernstein himself acknowledges, 'risk and variance have become synonymous'. The reality is that today every investor, every finance student, and every equity analyst believes that all the material risk of an investment may be measured by the standard deviation of its past returns. This is not what Knight and Keynes said at all. On the contrary, they expressly disagreed. So, far from

---

[23] Harry Markowitz (1952) 'Portfolio Selection', *Journal of Finance* 7(1), page 252.

holding Bernstein's statement true, we must instead treat it as puzzlingly false.

It may be significant that most of Bernstein's book is a paean to mathematics, statistics, and probability, and that he studiously avoids any mention of von Mises. This means that he never has to answer von Mises's contention of the futility of attempting to apply probability theory to financial outcomes. Von Mises would however be one of many writers to be cited in a landmark article in 2004 by Holton.

In his 2004 paper Holton notes that everyone seems happy to measure risk, but not to define it. He suggests approaching a possible definition from two different approaches: subjective probability and operationalism.

Subjective probability is in a sense what Jeffery was moving towards in his 1984 article. Any consideration of risk must include the notion of a consequence. Not just probability, but the probability of what? The 'what' is important, and is unlikely to affect any two investors in precisely the same way. Subjective probability goes further. Even if both the probability and exposure (the possible consequence) were in fact the same, it is unlikely that any two investors would perceive them to be the same.

This is partly because of what Jeffery referred to as differing 'emotional needs', which would include the extent to which investors may be affected by short-term gains or losses, and their readiness to hold an investment for the long run as against their instinct to cut their losses and sell. Remember, he notes that such factors are incapable of quantification, and gives this as his reason for not proceeding to develop further his notion of 'owner's risk'.

It is also partly because of what Holton calls an objective approach to risk, which focuses on probability – even if, as in the case of Knight, it is acknowledged that there are some situations which are not capable of calculation – but not on exposure. A subjective approach would instead look at how any individual investors might view that possible exposure as affecting them in the light of their own particular circumstances. Knight, he argues, views any proposition as being inherently true or false, and the extent to which one may be able to determine this as being dependent on the state of knowledge or ignorance of the relevant facts.

In fact, Holton does not make this argument terribly well when he goes on to quote Knight's famous distinction of what is measurable ('risk') and what is not ('uncertainty'). While it is true that Knight sees risk in somewhat binomial terms (will happen/will not happen) and ignores exposure, it is possible that Holton is getting caught up in the linguistics of the situation. Surely Knight's basic case is that much of what the world of finance sees as 'risk' is in fact just 'uncertainty', and that the basic error into which they fall is in believing it all to be measurable when in fact it is not? It is not clear why he feels the need to attack Knight's theory rather than just advancing his own, which is a very strong one and which comes at the problem from a very different direction.

Similarly he attacks Keynes, though only to open a window to use Ramsey,[24] a writer whom he clearly admires as 'ground-breaking' in subjective probability, to attack some of the more arcane aspects of Keynes's view of risk, claiming that they do not stand up when subjected to mathematical analysis.

Of Knight, he says:

> If we adopt a subjectivist interpretation of probability, Knight's definition of risk becomes empty. In the absence of objective probabilities (however defined) there can be no risks under his definition.

Not only is this intellectual sleight of hand (if we adopt a subjectivist view of probability then naturally there can be no objective probability), but it is also arguably unnecessary. Neither Knight nor Keynes claimed to have arrived at a universal definition of risk. Their central message was that whatever it was, it could not be measured. Indeed, Knight's view

---

[24] Frank Ramsey 'Truth and Probability' in *The Foundations of Mathematics and Other Logical Essays*, Harcourt Brace, New York 1931.

of 'risk' was a very narrow one based on a simple binomial situation, and even so he was careful to point out its weaknesses and limitations.

Holton then quotes a passage from a 1970 paper by Finetti,[25] which takes the subjectivist approach to what some may view as its *reductio ad absurdam*:

> My thesis, paradoxically, and a little provocatively, but nonetheless genuinely, is simply this:
>
> PROBABILITY DOES NOT EXIST,
>
> The abandonment of superstitious beliefs about the existence of Phlogiston, the Cosmic Ether, Absolute Space and Time,,,, or Fairies and Witches, was an essential step along the road to scientific thinking. Probability, too, if regarded as something endowed with some kind of objective existence, is no less a misleading misconception, an illusory attempt to exteriorize or materialize our true probabilistic beliefs

To say that risk cannot be measured is one thing. To say that probability as an intellectual approach is empty and invalid is quite another. Is it really necessary for Holton to go as far as this in seeking to debunk the traditional risk model? Particularly as he did not seem to have any problem with using variance as a mathematical measure in his 1992 paper?

Surprisingly he goes on to claim that Markowitz 'wrote as a subjectivist'. His grounds for this belief are that Markowitz was taught at the University of Chicago in part by Leonard Savage, 'a leading advocate of the subjectivist interpretation or probability'. Also, that Markowitz notes in a footnote that probability may be 'in part subjective', though this is misleading: Markowitz is there describing probability *beliefs*, an important difference, and is expressly suggesting that these will *not* impact probability outcomes to any great extent

[25] Bruno de Finetti an Italian work from 1970 translated as *Theory of Probability*, John Wiley & Sons, London 1974.

because 'we can, however, expect [any investor's] probability beliefs to be roughly consistent on important matters which have been carefully considered.'

That he knew Savage and devoted a chapter of a later book[26] to subjective probability surely does not make Markowitz a subjectivist. There is no evidence that he disbelieved in mathematical probability theory, nor that he disbelieved that the risk of an investment can be measured by its historical validity. On the contrary, his 1952 paper would be a nonsense if even one of these propositions was true, let alone both. Furthermore, as already noted, he had many years in which to protest that his work had been misunderstood, but entirely failed to do so. As Bernstein later pointed out, risk had become synonymous with volatility, and Markowitz had put a number on it.

If Holton's flirtation with subjective probability is unconvincing, he is on slightly firmer ground when it comes to operationalism, at least if you believe in operationalism, which is however a major caveat as we will see.

Holton initially cites Rapoport (from a 1953 article)[27] who talks about:

> the delusion ... that anything which is talked about is real ... Indeed, nothing is easier than to 'define' these noises so as to make it appear that they mean something.

Unfortunately the examples which Rapoport then gives do not really take matters much further and, as Holton goes on to cite the founder of operationalism Bridgman (who wrote in 1927)[28] without actually explaining what he said, we are left wondering exactly what he is talking about.

In fact Bridgman argued that we can only properly understand something in terms of what operates upon it. The

---

[26] Harry Markowitz *Portfolio Selection: Efficient diversification of investments*, John Wiley & Sons, New York 1959.

[27] Anatol Rapoport *Operational Philosophy*, Harper, New York 1953.

[28] Percy Bridgman *The Logic of Modern Physics*, Macmillan, New York 1927.

Stanford Encyclopaedia of Philosophy[29] ('*SEP*') gives the example of the concept of length. We can only have any real grasp of the meaning of length, Bridgman would argue, if we can find some way of measuring it. The act of mensuration 'operates' upon the concept of length. Thus if you cannot find a valid operator for any given word then you cannot define, as opposed to describe, what the word really means.

This view should be subject to one obvious qualification and at least three objections. The qualification was that Bridgman was writing specifically about the application of the scientific method is physics and never intended his thinking to be stretched into some sort of general theory of knowledge. He would later say:

> I have only a historical connection with this thing called 'operationalism'. In short, I feel I have created a Frankenstein which has certainly got away from me. I abhor the word 'operationalism' or 'operationism', which seems to imply a dogma, or at least a thesis of some kind. The thing I have envisaged is too simple to be dignified by so pretentious a name.[30]

The first objections came, perhaps predictably, from the logical positivists, who insisted that this 'non-thesis' did not go far enough. Being able to measure something, for example, was only part of the story. You must be able to go further and 'state' it as Wittgenstein might do. Perhaps wary of tangling with so powerful an ego with so devoted a following, Bridgman would draw back from any direct intellectual confrontation, as we have seen, arguing that his views had either been taken out of context or stretched beyond the rather limited span which he had intended for them.

The second objection is that there are circumstances in which knowledge, and thus also meaning, may be derived otherwise

---

[29] Online at http://plato.stanford.edu/entries/operationalism/.

[30] Quoted in Philip Frank *The Validation of Scientific Theories*, Beacon Press, Boston 1956 and noted in *SEP*.

than by operationalism. This debate centres around another major intellect, that of Albert Einstein. His theory of relativity could not be derived using operationist principles. This conflict between empirical observation and experimentation on the one hand and conceptual analysis on the other might be viewed as some sort of equivalent of the Methodenstreit, except that Bridgman himself again disavowed the strict way in which others were trying to apply his ideas:

> there need be no qualms that the operational point of view will ever place the slightest restriction on the freedom of the theoretical physicist to explore the consequences of any free mental construction.[31]

The third objection noted by the *SEP* is that there is no general agreement on exactly what things may properly be regarded as 'operators'. If one stays with the idea of physical measurement, for example, then very little indeed could be properly defined.

Thus it is slightly surprising that Holton should as late as 2004 seek to invoke what the *SEP* says 'is nowadays commonly regarded as an extreme and outmoded position'. While Bridgman made a valuable contribution to epistemology by stressing that there were limits to what we could properly know, in the sense of fully understand and comprehend, there seems to be general agreement that he tried to go too far too quickly, and that his ideas rapidly started to unravel when exposed to the forensic attentions of professional philosophers.

For the record, Holton goes on to explain that many of the elements of what we should be attempting to understand or convey when we use the word 'risk' are not capable of an operationalist approach. What 'operates', for example, on materiality, the extent to which any individual investor may be affected by any particular outcome? Certainly nothing universal, or capable of measurement. Then again there is the issue of perception. We may perhaps be able to define what

---

[31] Philip Frank *The Validation of Scientific Theories*, Beacon Press, Boston 1956.

we perceive risk to be in any situation, but we cannot attempt to define risk as it really is, because that is something else, and something the true nature of which is hidden from us behind the filter of perception.

So, just as Jeffery drew back from moving onwards with his definition of risk because he recognised that he was moving into largely conceptual territory, so too did Holton, concluding that there is no such thing as true risk. Incidentally, this is surely intellectually suspect: just because you cannot know what true risk is does not necessarily mean that it does not exist. Holton concludes:

> What is risk? How can we quantify risk that cannot be perceived? If a trader or a business manager has knowledge that is not reflected in a risk metric, does the risk metric misrepresent risk? In the absence of true risk, these questions are empty.

Bridgman's acknowledgement, adopted by Holton, that there are limits, and possibly severe limits, to the human ability to gather true knowledge could be usefully applied to the world of finance, as could the intellectual humility that such a view would impose. Instead of seizing upon a simple statistical factor which is capable of calculation and holding this up as 'risk', academics would be forced to admit that they did not know what risk really was, and were likely never to know. Within such parameters, useful discussion could then take place as to ways in which at least some aspects of risk may be glimpsed and grasped at.

Jeffery's contribution too should not be overlooked. His message that risk must be essentially subjective and individual has been simply ignored. Holton recognises this, urging that risk metrics should be set operationally within individual organisations, as I have advocated in earlier works, taking account of their own particular circumstances, target return, time horizon, and Jeffery's 'emotional needs'.

Holton's most important contribution comes right at the end of his paper when he points out that:

we can never operationally define risk. At best we can operationally define only our perception of risk.

A more manageable task is to operationally define some aspects of perceived risk. Risk metrics, such as variance of returns, are used for this purpose. It is meaningless to ask if a risk metric captures risk. Instead, ask if it useful.

Chapter 10

Things fall apart

Having seen how Markowitz's view of risk has come to exercise such a stranglehold on the financial imagination, let us turn to discussing its limitations in more depth. We will begin by showing the falseness of the various assumptions on which it is based. Then, in a separate chapter, we will discuss its fundamental weaknesses as a concept. Put another way, let us examine it first as the mathematical process which it purports to be, and then as a philosophical construct.

Remember that the former was something which was never used before the Second World War, its very validity being denied, but which was universally adopted without question or explanation thereafter. By contrast, the latter formed the basis of all pre-War discussion, but has since been largely ignored.

So-called Modern Portfolio Theory believes that the material risk of any investment asset is the same as, or at least can be calculated and expressed as, the variance of its historical returns (what we call colloquially 'volatility') measured by standard deviation. So-called because it dates from as long ago as 1952 and therefore is hardly 'modern'. So-called because it deals only with what happens within a portfolio of a single asset class (equities) rather than ranging across the different asset classes which exist within most truly modern portfolios. So-called because, as we will see later, it is not really a 'theory' at all, at least not in any recognisably scientific sense. We will return to all these issues.

A belief that risk and calculated volatility are the same thing rests on various implicit assumptions, among which are:

- that risk is capable of mathematical calculation;
- that variance of return is indeed a valid risk proxy;

- that periodic return is a valid measure of performance;
- that normal distribution applies to investment returns over time;
- that the past is a good guide to the future; and
- that we may safely ignore the time value of money.

In addition, Modern Portfolio Theory itself expressly states various assumptions which we are required to make in order for its mechanism to produce valid results when we pull its various levers. Chief among these are:

- that all investors are rational;
- that all investors have access to the same information at the same time; and
- that all markets are perfect.

Just to be clear, if you want to accept Modern Portfolio Theory as valid then you have to believe in *all* these assumptions, both implicit and express. Should you come to the conclusion that even one of them is flawed, then Modern Portfolio Theory, the bedrock of Finance World, crumbles away and the whole rotten edifice starts to totter. In fact, the avowed aim of this book is to persuade the reader that *none* of these assumptions may safely be made.

Risk is capable of mathematical calculation

This is perhaps the most fundamental assumption which underlies the traditional view of risk. After all, there is no point embarking on any mathematical calculation to measure anything, no matter what it may be, unless you believe that it is in fact capable of such calculation. It is therefore startling that nobody from Markowitz onwards has ever challenged, tested, or even stated it.

All the more remarkable since, as we have seen in earlier chapters, until Markowitz's seminal paper it was the accepted conventional wisdom that it was *not* capable of calculation.

That such a sea-change in people's beliefs could occur apparently invisibly and for no good reason is literally incredible, and yet it happened. It was as if, at sometime around 1952, the whole population of Italy went to bed one night as Catholics and awoke the next morning as Jews.

There are two things which need to be noted here. The first is that it could be argued that this assumption does no more than re-state some of the following ones, but not so. Saying, for example, that if normal distribution does not apply to investment returns then variance is not a good measure of risk, does not exclude the possibility that there may be some other mathematical measure which is. Statistics has other weapons in its armoury for different types of distribution. Challenging this present assumption raises a much more fundamental objection, namely that risk may simply not be capable of precise calculation *at all*.

Is it not possible, as the great pre-War thinkers argued, that risk is one of those things for which we cannot attempt a mathematical calculation, such as how happy someone feels, how much in love they may be with someone else, or how overcast the sky may be? In Finance World, such thoughts are of course the darkest heresy. Finance is a branch of mathematics, mathematics is a process of calculation, risk is the foundation of finance theory, therefore risk has to be capable of calculation. Even if it isn't.

Variance of return is a valid risk proxy

Here baldly stated is the central premise of Finance World. That what investors should be thinking of as the risk of any investment is the volatility of its historical returns.

Let us remind ourselves of what volatility measures: a range both above and below the average return within which the mean return of any new sequence of periods is likely to fall. In fact, in deference to one of the following assumptions, we should re-state this: the range within which the mean return of any sequence of periods has been calculated to fall in the past.

There are a number of problems with this approach. For a start, it does violence to the English language. If you are going to talk about risk then it is surely a sound starting point to make sure you are talking about what your listeners think of as 'risk' and how they apply the term in their day to day lives, rather than something totally different, some artificial construct which forms part of the jargon of a secret society that you have not invited anybody else to join.

A quick glance at the dictionary reveals that what most people would understand by the expression 'risk' is the chance that something unpleasant or unwelcome would occur. Volatility does not do this. It measures a range both below *and above* the average return. Receiving a return which is above average would generally be considered a pleasant and welcome thing, and not therefore a 'risk' at all. Many practitioners now recognise this by taking into account only downside risk, but this understanding is by no means universal.

Even then there are still problems. Finance World believes that a low spread of volatility betokens a low risk investment. Take, for example, an investment whose returns only fluctuated 1 per cent either side of the average compared to one whose returns fluctuated 8 per cent either side. Yet surely the common sense view would be to look not only at what the spread might be, but at where it occurs? If the average return of the former investment was 0 per cent, while the latter was 9 per cent, then surely it is the latter which is a low risk investment, not the former? In fact on one view (risk as capital loss) you could even argue that it carried no risk at all.

Periodic return is a valid measure of performance

We have already discussed the limitations of periodic return measures. By way of recapitulation, they force us to take account of unrealised gains and losses, they do not match the way in which an investor does, or should, view an investment, they cannot be applied validly across all different asset classes, and they take no account of the time value of money, a point with which we will deal separately.

Having dealt with these issues at length in an earlier chapter we can hopefully conclude without further discussion that periodic returns are certainly not a good measure of performance in respect of all asset types all of the time, and probably not even a good measure in respect of some asset types for some of the time. So why does Finance World persist in using them?

Again, we have already dealt with this point. Finance World believes that risk can and should be calculated mathematically. Therefore it follows that as their measure of risk they need something which is the output of a mathematical process. Equating risk, as they do, with pure uncertainty of outcome then there is really only one measure which seems appropriate, namely variance (volatility) of return. Variance can only be calculated using periodic return (or so they believe), and therefore periodic return is adopted without question as the standard measure of performance. Voila! The tail is wagging the dog.

So it can be seen that not only did Markowitz choose a phoney measure of risk, but that the required method of calculation makes use of return data which are less than optimal.

Normal distribution applies to investment returns over time

Various writers such as Niall Ferguson[1] and Nicholas Taleb[2] have already pointed out that we can see quite clearly from historical data that normal distribution demonstrably does *not* apply to investment returns. As Ferguson points out, after referring to the classic 'bell jar' of normal distribution:

> But in financial markets it doesn't look like this. If you plotted all the monthly movements of the Dow Jones Index on a chart, there is much less clustering around the average,

[1] Niall Furguson *The Ascent of Money*, Penguin, London 2009.
[2] Nicholas Taleb *The Black Swan*, Penguin, London 2007.

> and there are many more big rises and falls out at the extremes ... If Stock Market movements followed normal distribution ... an annual drop of 10% or more would happen only once every 500 years. And stock market plunges of 20% or more would be unheard of ... whereas there have been nine such crashes in the past century.

Taleb too challenges the view that Gaussian (normal) distribution governs financial returns. He believes that the only reason this assumption is made is that if normal distribution did not apply, Markowitz's chosen measure of risk, false though it is, could not be calculated, or at least could not be calculated with the available data. So again the tail is wagging the dog. A perceived need to be able to calculate something (with volatility chosen as the 'something') leads not only to selection of periodic return data, but also to having to assume something which is not true, namely that normal distribution applies.

At another point in his book he says, talking of his own experiences as a quantitative analyst:

> the foreign scientist with the throaty accent spending his nights on a computer doing complicated mathematics rarely fares better than a cabdriver using the simplest methods within his reach. The problem is that we focus on the rare occasions when these methods work and almost never on their far more numerous failures.

The past is a good guide to the future

Anyone who believes that future returns, or at least the range within which they are likely to fall, can be calculated using past data must necessarily believe that returns in the future are likely to behave in much the same way as they have in the past. Implicit in such a belief system would also have to be an expectation that returns are likely to fall within the same sort of range as before, and that the various systemic drivers of return are likely to remain largely unchanged.

Yet how realistic are such assumptions? Even if we look only at equity returns, the composition of market indices has changed dramatically over the decades, being driven at different times by sectors such as railways, banking, IT, oil, and telecommunications. It goes without saying that different drivers will impact on each sector. Even if one looks at things in the round, there is common consent today that equity markets are driven not by investment fundamentals but largely by emotive reactions to central bank statements on monetary policy. This was not the case in the past; at different times factors such as inflation and interest rates may have played a similar role.

At the level of mathematical calculation, chaos theory tells us that a relatively small change to one of the inputs of a process may produce a disproportionately large change in the value of the output. So if the range or distribution pattern of returns changes even slightly, then calculated 'predictions' as to future returns may vary hugely.

At the macro level, surely nobody would suggest that exactly the same drivers will operate in the future in exactly the same way and to exactly the same extent. Yet without such a belief, how realistic is it to assume that the future will be a perfect repeat of the past for those who were unlucky enough to miss it first time round?

Finally, let us remember the discussion of normal distribution. If normal distribution does not apply, then it must follow that the past cannot be a good guide to the future as measured by standard mean/variance analysis. Yet this is the chosen method, thus rendering the attempt meaningless. So even if one is not ready to accept the wider proposition that the past can rarely offer any meaningful insight as to the future, one has no choice but to concede that, at least as presently calculated, past returns are no valid guide to future performance.

We may safely ignore the time value of money

As we saw in an earlier chapter, the time value of money is one of the most important and basic concepts in finance. Given a choice, we would all rather receive money today than a year hence, and we would all prefer to defer paying a liability for as long as possible rather than paying it today.

Though a future cashflow may have the same nominal value as a cashflow today, its present value is less than that nominal value since by the time we receive it its purchasing power will have been diminished by inflation. In fact, as we have seen, there are other reasons as well such as cost of capital and opportunity cost. Whatever the case, we will value more highly a stream of cashflows which features gains in the early years and losses in the later ones, than one which contains exactly the same numbers but with the gains and losses differently arranged.

Nowhere is the concept of the time value of money more clearly demonstrated or widely accepted than in the case of a bond, that most basic of investment assets, whose price is calculated as a net present value, and whose yield to maturity as an IRR.

Yet despite the fact that bonds and their predecessors had been around for hundreds of years and that they formed a large part, or even all, of the portfolios of many leading institutional investors in 1952, Markowitz chose simply to ignore the time value of money as a relevant factor. Perhaps this is one more reason why he failed to advance any discussion of the nature of risk, choosing instead to follow his own rather tortured logic trail to a made-up proxy which could be calculated rather than being forced actually to think about what he was doing.

As we will explore in Chapter 11, the time value of money, and more precisely of cashflows, matches the reality of how an investor should view an investment whereas an approach which values the cashflows of each year equally, regardless of how far into the future they may occur, does not. In failing to recognise this, Markowitz produces a version of risk which apparently succeeds brilliantly as a mathematical construct, yet which has little relevance to what happens in the real world. Time is just as much a pillar of finance as risk and return, and none can usefully be viewed in isolation.

All investors are rational

This is a huge statement but, in fairness to Finance World, let us first consider it only in the rather narrow way in which it is advanced. Incidentally, you may be realising by now that Finance World specialises in using words and phrases in a different, sometimes very different, way to that in which they are understood by we boring everyday folk. To what extent this is just a rather sad consequence of mathematicians trying to communicate using language, and to what extent it represents a deliberate ploy to deter discussion and understanding is unclear.

Essentially what Finance World says is that a rational investor is one who will always accept the approach advocated by Modern Portfolio Theory. This is surely akin to a politician saying that only sane people can vote at the next election and that the only way in which they can demonstrate their sanity is by voting for him.

Specifically, the proposition is usually expressed by saying that the rational investor is one who will seek always to maximise his risk-adjusted return by accepting the outcome of something called the Capital Asset Pricing Model (CAPM). This model calculates the return and volatility of an individual stock relative to the stock market as a whole. It is not necessary to understand how this works save only that it is subject to all the assumptions we are here discussing, and therefore obviously flawed.

Again, there is a very tortuous trail to follow here. Let's take it one step at a time. In order for volatility as risk to be calculated, normal distribution must be assumed to apply, and the pattern of future returns to be likely to be roughly the same as in the past.

In order for both these things to be held to apply, it must also be held that there is never likely to be some unexpected external event which might suddenly impact returns and push them out of their 'normal' range.

In order to assume this, it is helpful to presume that the market is driven only by the actions of individual investors who are unaffected by external factors. The easiest way to do this is to assume that all investors will be running their CAPM calculations and abiding by the results, seeking to maximise their return for any given level of volatility as risk.

In fact every chain of this argument falls apart as soon as we subject it to the slightest scrutiny. As we have already seen, normal distribution does not apply, and nor can the past be taken to be a reliable guide to the future. Unexpected external events ('externalities') can and do occur, and impact financial markets when they do. Investors are not 'rational' even in the very narrow sense proposed by Finance World, being influenced by many things other than the supposed 'risk adjusted' return of individual assets. Finally, investors do not generally target levels of volatility, at least not in isolation; indeed for some investors volatility is largely irrelevant.

When we turn to the wider meaning of 'rational', the everyday common sense meaning, it is as if we turn a key and open a door into a sunlit world of real understanding of just how deficient Finance World is in its ability to recognise finance for what it is.

For, of course, investors are human beings, and human beings are not really rational in any sense of the word. We are animals, and like all animals are driven largely by strong and primitive emotions. In the case of investment these are chiefly fear and greed, though influenced also by issues of ego, competition, and affiliation. Anyone who has ever made an investment decision, or observed them being discussed and made by others, will be only too aware of this. Far from accepting the outcomes of financial modelling and using them to drive their decision making, investors are quite capable of ignoring them entirely or even of changing the results to made-up numbers to justify whatever conclusion it is they wish to reach.

As Keynes said, it is often 'animal spirits' which drive stock markets. If that were not the case then why, in the absence of some sudden unexpected macro event, would there ever be stock market crashes? As von Mises states, it is 'human action' which constitutes investment decision making and therefore to use financial data, which are simply a record of what lots of individual human beings did at a certain moment in time, to try to predict what many other human beings will do at a different moment in time is a futile exercise.

We will have a great deal more to say about this subject as we move towards hopefully a deeper understanding of finance, for it is perhaps the most important argument of all against Finance World's traditional view of finance as a branch of mathematics, with formulae and models as its predictive tools. If finance is not the workings of a giant mechanism but rather the sum total of human action, then how can we hope that mathematics, rather than disciplines such as psychology, can offer us any real understanding?

For the moment, it is sufficient to note that this assumption too, namely that investors are rational, simply fails, whether in the narrow sense of 'rational' intended by Finance World or in the wider, everyday sense.

All investors have access to the same information at the same time

To be fair to Finance World, this is probably less untrue than it used to be. At one time some institutional investors could have a large advantage over others if they had recently had the benefit of a briefing from the CEO of a business. However developing regulation has both widened the definition of insider knowledge and made much more dangerous such briefings for both business and investors alike.

That said, it is still difficult to accept. A private investor dealing online with only the internet as a research source will not be in the same position as a professional fund manager with a team of analysts upon whom to draw. This can and does make a huge difference since in investment matters knowledge is usually power.

Nor does it end there, depending on how you define 'information'. For many now deal not on investment fundamentals, communicated by the likes of published accounts and annual reports, but on 'quant' factors, whether asset specific or market wide. Here many investors will lack the financial models required, the detailed data to drive them, or the expertise to interpret the results.

Speed of transmission and access must be taken into account as well, since the assumption says 'at the same time'. Data such as company press releases will be disseminated to a professional through a Bloomberg or Reuters system far more quickly than they are likely to reach the retail investor or small wealth manager. Even were that not the case, a professional dealer will be at their desk checking incoming information second by second while the small investor may not become aware of it until they read the financial press the next morning. So, in reality, there will frequently be what is called information asymmetry

All markets are perfect

Let us be quite clear what is meant here. Market theory talks of price takers and price makers. In a market which operates freely all participants are essentially price takers, transacting at the prevailing market price, which will move up and down in search of the price allowing the market to 'clear'; that is for all sellers who wish to sell to be able to find buyers who want to buy. If there are insufficient buyers, then sellers will have to tempt them into the market by lowering their offer price, and so on.

The definition of a perfect market embraces this idea, but also includes the requirement that buyers and sellers will be 'willing', or in other words to be dealing in the market of their own free will rather than being forced to do so.

In the case of the first limb of the assumption it is also implicitly assumed that the actions of any one investor or group of investors will never be so large as to influence market prices other than by a normal (very small) incremental effect as it acts upon supply and demand. However this is no longer the case, even if it once was. Various investors, such as pension funds and sovereign wealth funds, are sufficiently large that their actions can and do move prices, particularly as the details of those trades are made public, allowing others to digest and analyse them.

So far as the second limb of the assumption is concerned, many investors can now be forced, rather than willing, purchasers. Increasingly regulations such as Basel III and Solvency II effectively force certain types of investors, such as banks, pension funds, and insurance companies to hold certain types of assets, such as government bonds. Some investors are even expressly ordered to buy the bonds of their domestic government. Thus bond markets are no longer free, and this has an indirect impact on equity markets. Investors may need to sell equities, or be unable to buy them even if they want to, in order to buy bonds. Artificially low bond yields in turn place an artificial floor under equity yields because of the obsession with 'the risk free return' which bonds are deemed to offer, and which is adopted without question by CAPM.

Things fall apart, the centre cannot hold

This was a phrase originally penned by the poet Yeats but subsequently borrowed in whole or in part by E.M. Forster and Chinua Achebe, and which seems perfectly to describe how we should view Modern Portfolio Theory and the Markowitz view of risk. Interestingly, a few lines later Yeats talks of the best lacking all conviction while the worst are full of passionate intensity. Again this could be applied directly to Finance World, whose blinkered inhabitants seem absolutely confident in the certainty of their knowledge, while those who wait outside doubt that matters such as risk can ever be properly understood at all. The latter can at least take comfort from Socrates and Confucius, both of whom said that true knowledge consists of admitting what you do not know.

We have seen that the various assumptions, both implicit and explicit, which buttress the traditional view of risk are untenable. In other words, the centre cannot hold. It would therefore seem obvious to accept that this particular view has fallen apart, abandon it, and settle upon a new hypothesis which could in its turn be tested and analysed. We will examine later why this has not happened. As we will see, this raises very fundamental questions not just about risk but about the very nature of finance itself.

In Chapter 11 we will begin digging into the whole conceptual framework of risk, but before we do so let us take one further look at the methodology employed by Modern Portfolio Theory, for we have so far examined its nuts and bolts but not its overall purpose and structure.

Is finance just a game of dice?

Jacob Bernoulli, one of the grandfathers of probability theory, wrote to his friend the philosopher Karl Leibniz in 1703 musing on using the methods of predicting the outcomes of dice throws to other subjects of study. Incidentally, even this basic probability theory was revolutionary at the time, and little known outside mathematical circles. The adventurer John Law, for example, who brought paper money to France with predictable results (asset price bubble followed by economic collapse), was able to make money consistently at gambling because he knew the odds whereas other people did not.

Bernoulli wanted to apply what we might call 'dice theory' to other topics, such as assessing human longevity. Surely, if probability theory held true, then all one needed was a sufficiently large body of observed data upon which to base one's calculations?

Leibniz was unenthusiastic, pointing to the incidence of new diseases, and the difficulty in gathering sufficiently large amounts of data. In addition, longevity was something which could properly only be recorded when death occurred, and thus could only be 'known' in retrospect, and even then would not necessarily give a good answer in respect of those who were still alive.

Bernoulli was unable to advance his specific aim although he did come up with the idea which today we know as the

Law of Large Numbers, namely that the larger your sample of data, the closer the observations will cluster around the average. He also suggested that in order for any probability calculation to be meaningful, it is necessary to assume that past data are a good guide to the future.

It was left to the French mathematician de Moivre to advance the idea of what we today call Normal Distribution, which allowed the standard deviation of a distribution to be known, and thus also exactly the sort of annuity and longevity calculations which actuaries have performed ever since. It was of course precisely these ideas which Markowitz employed in arriving at his view of risk.

There are however a number of problems in approaching the situation in this way. Bernoulli anchored the problem in dice theory. It will hopefully be common ground that one cannot apply this sort of methodology to financial data. With dice there are a limited number of possible outcomes, all of which are known in advance. Incidentally, this gives rise to what von Mises calls Gambler's Fallacy: just because we know in advance what the odds are of any individual number coming up on the roulette wheel, it does not necessarily mean we can predict when, or even if, that particular outcome will occur.

However in moving on to longevity there are still certain similarities. Data can be gathered and the distribution of results collated, though whether enough data can ever be gathered to produce meaningful results in a pre-information age society was a concern which even Bernoulli himself expressed. One similarity is that, like dice rolls, ages at death are largely independent events which, excepting suicide pacts, do not impact the result of other outcomes. Another is that, ignoring war or murder, the outcomes themselves are divorced from human cause and effect, just as dice rolls are. With dice, the dice rolls are initiated by human action but what then occurs is a matter of pure chance.

Where Markowitz goes wrong is at the very earliest stage of his task. As von Mises pointed out, financial data do not arise in a vacuum. Unlike dice rolls, economies and markets are not independent actors causing their own outcomes but what von Mises and Hayek called catallaxies, the expressions of collective economic exchanges between human beings. A financial data set has no relevance in itself other than as a record of what particular human beings were doing at particular times. It might just as well be a data set recording how many people in Manchester ate an apple one Monday morning, or how many people cleaned their teeth in New York before seven o'clock one Friday.

As von Mises makes clear, but Markowitz ignores, you cannot use mathematical models to predict future human action. Human action is the result of human decision making, and human decision making is driven by emotions, not probability theory. Emotions change, act upon other people's emotions, and may in turn be affected by what others say, or externalities. We all know about 'market sentiment', yet to believe in the power of mathematical analysis to predict future market outcomes then you must deny it exists.

To understand what is happening in financial markets, whether formal or otherwise, you need to know not just *what* is happening but *why*. Who or what caused it? Is the data the manifestation of a logical response to external events or have people over-reacted? If so, in what way is the market likely to correct itself, and when? Probability ignores all of this. It assumes that a financial data set has some significance in and of itself, divorced from its function as a record of human action, and it doesn't. Markowitz just got it wrong. Finance is not a game of dice.

Chapter 11

Risk and subjectivity

So why on earth did Markowitz not begin his 1952[1] paper by discussing what people viewed as the risk of an investment, or even by taking a look in a dictionary?

The only person who could answer this question would be Markowitz himself. We do however have a number of clues, including from Bernstein, who knew Markowitz. First and foremost, at the time he wrote the article Markowitz did not really know anything about finance.

The way Bernstein tells it:

> Markowitz had no interest in equity investment when he first turned his attention to the ideas [in his article]. He knew nothing about the stock market. A self-styled 'nerd' as a student, he was working in what was then the relatively young field of linear programming ...
>
> One day, while waiting to see his professor to discuss a topic for his doctoral dissertation, Markowitz struck up a conversation with a stock broker sharing the waiting room who urged him to apply linear programming to the problems investors face in the stock market. Markowitz's professor seconded the broker's suggestion enthusiastically, though he himself knew so little about the stock market that he could not advise Markowitz on how or where to begin his project.[2]

---

[1] Harry Markowitz (1952) 'Portfolio Selection', *Journal of Finance*, 7(1).

[2] Peter Bernstein *Against the Gods: the remarkable story of risk*, John Wiley & Sons, New York 1996.

In passing, though, it is curious, even if the professor knew little about the subject matter of what became the famous article, that he did not at least advise Markowitz about standard academic practice, such as citing authors who had discussed similar issues in the past.

So neither Markowitz nor his professor had any experience of investing. Markowitz was not a finance academic but a mathematician, and his article is essentially an exercise in mathematics. He did not go looking for an answer to the question 'what is investment risk?'. He went looking for something he could measure.

Thus he was in the direct intellectual line from the logical positivists. If something cannot be 'stated' it is not something which one should waste time considering. It is a non-thing. It has no intellectual substance. As Wittgenstein said 'there are no questions, only puzzles', the 'puzzle' being how to 'state' something. For Markowitz as a mathematician, simply substitute 'calculate' for 'state'. As Aldous Huxley, himself from a family of distinguished scientists, said in a letter to a friend, science simply ignores anything which it cannot measure.

Yet this is clearly nonsense. We cannot calculate or measure love, yet most of us spend our whole lives in search of it. We cannot calculate or measure whether God exists, yet for many this is the single most important question which they face. We cannot calculate or measure whether an action is good or bad, yet ethics is today not only an important area of study but also provides the guiding principles by which all conduct, whether personal, business, or financial, will be judged.

Perhaps if Markowitz had been trained in a different discipline, such as philosophy, psychology, or law, he would have approached his task in a different manner. Rather than assuming that it was pointless holding risk to be something which could not be calculated he might have started by attempting to define, or at least describe, his terms.

So let us pose the question with which Markowitz should have started, but which he totally ignored. What is risk?

What is risk?

A simple glance at a dictionary would have shown Markowitz that whatever risk may be, it could not be what he was attempting to calculate. Most dictionary definitions talk about the chance of something unpleasant or undesirable happening. Markowitz seized upon variance of return, which embraces volatility both below *and above* the average. Above average performance is neither unwelcome nor undesirable to an investor. Thus Markowitz's view comes crashing to earth at the first hurdle. It equates risk with uncertainty of outcome and, as Knight pointed out, that simply will not do. Risk is a far more complex animal than Markowitz would have liked it to be. The central principle which he espouses (portfolio diversification) is sound, though he stops halfway and only states it partially. The basis on which it purports to rest, that variance of return must always be 'an undesirable thing', is not.

The 'halfway' point is important, incidentally. Even if you accept for the sake of argument the 'volatility as risk' approach, Markowitz only deals with diversifying away what is called the 'specific' risk of holding one individual stock as opposed to a portfolio of numerous stocks. He makes no mention of how to diversify away the 'systemic' risk of holding stocks in the first place as opposed to a selection of different asset classes such as bonds, real estate, and so on.

Though it is difficult to be sure, this approach may have been a major influence on investors around the world developing a blinkered view that nothing other than bonds and equities (stocks) were acceptable investments. Ironically, this in turn led to them running very high risk (volatility as risk) portfolios, volatility which might have been diversified away to much lower levels by use of the uncorrelated returns which can be produced by a Multi Asset Class approach.

So if, contrary to Markowitz's view which has gone largely unchallenged for sixty years, we cannot use variance of historical periodic returns as risk, what can we use? If risk is not pure uncertainty of outcome, what is it?

There is undeniably a close relationship between risk and uncertainty. Uncertainty of outcome must form part of whatever view of risk we might adopt. Where anyone has attempted to calculate risk it is probability, a measure of uncertainty, which they have used. Where they have gone wrong is not in assuming that uncertainty forms part of risk, but in assuming that risk can be calculated at all.

Yet if we are to square the concept of uncertainty with the widely held definition of risk we must restrict the extent of the uncertainty which we consider to that which may result in something unpleasant or undesirable. To put it another way, might risk be the possibility of a future outcome actually causing us harm?

What causes us harm as investors?

This seems a simple, perhaps even an obvious thing to suggest, but in fact it opens up an intellectual can of worms. As we will see, to enquire what might cause us harm as investors forces us to deal with various other questions. For example, what do we mean by 'investors'? The answer may surprise you.

It seems a truism to say that investors make investments. Thus if we can define what we mean by an investment we can use this to help us to a better view of investors.

The *Oxford English Dictionary* defines investment as 'a thing which is worth buying because it may be profitable or useful in the future'. This is undoubtedly correct, but too vague for our purposes. It would include a torch or even a pair of sensible shoes.

Investopedia defines it online as 'a monetary asset purchased with the idea that the asset will provide income in the future, or appreciate and be sold at a higher price'. This is better, but still not enough. It describes what it is we are buying, but not really why. It is submitted that in the case of an investment our motivation in wishing to buy it may actually form part of the definition. We buy a tool not because of what it is but because of what we hope it can do for us. A simple hope that it may provide income or appreciate in value may be part of this but does not go far enough.

We invest to make provision for future expenditure. An asset represents the expectation of a future cash inflow. Whether explicitly or not, when we invest it is to set aside monetary value with which to pay liabilities, cash outflows, as they arise in the future. In other words, we invest in order to be able to match our future cash outflows with our future cash inflows. We invest in assets today with which to pay our liabilities tomorrow.

If we accept this premise then it suggests that a fuller and more accurate definition of an investment might be 'an asset which we consider purchasing in the hope that it will produce sufficient value to be able to discharge some specific part of our liabilities in the future'.

We can refine this view still further by amplifying what we mean by 'value'. In this case the 'worth' of an asset is measured by the 'worth' of a liability which it may discharge. This is in fact always the case. The worth of an asset is measured in money, and the worth of money is in turn measured by some quantity of another economic good for which it may be accepted in exchange. Here it is as if the owner of a liability is agreeing to accept an asset in exchange for it. Put another way, the value of an asset is represented by its purchasing power.

This raises the obvious consideration of inflation. As we all know, the purchasing power of money declines from one year to the next. Largely this is due to the amount of money present within the economy and/or the speed at which it circulates. Thus while the apparent 'value' of an asset may seem to rise, as measured perhaps by its market price, its value will only really have risen if this new 'value' will actually purchase more of another specific good, be it gold, or coffee beans, or residential property, than did the old 'value'. Or, in terms of our discussion, if the new value will actually discharge a higher amount of our liabilities than the old one would have done.

So a fall in purchasing power should be thought of in exactly the same way as a capital loss. Our asset is now worth less than it was before even though its market price may have risen. Contrary to popular belief, the value of an asset and its price are not the same thing. The value of an asset is its purchasing power, particularly when applied specifically to the discharge of liabilities.

This also means that the everyday perception of risk that it represents the chance of actually losing some part or all of one's capital is, though instinctively appealing, incomplete. If the purchasing power of your capital declines then you have made a loss, irrespective of what the outward monetary value of your capital might be.

Thus an even fuller definition might be 'as asset which will both preserve its initial purchasing power and produce sufficient additional return to discharge some specific part of our liabilities'.

So, if we are to ask 'what causes us harm as investors?' then the answer must be 'anything which might lead to an asset not performing the function we have just described'. Our risk is the chance that an asset may not both maintain its purchasing power and produce sufficient additional return.

This point appears to be lost on many so-called 'investors'. If, for example, a government bond produces a gross return which is less than the rate of inflation then it is not an 'investment' but simply a way of holding cash. Similarly, far from being the fabled 'risk free' asset, it carries 100 per cent risk since it absolutely guarantees that the purchasing power of your assets will be diminished, leading to you being less able to discharge your liabilities at some stage in the future. Yet most investors, because they misunderstand the nature of risk, will regard a government bond portfolio as risk free simply because Finance World tells them to.

As was pointed out in Chapter 1, Finance World would have us believe that a certain level of return may exist in isolation, not accompanied by any risk. This is simply a confidence trick. Rather sneakily, Finance World uses a different definition of the risk of a bond than it does for the risk of a stock (equity). As we have already seen, the latter is seen as the volatility of historical returns. The former is seen as the default risk of the issuer, and certain governments are regarded by

Finance World as being so unlikely to default that their bonds can safely be regarded as 'risk free'.

Even more sneakily, they then use this 'risk-free rate' as the comparator in the Capital Asset Pricing Model (CAPM). Yet if you are considering the volatility as risk of a stock, then surely you should be looking for a rate with which to compare it which represents zero volatility as risk, not zero default risk? Incidentally, no such thing exists. Even prime government bond yields and prices are volatile when viewed against themselves over time.

Once we realise what risk really is, then even this tired old pretence goes out of the window however. Both volatility and default risk should be viewed for what they are: at best, but two needles on a highly complex dashboard, and at worst irrelevant. What an investor really needs to know is the material risk of an asset, the risk that it may fail to meet the investor's objective of discharging future liabilities. Default risk, for example, can indicate only a very small part of this, and even then only if it has been correctly assessed (a big 'if').

The definition of a 'risk adjusted' (or in reality 'volatility adjusted') return changes too. The question 'relative to what?' is no longer answered by 'the (largely notional) risk-free return' but 'the chance of not achieving your objectives'. Thus risk really is the other side of the same coin to return. Remember Derrida and 'différance'. What gives meaning to achieving our target return is the chance that we may not achieve it.

If we follow this line of reasoning then the process of investment must begin by identifying and, so far as possible, quantifying our liabilities. Since these will occur in the future we also need to assess so far as possible exactly when in the future each is most likely to occur. On this stream of future outflows we can then superimpose the stream of future inflows which we need to generate in order to match the two. The only logical investment strategy is then to select the portfolio which you believe offers the best possible chance of achieving this. This may sound a rational and straightforward approach, but none of the world's major investors currently does this, nor have they ever done so. Instead, asset allocation is set in a vacuum supposedly governed by the traditional risk model and, if determined by anything, likely to be clustered around a chosen level of volatility, not return.

One of the many problems caused by this traditional approach is that you never even consider the one thing which should be fundamental to your plans: the ability to pay your liabilities. Had a proper view of risk prevailed, rather than the artificial Finance World view of volatility as risk, then it would have been apparent years ago to many pension funds around the world that their investment decisions were actually making it not just more likely but a racing certainty that they would be unable to meet their liabilities. Instead of running low-risk portfolios, they were actually running high-risk portfolios, often with a heavy concentration on government bonds.

Had they undertaken the above exercise and calculated the target returns necessary to discharge their liabilities then they would also have realised that the target return, and thus also the chance of failing to achieve it (true risk), was in many cases unrealistically high, and been able to hold a proper informed discussion about improving their funding position or reducing their liabilities. Reducing the level of volatility in your portfolio when you are not already fully future funded will not reduce the chance of failing to meet your liabilities, but increase it. In fact for any true long-term investor such as a pension fund, which is most unlikely ever to be a forced seller of any asset, it is strongly arguable that volatility is actually not 'an undesirable thing' at all, but just the opposite.

A subjective approach

We touched earlier on Kant and Schopenhauer. The traditional view of risk is essentially objective, just like Kant's idea of the noumenal world, the world of things in themselves. Because risk is a mathematical value and is a calculated output of an arithmetic process, it has an objective reality of its own which sits within the asset to which it relates. One of the qualities of that asset is that it contains this calculated value of risk.

If this is so then it raises significant philosophical problems for our view of risk. If we view risk as the chance of failing to match the target return which you need to achieve in order to be able to discharge your future liabilities, then it follows that the level of that risk will be different from one investor to another, depending on their target rate of return and their investment timescale. If one investor is a pension fund with a target rate of return of inflation plus 3 per cent and a timescale of thirty years, then the risk to them of holding Coca-Cola stock will not be the same as it would to a second investor who may be an internet day trader looking to make 10 per cent in a single afternoon.

In fact Schopenhauer's view makes much more sense. Risk is not a fixed objective quality sitting within the asset, but a function of the relationship between the qualities of that asset and the circumstances of any individual investor. Since different investors will have different circumstances, then the risk of holding that asset will also be different for each. It is one of the saddest examples of the stubbornly dogmatic thinking into which Finance World has fallen that it fails altogether to recognise this glaringly obvious fact.

For Finance World is built on the assumption common to many mathematicians that there is always 'one right answer', and that all that is required to find it is the right methodology and the right data. Wherever the one right answer is as yet unknown it is because one or both of these ingredients is missing, not that the answer is incapable of calculation. In order for this always to hold true, Finance World reverts to the logical positivist technique of never asking any question unless you know in advance that it is capable of being answered (calculated).

Any possibility of a subjective view blows this whole assumption out of the water. In fact it torpedoes Finance World utterly and completely and leaves it sinking, irretrievably holed below the waterline. If the risk of an asset does indeed change from one investor to another, then there is no one right answer, let alone one which can be calculated based on the historical volatility of the asset's returns. There are not even lots of individual one right answers that can be calculated for each particular investor, unless, that is, you believe that the past is a good guide to the future, and in all the other assumptions which we demolished earlier. We can calculate the required target return, but not the chance of failing to achieve it.

If we believe in a subjective view, this does little harm. Just because we cannot calculate that the probability of us failing to match our target return is, say, 36.4 per cent does not mean that we cannot make a valid subjective assessment based on all available indicators, both qualitative and quantitative, and using our accumulated personal expertise. All of this is anathema to Finance World, though, since qualitative factors are incapable of calculation and, particularly when used in combination with subjective judgement, render any form of objective, quantitative approach impossible.

So a switch from an objective to a subjective view of risk makes a big difference. An objective measure of risk has intrinsic meaning, meaning within itself. In any subjective view, risk has meaning only when operated upon by the perceptions, values, and circumstances of the observer. An objective view of risk sits within the asset as one of its qualities. A subjective view of risk requires us to consider not the asset itself but its relationship with each individual potential holder of it. An objective view of risk is a calculated output of a mathematical process. A subjective view of risk can incorporate, or even consist entirely of qualitative assessment.

Seeing the big picture

Finance World will undoubtedly view such an approach as a grave threat, and brand it as dangerously misguided heresy. This is unfortunate, since in fact switching to a view of risk which more closely matches the basic reality of an investor holding, or deciding whether to hold, an asset is greatly liberating. It releases us from the tired old blinkers of having to view risk as volatility. More importantly, it allows us to view risk in the round.

For the mathematicians of Finance World the Markowitz view is convenient. It provides a pat, ready-made solution; a quick and glib response to any investor's concerns. Yet what is not widely appreciated is that this convenience comes at a very heavy price. For if you believe that volatility and risk are the same thing, then by definition anything other than volatility is not risk, and therefore need not be considered. At any rate, it is not material risk, risk which it is meaningful for you to consider, much less understand. Those in search of factors behind the events of 2007 and 2008 need look little further.

By coincidence, the writer was chairing an investment conference in Sydney on the very day in 2007 on which it became apparent that cracks were beginning to appear in financial markets (the Dow fell heavily, followed by other indices around the world). So concerned were investors that on this day, the second day of the conference, many failed to show up, being busy instead reassuring clients, directors, and trustees.

However on the first day of the conference a report had been presented. Commissioned by a global association of hedge fund managers, a survey had asked institutional investors around the world why, if they did not already have an allocation to hedge funds, this was so. Some of the researchers who were behind the report had spoken earlier of their puzzlement that so many investors had hung back. After all, had many hedge funds not delivered significantly enhanced risk-adjusted returns over the last several years?

The answers surprised everybody except perhaps those who already worked, or had worked, for institutions such as pension schemes and sovereign wealth funds. Chief among them was the desire not to have the institution named in the press as having been an investor in a high profile hedge fund failure. This was of course before Madoff and Stanford, so it is fair to assume that today the same would apply 'in spades'.

Others spoke of the fear of being associated publicly with funds which may produce market abuse or manipulation, whether real or imagined. Incidentally, surprisingly few spoke of lack of transparency, style drift, or levels of fees, all factors which those behind commissioning the report would probably naïvely have suggested.

So clearly the risk implied by soft issues, things like headline risk and reputational risk, weigh heavily with real life investors, and particularly so with those very large ones who handle much of the world's investment capital. Yet these cannot be calculated, and thus are disregarded by Finance World. It does not appear to worry them that in attitudinal terms a huge gulf appears to exist between how the process of investment is viewed by practitioners on the one hand and academics on the other. It is difficult to imagine such a situation appearing in disciplines such as medicine or engineering, where academic research is eagerly seized upon by practitioners who are keen to apply it in the real world of their day to day work.

Similarly, today other 'soft' risk factors play a very significant role, at times even an overpowering one. Good examples would be regulatory risk and political risk. Many investors would instinctively downgrade any business or project which is operating within a highly regulated environment. In cases such as healthcare, education, or financial services, the cost to the business of ensuring compliance, and the reputational risk for any investors should management fail in this task, can be very significant. In others, such as utilities, pricing is under direct government control and thus could theoretically be changed overnight on a political whim. Areas such as alternative energy are dependent on government subsidies which can be (and have been) unilaterally withdrawn.

Pure political risk exists in countries where the real risk of misappropriation of an asset has to be taken into consideration. It may also manifest itself in arbitrary and unpredictable legislation or regulation, sometimes even (as recently threatened by the Indian government) with retrospective effect. Sometimes this can even be a factor on a supra-national level.

Following the events of 2013 in Cyprus, many investors are now wary of holding any cash deposits at all with banks within the EU, or even with banks anywhere in the world which are registered in the EU.

All these are important issues. In fact, considerations of regulatory and political risk are now the main drivers behind many investment decisions. Yet none of these are things which are capable of quantitative calculation. Least of all do they bear any similarity with the variance of historical periodic returns.

Nor is this list exhaustive. People risk, for example, plays a huge part in areas of investment such as private equity, small cap stocks, energy, and infrastructure. Usually a large part of an investor's due diligence and discussion will centre around the people running the project or business, both singly and collectively, since it is acknowledged that their success or failure as a management team is likely to condition the success or failure of the venture itself.

Yet this risk cannot in any way be expressed as the variance of historical periodic returns. For one thing, the investment may not have exhibited any past returns. Even if it has, it may not in the past have been run by the same people as those who run it today. Even if it has, there is no guarantee that similar external factors will operate upon the business, or upon the team, in the future as they did in the past, let alone in the same way.

If we add into the mix things such as currency risk, weather risk, terrorism risk, inflation risk, and (in the case of pension funds) sponsor risk, then we have pretty much covered the most important issues taken into consideration when discussing a potential investment. Yet only one of these (currency risk) can be measured mathematically, and even that exercise will not be meaningful unless you assume that government policy, central bank actions, and economic conditions will operate in the future exactly as they have done in the past.

Yet perhaps the most startling example of the Markowitz view of risk being highly dangerous and misleading comes when we turn to the question of debt. For Finance World brandishes yet another shiny toy for its inhabitants to play with; it is called the Modigliani and Miller model, or MM for short. Needless to say, it does not actually work in practice, and since producing a financial model which doesn't work seems to be a prime requisite for being awarded the Nobel Prize for Economics both its creators were duly so honoured. Bearing in mind that Markowitz too was awarded the Nobel Prize for Economics, it seems clear that Economics is the only discipline in which one can win prizes for failure.

MM maintains that it is irrelevant from the perspective of an investor how much debt a firm carries on its balance sheet, and that accordingly this should not impact the value of the firm. The rationale is that if the firm is levered (geared) with debt then the investor can buy the shares and the effect of the debt will be to enhance the return on equity. If the firm is unlevered then the investor can buy the shares and borrow money himself.

This is of course nonsense. Even if everything else about it held true, it requires one to assume (sound familiar?) that everyone can borrow money equally easily and at the same price. It also ignores the effect of taxes. If the firm borrows money it will be able to offset the interest as a business expense before tax. If the investor borrows money, he or she must service the interest out of dividend payments, which are paid *after* tax. In any event, it is most unlikely that the firm and the investor will pay tax at the same rates or with the same allowances.

Not only nonsense, but dangerous fantasy. Any common sense real life investor would rate the amount of debt carried by a firm as a prime factor in its perceived level of risk, and thus also in its valuation. If you are unlevered and have a bad year then you simply skip the dividend and carry on, with some or shareholder value being preserved. If you are highly levered and have a bad year then you cannot make your interest payments and go bust, with shareholder value being destroyed.

But if risk is viewed simply as the volatility of past returns then this very real risk factor cannot be captured. In fact, where a firm is highly geared this will often have the effect of increasing the return on equity, so that its 'risk adjusted' (volatility adjusted) return may well look flatteringly high when compared to other stocks. As has been noted, why does Finance World think it a good idea to rate a bond entirely by its perceived default risk, and yet to ignore this completely in the case of equities?

So the Markowitz view of volatility as risk, to which many of the world's investment advisers continue to subscribe slavishly and unthinkingly, is not just wrong but very dangerous indeed. Dangerous because it focuses analysis on volatility, which for some long-term investors can be almost entirely irrelevant, rather than on other highly relevant risk factors, which should be given significant weighting but are frequently afforded none. Dangerous too because when asset types are encountered for which volatility is clearly not a valid risk measure the easy response is to refuse seriously to consider the asset class for investment, leading to dangerously undiversified and highly liquid portfolios, which offer little protection in times of extreme market turbulence.

So, in having put, as Bernstein says, 'a number on risk' Markowitz did not after all perform a huge service to the world of finance, offering it an infallible compass with which to navigate its way through the uncertainty of investment outcomes. Rather, he led it up a blind alley from which it is still struggling to extricate itself.

Chapter 12

The shock of the new

Sweden in the seventeenth century was a small and not particularly prosperous country which would however develop over the course of the next hundred years or so into the major European producer of naval stores, such as the long, straight fir trees which were much in demand for the masts of warships, as well as the hemp rope and tar (produced from pine wood), without which no wooden-hulled sailing ships could function.

Her main problem, from an economic point of view, was the almost total lack of deposits of precious metals with which to make high value coins. Sweden's currency was thus perforce almost entirely minted in copper. Since in those days the value of a coin was assessed by the value of the metal which it contained, this meant that high denomination Swedish coins were actually large copper sheets weighing several kilos and having to be transported by pack horse. For this reason, it would be in Sweden that Europe's first experimentation with paper currency would begin in 1661.

As we begin our story thirty years earlier, Sweden had grown to dominate its own immediate surroundings but was not generally reckoned to be a major power on the European stage. Certainly she had thus far played little active part in the Thirty Years' War which had begun in 1616. Though nominally a member of various of the constantly shifting alliances which existed between the different Protestant powers, she had preferred to restrict herself to expanding and strengthening her possessions around the Baltic Sea. By the end of the war however Sweden would be recognised not just as one of Europe's great powers, but as the de facto leader of the Protestant states of Northern Europe. The reasons for the rise of what would become known as 'the Swedish meteor' can be traced to what happened on 17 September 1631, and to the remarkable man who shaped those events: Gustavus Adolphus.

We are not concerned with the wider details of the Thirty Years' War, a war which began ostensibly as a religious conflict between Catholics and Protestants, but degenerated into a naked power struggle which saw at one time, for example, Catholic France allied with Protestant Sweden. We *are* concerned with what happened that day in 1631 however, since from its events we can draw a direct parallel with the world of traditional finance.

When Gustavus had invaded what is today northern Germany in 1630, his nominal allies had been lukewarm in their support, and, still more disturbingly, his Imperialist enemies had largely ignored him. Early in 1631 however the situation changed when the Imperialists won a decisive victory in Italy, leading to a peace treaty and the opportunity to march northwards with their large forces, which had until now been tied down south of the Alps, and crush this troublesome little invader once and for all.

As the Imperialist general, Tilly, marched north and Gustavus marched south, they found themselves on opposite sides of the Electorate of Saxony, which had been attempting to remain neutral. Tilly peremptorily demanded free passage for his troops. The Elector courageously refused. Tilly ignored his refusal, and marched his troops across the border anyway. The Elector now sided with Gustavus and invited the Swedes to advance into Saxony in their turn to confront Tilly. Thus it was that the two armies drew up opposite each other near the small town of Breitenfeld which was to give the ensuing battle its name. The Saxons were to fight alongside the Swedes, but will play little part in our story.

Warfare in Europe had become a scientific matter much studied and discussed, not least because of the lengthy Italian Wars of the previous century. Crossbows had given way to firearms, increasingly sophisticated cannon made possible large set-piece sieges, and cavalry were being gradually relegated by well-trained and well-armed infantry into a peripheral role, protecting the flanks of infantry formations, and charging home only when an enemy was already weakened, or even already in flight.

Tilly had disposed of his infantry in the usual manner, based around about a dozen deep blocks of mixed pikemen and musketeers.[1] These blocks were more developed versions of something called a tercio, a formation which had dominated the Italian wars. Defensively, the qualities of the tercio were undoubted. Used offensively, it could still prove a fearful adversary, though its mobility could be impeded owing to the need to hold strict formation while carrying very long, heavy pikes. Also, as was usual at the time, Tilly had about twice as many pikemen as musketeers in each tercio, and each tercio was about ten ranks deep.

The battle opened, as was customary, with an artillery duel, and here Tilly received the first of several unpleasant surprises which he was to experience that day. Gustavus had developed lightweight cannon, expertly cast from prime Swedish copper, which could be easily moved around the battlefield by teams of horses, and had a higher rate of fire than their heavier counterparts in the Imperial army. Consequently he was able to deliver about three shots to every one fired by the enemy.

Tilly now tried a series of cavalry charges. These failed, largely because Gustavus had trained his men to aim for the horses rather than their riders, whom he rightly reckoned would prove largely useless once unhorsed. It is also worth noting that these were 'charges' in name only, the favoured tactic of the time being something called a caracole, whereby the riders would draw up a short distance from the enemy line and fire their pistols. Though theoretically they were supposed then to close with the sabre, few chose to do so.

---

[1] We will use the term 'musketeers' for convenience, but strictly speaking the weapon which was used at the battle was an arquebus, an early form of musket. They differed from later weapons in being either matchlock or wheel-lock instead of flintlock, and being supported on a firing stick rather than being held unaided to the shoulder.

Against the Saxons on the Swedish left, Tilly's tactics were more successful, and the entire Saxon army started to fold up and disappear from the field. Intending to roll up the Swedish army starting with their left flank, he ordered his tercios to move diagonally across the Swedish positions. This was in fact a very difficult manoeuvre for them to undertake, burdened as they were by their long pikes.

Gustavus, on the other hand had issued his men with much shorter pikes specifically so that they could manoeuvre more easily. They were also drawn up in line rather than in tercios. As the unwieldy tercios crabbed clumsily across the battlefield the more nimble Swedish infantry simply pulled back the flank that was being attacked while advancing with the other one, thus keeping all the Imperial troops in their line of fire (called 'oblique order', this tactic would later successfully be copied by Frederick the Great amongst others). As Gustavus had boosted the number of musketeers in his formation to rough equality of numbers with the pikes, and was using many fewer lines than his opponents so that all of his muskets could be brought to bear, the tercios now found themselves coming under a withering fire.

To make matters worse, Gustavus had also infiltrated light cannon into his infantry units (a tactic that would later be copied by Napoleon), and these had been trained to fire low, sending cannon balls into the tercios at knee height, inflicting terrible wounds.

As the tercios struggled desperately on with great holes opening up in their ranks, Gustavus saw an opportunity for a master stroke. As the Imperial infantry moved to the right it left their cannon, which had previously been roughly in their centre, exposed. With a roar, the Swedish cavalry, which had been taught to ignore their pistols and charge home with the sabre, swept round the Imperial left flank and captured them.

Ordinarily, this would have been a bad blow, but not a disaster. Cavalry would slaughter any gun crew they could catch, and then move on. They were supposed to spike the enemy cannon by hammering nails, which they carried specially for this purpose, down the touch-hole, but frequently they would forget to do so in the heat of the moment and it was not unknown for cannon to be subsequently re-captured and brought back into use. Gustavus however had trained his cavalry also to act as artillerymen, and rather than pursuing their fleeing adversaries they jumped off their horses and brought the guns into use against their former owners, delivering a devastating cannonade into the rear of the tercios. After resisting bravely for some time, they broke and what was left of Tilly's army routed and disappeared into the surrounding countryside.

Tilly could be forgiven for being dazed. Dazed physically, since he was escorted from the field unconscious having been struck on the head, but also mentally. By the standards of the time he had done nothing wrong, yet at every turn he had been met by some totally unexpected innovation which was outside his experience and which he accordingly had no idea how to counter. He had been undone not by any incompetence on his part, but by the shock of the new.

His only mistake was a failure of imagination rather than a lack of competence, a failure to grasp that what had occurred routinely in the past would not necessarily occur again in the future. Yet this failure of imagination is made on a daily basis by those in the world of traditional finance, as they analyse masses of historic data and use them and their magic formulae to calculate likely future outcomes. It all depends on a basic assumption which we have already considered, namely that past results will always be a good guide to future performance and, as we have seen, like most of the basic assumptions which underpin traditional finance, this one is false, or at the very least open to serious question.

Aficionados of TV sci-fi will know of the 'prime directive' in the various *Star Trek* series which prohibits any interference, no matter how seemingly trivial, in the affairs of the present, since any such interference could have dramatically enhanced and completely unforeseen consequences upon the future. This is of course fiction, but it states a serious proposition. As students of chaos theory (on which we touched briefly in an earlier chapter) will know, a very small difference in the starting circumstances in any given situation can give rise to a large difference in final outcome. This is sometimes stated as 'the butterfly effect',[2] an image conveying the idea that even something as inconsequential as the beating of the wings of a butterfly might cause some significant effect on the other side of the world.

Chaos theory divides series of events into two different types: deterministic and non-deterministic. A deterministic system is one which is sensitive to its initial conditions but thereafter evolves on its own in a completely independent way, sealed from any further external influence. In other words, its initial circumstances may effectively set a range within which possible outcomes will occur, but those outcomes are determined by the system itself.

This is where the butterfly effect comes in. Research seems to suggest first that a very small change in the initial conditions can produce very significant changes in the final outcome, and second that the nature and degree of such change is essentially unpredictable.

Note that this applies even where a system is deterministic, in other words when you can simply plug in the starting circumstances and then stand back and watch events unfold in a hermetically sealed environment. Is this true of finance? No, surely not. Finance is dynamic, or at least operates within an environment to which it is continually sensitive, and that environment is dynamic.

In other words, finance is sensitive on an ongoing basis to changes in circumstances, and those circumstances are themselves constantly changing, and acting upon each other as they do. So if it is true that it is impossible to use the initial circumstances to predict the likely outcome even of a series of events which is self-contained (deterministic), how much more true must it be that it is impossible to do so in respect of a series of events which are *not* self-contained but which are, on the contrary open to constant influence and contamination by external forces?

---

[2] A phrase reputed to have been coined by Edward Lorenz.

Yet, like Tilly at Breitenfeld, investors behave as though what has held true in the past will continue to hold true in the future. A couple of examples may serve to illustrate this.

We saw in a previous chapter how traditional finance came to adopt the volatility of historic returns as representing risk, and that based upon this idea the Capital Asset Pricing Model (CAPM) was developed. It is not important to know how CAPM works, but basically it claims to measure the risk of one share within a portfolio relative to the risk of investing in a 'market portfolio'.

This is not nearly as complicated as it sounds. Let us consider two different situations. Two different investors each want to invest on the stock market. One decides that they are happy to take whatever return the market as whole offers, and so they invest in something like an index tracker fund, one where the manager has no discretion as to which shares to buy, but must reproduce exactly the composition of the relevant stock market index at any time. This is known as passive investing. The other investor wants to be free to choose individual shares, since he believes that he can out-perform the market as a whole. This is called active investing.

Instinctively, the first strategy, passive investing, sounds less risky than the second, active investing, and of course it is, since whatever 'risk' may be, we have clearly diversified away the risk of investing in any individual share. Investing in a broad, diversified portfolio carries less risk than investing in a small number of shares, or perhaps even one individual share. An obvious question then arises: what is the additional risk which the second investor accepts as a result of an active, stock-picking strategy?

This is actually a very difficult question to answer, since it would differ from one portfolio to another and, of course, it all depends on what you mean by 'risk' in the first place. CAPM is traditional finance's attempt to crack the problem, which it does, as we have seen, by calculating (of course!) the 'risk' (historic volatility) of any one individual share relative to the market, or market index, as a whole. For the curious, or the technically minded, it does this by measuring the covariance of the individual asset against the market, then the variance of the market return, and dividing the first by the second. In practical terms, it is calculating in effect the volatility of the individual share, relative to the volatility of the market.

This mathematical output is referred to as beta and, as we have just seen, there is no magic about this. It is simply an arithmetic function whose existence is required to make CAPM work. The market itself always has a beta of one, so the beta of any individual share will be a number bigger or smaller than one. So much for the theory. As we will see shortly, there are a number of very large objections and obvious limitations that need to be considered when discussing CAPM and its various cousins, but let us leave that for now, and return to our first example.

As we have noted before, whatever CAPM claims to measure it certainly cannot be risk, since it includes the possibility of out-performance, and risk is the possibility that something unpleasant may happen not something pleasant. It does however undoubtedly measure relative volatility, and this fact has been used by institutional investors for many years as a basis for investment strategy. Let us just think for a moment about the implications of CAPM beta and then the thinking behind this particular strategy will become clear.

Shares which have a beta in excess of one will tend to move by more than the market; in other words, when the market goes up they will tend to go up even more, and when the market goes down they will tend to go down even more. Shares which have a beta of less than one will do the opposite.

You will probably have guessed the strategy already. It is to divide shares into two different types: 'cyclical', which have a high beta, and 'defensive', which have a low beta. If you think that the market is more likely to go up than down then you favour cyclical shares, while if you think the market is more likely to go down than up then you favour defensive shares. Cyclical shares were traditionally retail companies such as chain stores, department stores and supermarkets, particularly those towards the luxury end of the market, while defensive shares were typically things like banks and utilities. This was a strategy that had always worked reasonably well – provided of course that you were always able to call the market correctly!

However consider what would have happened if, on becoming nervous about the stock market in mid-2007, you had assumed that the old truths would always apply and had rebalanced your portfolio heavily in favour of the banking sector. Suddenly, instead of being one of the safest places to be, it would in fact have been one of the most disastrous.

The second example is drawn from the world of private equity, often viewed as rather shadowy and sinister. In fact, it is not, and much of the ambivalent feelings towards it spring from a lack of understanding of what the various types of private equity (and, yes, there are indeed several different types) are, and what they seek to achieve.

Let us focus on one particular type of private equity, namely early stage venture capital in the United States. During the latter part of the 1990s, the leading firms in this area made staggeringly high returns for their investors, with venture funds occasionally even returning more than twenty times their original capital. On the back of these performance figures, many, many more investors were drawn into the asset class, which ballooned alarmingly in size. In 1991 less than $2 Billion a year was raised by US venture funds. By 2000, most estimates place the corresponding figure in excess of $100 Billion.

Common sense would have suggested that no asset class, regardless of what it might be, could possibly absorb such an enormous increase in capital without a very severe decline in returns. Yet common sense took a back seat. Investors assumed that what had happened over the past decade was a good guide to what was going to happen in the future. With the infallible benefit of hindsight, this was of course doubly blind, since an enormous bubble was underway in both the technology and internet sectors, which was driving a related stock market bubble. As we now know, valuations had reached unsustainable proportions, and were being maintained only by the weight of all the new capital flooding into the market.

What had happened in the past was *not* in fact a good guide to the future at all.

Many other examples could be drawn from investors' experience. In some cases the error is a straightforward one, where things appear, at least at first glance, to be the same as they always were. In others, things are more complex. In particular, investors have demonstrated that they are not very good at recognising when some structural shift has occurred within the asset class, or where there have been changes in the surrounding environment. Remember, that even the slightest change in the starting circumstances can result in a significant change of outcome. Where that initial change is itself a large one (perhaps the rash of 'cov-lite' lending and credit derivative transactions which each played such a major part during the period leading up to the crisis that began to affect the banking sector from 2007), then naturally the final outcome becomes even more difficult (impossible?) to predict.

There are various reasons for this. One is that, as we will see when we look at the behavioural aspects of finance, investors tend to give undue weight to data which appear to validate their beliefs, and discount that which cast doubts upon them. Another is undoubtedly that investors find comfort in doing what has been done before, not just by them but by the great majority of investors, and are instinctively nervous of being the first to depart from an accepted view or approach.

As Shaw's Joan says when someone in *Saint Joan* claims it is 'a great responsibility to depart from the usual practice':

> Thou art a rare noodle, Master. Do what was done last time is thy rule, eh?

More prosaically, humans make mistakes. We are quite often just not very good at noticing that things have changed, and considering how this might require us to act differently. Did it not occur to Tilly, for instance, when he saw that Gustavus had drawn up his men in line rather than grouping them into tercios, to stop and think about what this might imply? Yet even the great Napoleon was to prove strangely unable or unwilling to change his tactics as the enemy gradually adapted to them, which is why many of his later battles degenerated into ugly, and very bloody, slugging matches.

Change is endemic. It is the one thing with which we can be certain that we have to deal, and yet the one thing with which we seem consistently unable to do so, particularly if the required reaction is either immediate or radical. As long ago as 1970 Alvin Toffler was moved to write *Future Shock*[3] by the recognition that huge change was taking place in the world, but that mankind seemed both largely blind to it, and largely unable to cope with it. Since then a whole body of management theory has grown up around change management, recognising that not only is there always resistance to change but also instinctive human hostility.

It seems highly probable therefore that there are deep-seated psychological reasons for this desperate search for comfort in tradition. We need the reassurance of believing that the past is a good guide to the future, even though this has been described as being akin to driving a car at high speed while looking only in the rear view mirror. We need to feel that what has happened before is likely to happen again, and in substantially the same way.

So, traditional finance is pushing on an open door here. We welcome the idea that we can use historic data to calculate likely future performance. It is the comfort blanket to which traditional finance clings, particularly if and when things start going wrong.

Of course, many times it *is* a reasonable guide to the future. We have already referred to one example, stock market crashes tend to follow inescapably from a sustained rapid rise in earnings multiples. Yet ironically it tends to be in these very situations that we ignore the warning signs of a price bubble and kid ourselves that we are locked into a rising market which can sustain itself for ever.

The key here lies in the use of the word 'guide' however. It is a dial on the dashboard which gives us some idea of how

[3] Alvin Toffler *Future Shock*, 1st edition Random House, London 1970.

our car might be likely to perform. Yet there may be other dials we can look at as well, or information which can be gained by looking out of the window, or listening to how the engine is running. It is here that common sense and traditional finance part company.

Common sense suggests that past data is one means of assessing what might be the range of outcomes most likely to occur. It would however yield to our judgement when it came to considering whether changes in the surrounding circumstances had occurred, and in the case of a major structural shift having taken place then it may be that it would actually be very little use even as a rough guide.

Traditional finance, on the other hand, has no place for 'assessment' or 'judgement'. It is concerned with calculating, not assessing, and no judgement is required, since calculation will always produce the one right answer. Traditional finance has no place for a subjective or a qualitative approach, or for the open questions which they involve. Remember, traditional finance only asks questions to which it can calculate an answer, and any such calculation is impossible (or, at least, invalid) unless you assume that the past data are a good guide to future performance, since the historic data are all you have available.

Of course, all finance writers give a passing nod to this objection. Finance books and investment circulars alike all state somewhere that past performance may not necessarily be a good guide to the future, yet this is usually done as a matter of form rather than because they actually believe it may be misleading. The reality is that they are unwilling, and probably unable, to come to terms with the fact that their workings may actually just be a soft, fuzzy part of a soft, fuzzy whole rather than a crisp, clear, snappy calculated solution.

This has other implications as well, for this obsession with using historic data, and applying statistical techniques to them, tends to force upon investors a particular view of financial returns, and of how these are measured and analysed. We have already seen how this view may be artificially narrow and be less helpful to an understanding of the needs of investors, particularly long-term investors such as pension funds and life insurance companies, than some alternative approaches.

It seems that in whichever direction we pursue our discussions we always come circling back to the fundamental issue of how people should best approach finance. It is as if we are trapped in an intricate maze and keep finding ourselves back in the centre, where this question keeps confronting us. There is a reason for this. It *is* the central question, or rather it is the fundamental question, the one which people should tackle first before they open their books on corporate finance or investment theory, but which they don't, and never do.

For in order to understand how we should approach finance, how we should treat it, we have to answer the question which we posed right at the beginning of the book. What is finance?

It is time that we faced up to this issue once and for all. Just what is finance? What sort of animal is it – fish or fowl? For unless and until we know the answer to this we cannot possibly hope to evolve a coherent way of approaching it and dealing with it. So, let us find the answer to this question. We will begin in Vienna before the Second World War.

Chapter 13

Finance and science

In examining the relationship between science and finance it would be helpful if we could first answer the question 'what is science?', since until we can do this we have no real frame of reference. Fortunately we have a lot of help here from one of the greatest modern philosophers, Karl Popper, who did his early work in the intellectual hot-bed of Vienna between the two World Wars. In his book *The Logic of Scientific Discovery*[1] published originally in German in 1934, he addressed this very question. What is 'science'? What makes one approach or area of study 'scientific', and another not?

Incidentally, two of the spurs to this line of discussion were physics and the relatively new 'science' of psychotherapy. Though Albert Einstein had emigrated from Berlin to the United States shortly before Popper's book was published, he still cast a long shadow in Europe. Actually resident in Vienna at the time, though both he and Popper would shortly follow Einstein into exile in flight from Nazi anti-Semitism, was Sigmund Freud. So, on the one side you had Einstein and physics, surely a science if anything was, and on other side Freud and psychology, or more properly psychotherapy. What was there about them, if anything, that might distinguish one from the other?

Something very important, said Popper, something which he chose to call 'falsifiability'. Though he gave it a complicated name, this is really quite a simple concept to understand. Scientific rules, he said, are not verifiable. You cannot

---

[1] Karl Popper *The Logic of Scientific Discovery*, Taylor & Francis, 2005, Kindle edition. First published as *Logik der Forschung*, Verlag Julius Springer, Vienna 1935.

prove that they are true, but only that they have never yet been proved false. If we say that iron is capable of being magnetised by wrapping an electric coil around it, what we really mean is that we have never yet found a piece of iron that does not behave in this way. So, if we conduct an experiment based on the hypothesis that the iron will be magnetised, and the result is consistent with the hypothesis, it does not prove that it is true. It simply means that we can adopt the hypothesis as valid for the time being, unless and until somebody somewhere conducts an experiment which gives a contrary result. When that happens, the rule or hypothesis will have been falsified and must be abandoned in favour of something else.

This, he said, is the nature of a truly scientific approach. Scientists are engaged in a constant testing of the rules of their area of study by experimentation, and are engaged in an ongoing effort to prove them wrong. Why? Because they recognise that this is the way progress lies. Once you have to abandon a rule you must think up some possible alternatives, and test these in their turn. Sooner or later you will find one that you cannot falsify, at least not for the moment, and which can be adopted as the new rule.

As the great physicist Dick Feynman, who claimed to be the only man in history ever to be both declared mentally unfit for military service and to win a Nobel Prize, said: even if a rule is found to be a little bit wrong, it makes a big difference to how we view the world.

Scientific rules share two characteristics. As we have just seen, they must be capable of falsification, but they also must be of universal application, at least within the class of objects or events to which they apply. The rules which govern the way in which the universe operates do not differ from one solar system to another, though their interaction may have produced very different results. The rules themselves are universal (no pun intended). They must work in exactly the same way every time.

For both these reasons, Popper concluded that psychotherapy was not a science. What was being studied in each case was one individual human being, and there was no way of falsifying any rules which anyone wished to advance based on such observations, not least because, as Jung pointed out, the results of each observation were in any event filtered through the individual perceptions and prejudices of the particular therapist. Nor was there any suggestion that such rules would apply to every person in every case. On the contrary, sometimes results were observed which were consistent with them, but often not. In fact, many psychotherapists today believe that some of the principles which Freud adopted as settled truths were in fact highly questionable, not least his whole theory of the subconscious.

So psychotherapy was not a science, and therefore not a suitable subject for study by use of the scientific method of seeking to falsify its rules. Unlike finance, which is a science, and probably a branch of applied mathematics.

Yet just how valid is this assumption? Is finance really a science?

What is finance?

Having asked ourselves 'what is science?', it is logical now to ask the question 'what is finance?' Does finance actually manifest the characteristics of science, or is it in fact something else, like psychotherapy?

One could dive into lengthy discussion as to whether the rules of traditional finance are both falsifiable and universal. If finance is indeed a science, then both these things must be true. Yet as we will see later, both these things are highly questionable. In fact, the situation is rather more bizarre than that. In practice, it is precisely those people who claim to approach finance as if it *is* a science, by way of mathematical responses to closed questions, who do *not* treat the concept of falsification as applying to it. We know, for example, that the risk of an investment cannot be calculated by reference to its historical returns, and perhaps not at all, yet continue to do so. We know that normal distribution does not apply to stock market returns, yet continue to assume that it does. We know that investors do not act rationally, and so on. In fact, any traditional view of finance requires intellectual dishonesty on a huge scale.

Yet there is one massively important observation that we should make straightaway. Think for a moment about physics compared to finance. On the one hand you have rules which govern the way the universe operates. On the other hand, you have rules (and let us suppose just for the moment that they are indeed 'rules') which govern the way finance operates. There is nonetheless one basic and hugely significant difference between these two areas of study.

Just suppose that mankind was suddenly to vanish from the face of the earth. The universe would still carry on functioning, and functioning moreover in exactly the same way in response to exactly the same rules. Finance, on the other hand, would not. Finance would cease to exist. For finance relies on human actions and interaction. Its workings are determined by human decisions, and those decisions are in turn influenced by a whole range of emotional, behavioural, and environmental considerations.

In studying finance, we are studying manifestations of the thoughts and behaviour of individual human beings, and so finance cannot be a science any more than psychotherapy can be. There is no guarantee at all that any two human beings will make exactly the same financial decision when faced with the same facts. Indeed, if they did, then no financial transactions would be possible. If one investor sells a share to another for $1, then one of them must surely expect it to go up, and thus that $1 is a good price at which to buy, whereas the other will tend to expect it to go down, in which case $1 is a good price at which to sell. They cannot both be right.

Any scientific rules, such as those expressed by way of mathematical formulae, are of course capable of being falsified when they are applied to finance in exactly the same way as they would be in any other environment, but they are not operators in the same way as they are in other areas of science. In physics the rules explain how the universe has always operated and will always operate; there is no need for human beings to execute the rules by pulling levers and pressing buttons at the right time. In finance, the rules might seek to explain how things *seem* to have operated in the past, but they cannot explain how they will operate in the future, because that will be an outcome determined by people pulling many different levers and pressing many different buttons at the same time, some of whom may be acting in a completely random fashion and not obeying any 'rules' at all.

So finance, if anything, appears to be much more a part of human behaviour, which is always unpredictable and frequently illogical, than it is of a science such as mathematics. Yes, it is possible to come up with rules which seek to explain how things have happened in the past, but we will see that when held up to the flame of falsifiability they are quickly burnt. Finance is not a subject that can be understood by asking closed questions, or at least not only closed questions.

So any study of human behaviour, such as psychology or sociology, can at best be what Popper classified as a pseudo-science, where we may attempt to take a scientific approach such as the gathering of data and recording of observations, but we cannot frame hard and fast predictive rules which posit that given the same inputs and conditions the same result will always emerge. We can at best suggest guiding principles that given certain inputs and conditions certain results are more likely to emerge than others. These rules cannot be falsified, and therefore cannot represent 'science' as properly described.

We can therefore conclude that finance is not a science, since its rules cannot be falsified, and certainly not a branch of mathematics. It is not 'about numbers'. Yet surely those who believe it to be a science would approach it as if it is? Well, no actually, and a consideration of why this is leads us straight back to Gallileo.

As scientists such as Dick Feynman and Stephen Hawking have pointed out, you can never say that a scientific rule is 'true'. It is simply a hypothesis which has not yet been disproved. It is the duty of scientists to attempt to prove that it is not true, since it is in this way that progress towards greater knowledge and understanding may be made. Since scientific rules must be universal and predictive, a hypothesis may be proved to be false by showing even one instance where the outcome was not as predicted. The hypothesis is then abandoned, and a new one formulated which is consistent with the actual result observed. This is then tested in its turn, and so on.

As Stephen Hawking says in *A Brief History of Time*:[2]

> [a scientific theory] is always provisional in the sense that it is only a hypothesis: you can never prove it. No matter how many times the results of experiments agree with some theory you can never be sure that the next time the results will contradict the theory. On the other hand you can disprove a theory by finding even a single observation that disagrees with the predictions of the theory.

Clearly this has not happened in the case of finance. Where reality refuses to match a hypothesis which has been laid out, then, like the inhabitants of Kriket whom we met earlier, Finance World sends out the killer robots to blast it into conformity. Instead of abandoning a hypothesis, comforting assumptions are imposed, even though these frequently are almost hilariously at variance with what actually happens in the real world. It is like creating a sterile environment, perhaps a vacuum, within which Finance World's delicate mechanism can function, but if the glass cracks and lets in the outside environment then it collapses and dies.

Even where a field of study qualifies as one of Popper's pseudo-sciences, there must be an attempt at a scientific approach, with rules being tested against observations, and modified or re-framed where appropriate. In other words, one needs to look not only at what is being studied, but how. The actions of Finance World in stubbornly clinging to old rules

---

[2] Stephen Hawking *A Brief History of Time: From big bang to black holes*, BCA, London 1998.

which have long since been discredited, the use of increasingly desperate assumptions with which to prop them up, and the discouragement of any dissenting voices surely fall far short of the required standard.

In fact finance much more closely resembles what Popper dismisses as simply 'dogmatic thinking', where beliefs are held automatically, without being challenged. It is effectively a religion, and a particularly unforgiving one at that, closely resembling the Catholic Church at the time of Gallileo. Even the word 'thinking' is perhaps inappropriate, since if we are told what to believe then thought is irrelevant.

So, finance would otherwise qualify as a pseudo-science, what we would today call a social science like psychology or sociology to distinguish it from the natural sciences such as physics and chemistry. However the way in which academics approach finance, refusing to abandon discredited hypotheses, reduces it to the level of a religion.

We will need to discuss what implications this has for the study of finance generally, and how finance courses might be organised and structured, but before we do so we must explore in more detail the effect of this unscientific approach to finance theory in so far as it washes across into practice.

As already noted, in a field such as medicine much valuable research is done in universities and hospitals. This research is then published and, where appropriate, doctors will try to apply it in practice. This is a natural and beneficial process. Yet when it comes to finance, little pure academic research seems to make any great impact other than on the first morning of its release. Funds built specifically upon academic research are few, and rarely successful. Perhaps one of the most high profile failures was Long Term Capital Management, among whose leading lights was the Nobel Prize-winning Myron Scholes, one of the inventors of the Black Scholes model.

Of course, funds built upon reducing volatility within a portfolio for a given level of return or boosting return for a given level of volatility are numerous and certainly most of them seem to succeed in their chosen aim (which in finance speak is usually referred to as 'extending the efficient frontier'). Yet this assessment requires us to accept either that volatility and risk are the same thing, or at least that reducing volatility must always be a good thing.

Whatever the case, when it comes to finance, a gap seems to have opened up between academics and their acolytes (the 'believers') and those who actually practice investment, many of whom are growing increasingly agnostic about this repressive old religion. The image of the Reformation, a clash between old and new versions of the same religion, comes instantly to mind and is one to which we will return.

It is submitted that the scale of this gap is set to increase steadily and perhaps dramatically in future years. The number of practitioners who seriously doubt the traditional view of risk is as yet small, though growing, and becoming more willing to speak out. In much the same way, in economics the accepted view that what we today call a Keynesian system is the only way of approaching public finances is beginning to be challenged by heretics who claim that an alternative approach, based in large part on the writings of the same von Mises whom we have already encountered, may be preferable. 'Keynesianism', they whisper, may itself be just a huge confidence trick just as we have already shown the Markowitz view of risk to be.

It is curious that this growing gulf between investment theory and practice should not have attracted more attention, for it is a fundamental issue which goes to the heart of what Finance World should be trying to achieve, and therefore the measure by which its success or failure should be judged. For it is important to ask not just what Finance World should be studying but why, and in this case things are more complex even than this distinction might suggest, since the answer to the latter conditions the answer to the former.

If a study of finance is to have any relevance, particularly if it is at best a social science, then surely it is to promote among investors a greater understanding of the techniques which they employ, and environment within which they work, so that they may perform their task more efficiently. Finance World seems to have lost sight of this, believing instead that financial research is an end in itself, and that the worth of an academic should be measured not by how well they assist investors to a greater depth of understanding, or even how well they teach their students, but how many articles they have published by peer reviewed academic journals. This would be sad even if it were not the case that, as we have demonstrated in earlier chapters, many of these articles are themselves of little practical value since they are concerned simply with creating more and more complicated mathematical models which are built on the flimsiest of conceptual assumptions.

Sadder still however is that academics should have fundamentally misunderstood the nature of what it is they are studying. The numerical quality of data gives a comforting illusion that what one is doing is scientific, just as if one was analysing the results of experiments in physics – but of course this is nonsense.

Unlike the outcomes of those experiments, financial data have no real relevance or meaning in themselves. Data simply record the outcomes of human behaviour which is in turn driven by human decision making, which is in turn driven largely by emotion. The fact that the standard deviation of the annual returns of a particular asset over a particular period was 14.6 per cent, or that the return patterns of two different assets showed correlation (a measure of the extent to which two things move in the same way at the same time) of 66 per cent may well be 'true' in the sense of 'not false'. A properly calculated mathematical outcome must always be 'true' in this sense. Yet it has no real meaning or validity to an investor.

The data that are being used as the basis of the calculations are not data in the sense of observed rainfall, or observed heights of schoolchildren. They are more analogous to the observed numbers of ice creams sold in a particular place on a particular day, and the price at which they were sold. The latter is simply a record of human action, namely the number of people who bought ice creams that day. If you want to understand why then you need to explore the motivation of the people involved, as well as all sorts of externalities such as the weather, and whether 26 July was a weekend or a holiday rather than just a boring old weekday. You would also need to explore how their decision might have changed at higher or lower price levels, as well as things like the availability of substitute products such a bottles of chilled Coke.

Quantitative analysis of financial data has no intrinsic value. It has value only if it is of use to some investors, and the only way it can be of use to them is if it assists them to a greater understanding of what it is they are trying to do, and therefore increases their chance of success. When you consider that some of the world's investors are large institutions upon which millions of people rely for pension or insurance protection then the importance of this point becomes clear.

So, if we really wanted to understand how likely a certain number of ice creams were to be sold on a particular day at a particular place and for a particular price, the best way of doing this would be not to analyse the numbers but to get out to that particular place and interview people about their motivation in buying ice creams, and how this might be influenced by externalities such as the weather as well as by personal circumstances. As always in finance, the numbers could usefully be used as one dial on the dashboard, but they cannot possibly tell the whole story. They record one particular outcome of human behaviour, but offer no understanding of how or why that outcome occurred.

So why is it, then, that when it seems obvious that to understand finance you need to understand human behaviour, Finance World continues to insist that finance is 'all about numbers' and can be fully understood using mathematics? Partly, perhaps, because so many of them are mathematicians to start with and they find it difficult to see things other than within a numerical framework. Partly, perhaps also, because many have Type-A personalities and they find it difficult to deal with uncertainty. Yet surely also because so many are reluctant to admit that they may have been wasting their time all these years basing their work on the Markowitz worldview, just as so many unrepentant socialists found it difficult to admit they had been used as Stalin's 'useful idiots' when the Soviet Union collapsed.

It is all a series of inter-locking delusions. Finance is a science and must therefore be about things which can be measured and calculated. In order to do this we need financial data. We need to understand risk, but because of the way in which we have defined our approach we need to be able to do this by measuring and calculating something. Therefore we will not concern ourselves with asking the question 'what is risk?' because it is inadmissible. Let us find something which we can measure and calculate and adopt that as 'risk'. Should anyone challenge this approach we will deal with this by insisting that this is the definition of 'risk' which they must accept, no matter how artificial it may be. If that fails, we will send in our killer robots.

You may find this last paragraph ridiculous, and indeed so it is, but it is true. This is in fact the approach which Finance World has adopted and the most ridiculous thing of all is that nobody should ever have challenged them before.

The reality is of course very different. Finance is not a science at all, certainly not if one accepts Popper's tests. Its rules are neither universal nor predictive, and therefore neither are they falsifiable. Furthermore if the proponents of the 'finance as science' point of view really believed that it was a science, then surely they would treat it as one, rejecting each hypothesis as it was found false, and adopting new ones for testing. Yet in fact they choose to retain them, propping them up with assumptions which attempt to force reality into conformity with theory, rather like creationists who refuse to accept the fossil evidence of evolution.

It is this defence of outdated beliefs and the unwillingness to tolerate any deviancy of intellectual approach which arguably prevents finance from qualifying even as a pseudo-science and relegates it to what Popper called dogmatic thinking.

At the heart of this failure of approach lies a failure to recognise what it is one is studying. Remember what von Mises says in his *Foundation of Human Knowledge*:[3]

---

[3] Ludwig von Mises *The Ultimate Foundation of Economic Science*, Van Nostrand, New York 1962 (Kindle edition).

> In the sphere of human action there are no constant relations between any factors. There is consequently no measurement and no quantification possible. ... Deluded by the idea that the sciences of human action ape the technique of the natural sciences, hosts of authors are intent upon a quantification of economics ... They try to compute the arithmetical relations among various of these data and thus to determine what they call, by analogy with the natural sciences, correlations and functions. They fail to realize that in the field of human action statistics is always history and that the alleged 'correlations' and 'functions' do not describe anything else than what happened at a definite instant of time ... as the outcome of the actions of a definite number of people. As a method of economic analysis econometrics is a childish play with figures that does not contribute anything to the elucidation of the problems of economic reality.

So if we really want to understand finance then we need to study psychology, not finance, but there is no place in finance journals for articles which do not ooze mathematical formulae from every pore. If we want to understand finance we need to understand not just what happens, but how and why. Yet, just as with Deep Thought, there are no Nobel Prizes in economics for qualitative assessment, only for quantitative calculation.

That this forces the study of finance into a narrow, mathematical path is tragic, because were Finance World to start examining finance as what it is, rather than as what they would like it to be, they would rapidly discover that it is a much richer and rewarding field than that of linear programming and simultaneous equations. An extremely different one, though, and we all share the very human characteristic of regarding change as a potential threat. The temptation must be to peer out over the walls of Finance World and regard everything outside as alien territory.

Finance World is under siege however. At isolated points just out of range of the defenders, small groups of subversive elements have set up camp and have started to undermine the ramparts by suggesting exactly what has just been outlined, namely that if you want to understand finance then you should study behaviour and decision making, rather than mathematics and financial data.

If finance really is just about numbers, their efforts are doomed, but if on the contrary a set of financial data is nothing but a record of human action and has no intrinsic meaning in itself, then sooner or later they will prevail, and breaches will start to appear in those once impregnable fortifications.

The mine which they are driving towards the walls is called Behavioural Finance. While this has been around a long time (one of the seminal articles was published in 1979) it has been slow to catch on among the mathematical inhabitants of Finance World. When one of the authors of that paper, Daniel Kahneman, won the Nobel Prize for Economics in 2002 it was for having 'integrated insights from psychological research into economic science'. Note the word 'science', making it quite clear that in the view of the Nobel Committee economics and finance remain firmly in the camp of universal rules and quantitative analysis. Finance World may be under attack, but it is fighting a very effective rearguard action.

The view persists that finance exists as a field of study to provide the reassurance of categorical solutions to questions which can be answered using mathematical calculation, and that this necessarily requires the use of historical data as a guide to future outcomes. There is not the slightest glimmer of recognition that an increasing number of those who practice investment understand all too well the degree of uncertainty with which they have to work, and regard with grave suspicion the attempts of Finance World to produce intricate models artificially to define its scope.

For financial markets are not clockwork models which can be wound up, and the results observed. They are, quite literally before the advent of electronic dealing, teeming groups of human beings all interacting with each other; a constant stream of human action driven by a constant stream of human decision making. Humans are not just receiving and analysing financial data, they are the economic agents whose actions create that data in the first place.

It seems obvious that issues such as emotion and perception must operate upon this process. Indeed some believe that matters are even more complicated, with emotion affecting the way in which we perceive things. Let us explore this area in more detail.

Chapter 14

It's all in the mind, you know

Readers of a certain age may recognise the heading of this chapter as a catchphrase from *The Goon Show*,[1] usually uttered by the character of Neddy Seagoon, played by Harry Secombe. It neatly encapsulates what many practitioners already recognise about the day to day business of investment, namely that, as pointed out at the end of Chapter 13, the making of investment decisions represents an example of human behaviour, and that both emotion and perception operate upon it.

A couple of points fall to be made for purposes of clarification before we consider this issue any further. We have thus far mentioned emotion and perception separately, and it is right that we should have done so, since they raise fundamentally different concerns when it comes to traditional financial thinking. The question of emotion challenges the assumption of the rational investor, while the role of perception argues for a subjective approach, embracing not just the qualities of any given asset but of its perceived qualities as part of a relationship between it and any given investor.

It is however far from clear to what extent perception may itself be influenced by emotional states of mind. We will in this chapter be considering what are called cognitive biases. There is clear evidence, and thus broad consensus, that they affect the way in which we make decisions. What is less clear is whether they do this simply by operating on our heuristics (our decision-making systems), or in a more subtle way by affecting our perception of external facts and circumstances.

---

[1] *The Goon Show* was a British radio show that started in 1951 and ran until 1960.

Some even argue that cognitive biases are actually heuristics themselves.

There is also a complex relationship between emotional states of mind, perception of externalities, and belief systems. Where there is a conflict between a belief and a perceived event, we will generally try to alter our perception, or at least interpretation of the event to accommodate our belief system. In general terms this is often what we mean by someone being 'in denial'. It is only where the gap between them becomes too great to bridge that we reluctantly change our beliefs. This is itself a painful process, often arousing other emotions such as grief, sorrow, or anger. So painful, in fact, that some people shy away from it altogether and head off down the path of prolonged delusion and fantasy, which can lead towards serious mental illness.

It is not necessary for us to explore these complex relationships, but we do need to be aware that they exist. Accordingly, it is proposed to deal with cognitive biases by explaining what they are and what their outcomes tend usually to be, without delving into the psychological nuts and bolts of how and why they operate.

The second point to make before we embark on this discussion arises from the chapter heading. It is proposed to use 'the mind' in a different sense to 'the brain'. The latter is an organ within the body which causes and handles the physical process of our thoughts and sensations. The mind is an amalgam of our emotional and imaginative state of being. Hence the expression 'in the mind' which implies a delusional belief, driven perhaps by strong emotions, not based on any accurate perception or rational appreciation of the facts. Finance World, with its dogged belief in the rational investor, would say that finance operates entirely within the scope of the brain, a human computer which processes mathematical analysis to arrive at the one right calculated outcome, and then acts upon it. It is submitted that such a view does not match the reality of how finance is actually practised, and that many of the necessary decisions are operated upon at least in large part by the mind.

Cognitive biases seem to take the normal path of rational thought and block it up, diverting the resulting decision away from its natural destination. We are as yet still at a very early stage of trying to understand how this happens and since psychology is in any event a social science (a 'pseudo-science' in Popper's terminology), the best that can be done is to observe individual outcomes and try to derive general principles from them; true scientific progress by way of repeated testing of universal, falsifiable rules is not possible.

Let us state, with appropriate caution, what we can advance by way of commonly accepted general principles. Cognitive biases do not rely for their effect on any lack of intelligence. On the contrary, many of the people who make these decisions are very intelligent, and usually also educated to a high standard. It therefore seems reasonable to assume that the emotional 'pull' generated by a cognitive bias is somehow capable of subverting what might otherwise be the purely logical outcome of a discussion.

The effect of a cognitive bias can be greatly strengthened by its operation across a group. They also seem to be highly contagious within groups, particularly where one or more senior members of the group are initially infected. Thus it seems reasonable to assume that it is far more difficult to counteract their effects when they operate within a group or organisation rather than simply within an individual.

Where a group is hierarchical in nature (and most groups are), then the task of any cognitive bias is greatly assisted by the natural tendency which seems to exist within most people to obey orders unquestioningly. At Yale in the 1960s Stanley Milgram controversially proved through experimentation that most people were prepared to administer a fatal electric shock to another human being, if placed in an authority situation and ordered to do so. 'Controversially' since it threw into doubt the refusal of the judicial authorities to accept the 'I was only obeying orders' defence of Nazis accused of crimes against humanity. Sadly, Milgram paid the price for the establishment's token lip-service to the concept of academic freedom of speech, and his later career suffered for it.

Though there has subsequently been much criticism of his methodology, and of attempts to link them directly to the perpetrators of the Holocaust, his experiments demonstrated (even if they did not 'prove') that the tendency to obey orders no matter what the surrounding circumstances was very significantly greater than anyone had anticipated. Even those few subjects who refused to administer the final fatal voltage still asked for permission to leave the room.

This is in turn exacerbated by the common tendency within organisations, particularly large ones, to view any members of the awkward squad who dare to question the conventional wisdom as dangerous subversives, and to weed them out as a matter of urgency. Where this is known, or at least assumed, by individuals within the group a 'spiral of silence' can quickly follow, making it less and less likely that the consensus view will ever be challenged.

These various factors come together to shape the dreaded 'groupthink', in which any view, if held by a large enough group, or one or two significantly influential people, will be accepted as the factual framework for discussion, no matter how implausible may be its assumptions, or how unconvincing its reasoning.

It may be that the effects of cognitive biases are so difficult to resist because they play upon very strong, deep human fears, particularly the dread of uncertainty. As mentioned earlier, this may in turn be so partly because we equate uncertainty of outcome with a state of not being in control of events, and partly because there is some instinctive transference between the fear of uncertainty generally and the sense of our own mortality, the one event in our lives which is both universally feared and totally uncertain, whether as to its timing, cause, or manner.

Ironically, as the Filipino novelist Jose Rizal pointed out, uncertainty may be the outcome of knowing too much rather than too little. The more you know, the more you know you don't know. (Aristotle Onassis was reputed to have turned this into 'the more you own, the more you know you don't own'.) The Nobel Prize-winning physicist Dick Feynman held that the true function and objective of science was to expand the frontiers of ignorance; the only time we can be sure to be right about something is when we know we don't understand it, while a certainty is just a hypothesis waiting to be disproved.

This emotional need for certainty would certainly be consistent with the general trend of cognitive biases to emphasise and boost existing belief systems, while exaggerating and resisting the possible effects of uncertainty of outcome, and to overvalue the present (the known) at the expense of the future (the unknown). It is almost as if they answer some deep-felt human need for reassurance and validation.

Identification and appreciation of cognitive biases grew out of the work of Kahneman and his fellow researcher Amos Tversky. Recognising that most people's powers of numeracy were limited, and that the brain functions of even talented mathematicians were not capable of calculating things like logarithmic scale outcomes unaided, they sought other explanations as to how and why people took decisions in situations of uncertainty where no 'rational' assessment of probability might be possible. For example, many people play games of chance without even understanding the basic principles of statistics – witness the number of players who religiously note down each number that comes up on a roulette wheel and target ones which have not occurred recently. There is a good reason why casinos are happy to supply pads and pencils for this purpose: each individual outcome has no effect on any subsequent outcome.

Where reason fails, we as animals must rely on intuition and instinct, and heuristics can be seen as short-cuts in the decision process to help make it manageable. A hunch as to what the right answer might be takes the place of a calculated outcome. This might, for example, take the form of remembering that we have seen what looks like a similar situation before, and assuming that what happened last time is likely to happen again. Or it may involve an instinctive belief that because a number has not come up on the last two hundred rolls of a roulette wheel it is now more likely to come up than one which has. The contribution of Kahneman and Tversky was in beginning to study how and why such an approach does not seem to lead to good decision making.

On the face of it there is no obvious reason why instinct need be incompatible with sound decision making. In sporting events, for example, we often see one player proving superior through successfully predicting what an opponent might do, or consistently choosing the right teammate to whom to pass the ball. So there must be something fairly specific to financial matters which causes cognitive biases to kick in and get in the way. We do not know the answer to this question, and perhaps we never will. It may in fact be the case that the same or similar biases are at work in other areas, though perhaps operating slightly differently. For example, both sides in the American Civil War (but particularly the Union) consistently over-estimated the forces available to the other side, and thus those required to defeat them.

In the case of finance, we do however know roughly what these biases are, and how they can distort the decision making process. In fact many different biases have now been identified. These are divided into (1) biases which affect our decision making and belief systems, sometimes called 'behavioural' biases; (2) those which affect the way we deal with our interaction with other people and their input, sometimes called 'social' or 'attributional' biases; and (3) those which interfere with the proper functioning of our memory, unsurprisingly called 'memory' biases.

Behavioural biases will include things like the tendency to cling to what is known rather than what is uncertain, to rely on one piece of data which supports our instinct while ignoring or giving insufficient weight to others which cast doubt upon it, and the tendency to believe something more readily the more often it is repeated and heard.

Attributional biases include the tendency to hear a speaker say what you want to be expressed rather than what is actually intended by the words, allowing the physical or professional impressiveness of a speaker to wash over into the perceived quality of what they are saying, and ascribing more weight to opinions expressed by members of your own group than to those of outsiders with comparable skills and experience.

Memory biases are partly to do with common sense biological outcomes, such as that more recent events are more easily remembered, as are those from certain periods of life (particularly our teens) and those which are for whatever reason more vivid. Others seem to have more to do with perception or even false memory, such as the tendency to remember ourselves as having been responsible for good outcomes but not for bad ones, and massaging past memories into consistency with our present beliefs.

Small wonder, then, that with all of these things operating upon our investment decision process there can be no such thing as a rational investor. Even if they wanted to be rational, and thought they were being rational, cognitive biases make that impossible.

Any comprehensive study of cognitive biases would require a book all to itself, but let us at least take a look at some of the more important ones. Since it is not possible to consider them all in isolation, the following discussion may sometimes blur two or three into each other, which it is hoped the purists will forgive.

I will focus on those which I have personally seen to distort the investment decision process the most often and the most significantly.

Confirmation bias

This is the tendency to cling strongly to data-points which support your preferred course of action and to ignore or downplay those which do not. In part this is a behavioural bias, but in part also a memory bias, in that it may be that it suppresses memories of past experience which would tend to undermine the preferred view. It is not uncommon, for example, to find that a potential difficulty or drawback contained in a meeting note which was circulated at the time is simply forgotten and disregarded for no apparent reason. A good way of combating this is to have one or two pairs of fresh eyes, who have not previously been involved in the process, conduct a rigorous *ab initio* review before a final decision is made. This apparent determination to ignore unhelpful information is sometimes known as the *Ostrich Effect*, for obvious reasons.

The other side to this coin is probably the tendency not sufficiently to test or validate assumptions and statements which are deal-positive, while eagerly and enthusiastically attacking those which might argue against the proposed course of action. Again, the sort of review process mentioned here can reveal that on various key points someone's word has been accepted without question whereas there was in fact ample opportunity for due diligence to have been carried out by way of enquiries with third parties. It may be that the issue was one which might have a critical impact on the outcome of the investment, but that confirmation bias stopped it being pursued for fear of undermining the essential belief that doing the deal was the right thing to do.

There are of course connections and relationships between many of these different biases, since they are all driven by the same psychological drivers. Confirmation bias can be particularly harmful when combined, as it almost always will be, with group-think and the spiral of silence. It is unlikely that a relatively junior member of a fairly large group will be eager to do anything to rock the boat by suggesting validating an unhelpful issue, or disproving a positive one. In recognition of this, some investment organisations appoint a specific 'devil's advocate' within each deal team specifically to challenge every assumption, but even this often does not work very well. *False consensus*, described further below, may also come into play here.

Hyperbolic discounting

We have discussed the importance of the time value of money at various points in the book already, and the important follow-on point that consequently compound return measures such as an IRR should always be viewed as more meaningful than periodic returns, whether annual or otherwise.

Hyperbolic discounting is the tendency to eschew the supposedly 'scientific' (though assuredly 'mathematical') technique of discounting future cashflows and instead arrive instinctively at a present value representing future financial outcomes. Effectively what one is doing is rejecting the discount value normally used, such as a firm's Weighted Average Cost of Capital, or inflation, or whatever it might be, and substituting it with some arbitrary discount rate which is very much higher.

In other words, one is giving much too little weight to what is yet to happen in the immediate future, and dramatically too little weight to what is yet to happen far out in the future. When one considers the very wide range of investment assets today which represent long streams of future cashflows this is a particularly serious failing: bonds, real estate, private equity funds, and infrastructure projects are but the most obvious examples.

Presumably if there was such a thing as a rational investor then a proper understanding of the time value of money would be built into the assumption. Yet another example, then, of how the assumption cannot hold in real life.

Perhaps this is all part of the exaggerated fear of uncertainty to which we seem to keep returning. Where an investor is somebody like a pension fund, who could and should be taking a long-term view of investments in order to match the long-term nature of their liabilities, hyperbolic discounting is a serious issue. What it does is basically to mis-price uncertainty, whereas a long-term investor needs to be able to embrace uncertainty and accept it, if not as a friend then at least as an inevitable part of the landscape. The more expensive they perceive it to be, the less likely they are to accept it.

Status quo bias

Just as we hate uncertainty, so too do we hate change. These psychological factors are obviously related. If no change occurs we are left with what we know, whereas if change occurs then uncertainty comes with it, for we all know that projects and investments rarely work out exactly as we had intended.

The smaller and more nimble an investor, then generally the less chance status quo bias has to exercise a stranglehold on decision making. The larger, more bureaucratic, or more closely part of the public sector, then the more enervating the effects. Among Japanese managers in particular it seems to be an unwritten but well understood point of honour to hand on one's department to one's successor exactly the same in every detail as it was two years earlier.

In investment, we see its effects in waiting too long to dismiss under-performing fund managers, and in extreme reluctance to consider meaningful allocations to new asset classes, even if what would be 'new' to the organisation is hardly so to the outside world. The Government Pension Fund of Norway, popularly still known as The Oil Fund, announced in late 2013 that it was mulling an allocation to private equity. What was not disclosed was why this move was being considered in 2013 rather than a couple of decades earlier, at which time it would have been a particularly smart investment decision.

Status quo bias has undoubtedly been partly responsible for driving investment organisations towards ever larger committees and a proliferation of sub-committees, consultants, and external review. If one is frightened of change then it makes sense to slow down the investment process as much as possible. It is difficult to think of any other reason for an investor believing that taking eighteen months to make a fairly straightforward decision is actually a good thing rather than a bad thing.

Loss aversion/endowment effect

In any room full of people, ask them to submit written bids to purchase some everyday item such as a bottle of wine from you for real money. The highest bidder will win the auction.

Now ask that person to write down how much they would accept for it were you to ask them now to auction it in their turn. What would be the reserve price? You will find that in every such situation without exception they will stipulate a higher price than the one they just paid.

You have just demonstrated the endowment effect. We all value the same item more highly when we own it than when we do not. That is why we feel that we are getting a lousy deal whenever we sell our house, or our car. It may be the same as the one next door, but we would all, if asked, offer a lower price to buy our neighbour's than we would to sell our own.

This manifests itself in public markets as an unwillingness to sell an asset because we believe that the market has somehow irrationally under-valued it. In private transactions it is often encountered when the owner of a business, particularly if they have a strong sentimental attraction to it because they were the original founder, or it has been in the family for generations, will resist selling it at a price which seems perfectly 'rational' when established financial techniques are applied to it. In such a situation, the potential vendor will also be prone to cling to a former valuation, which may have been reached on the back of totally different performance figures or market conditions (another example of *confirmation bias*).

Hand in glove with the endowment effect goes *loss aversion*. All this means is that we are psychologically more affected by a loss than by a gain of the same amount. You can test this very easily. Tell a room full of people that you are considering an investment which could result in a loss of 10 per cent. What likely gain would they require the investment to offer in order to compensate for a possible 10 per cent loss? Most will give answers in the range 20 per cent to 30 per cent.

Making a loss on an investment can be a harrowing experience, particularly if it occurs towards the beginning of someone's track record, since apart from anything else it can impact adversely on their career prospects. This may in many cases be unfair. Your mandate might be limited to a particular market which has experienced deeper losses than your own portfolio, so in effect you have out-performed rather than under-performed. Similarly you may have several previous periods of out-performance and only one of under-performance. Yet investors do not see things in this way.

This has a clear practical effect on investment behaviour since it can lead to both investors and investment managers becoming risk averse. This can itself lead to bizarre behaviour which is certainly not 'rational', such as selecting a particular asset mix which is extremely unlikely to achieve an investor's target rate of return simply because it is also unlikely (if past data are to be believed) to lead to a large loss. Choosing a portfolio which cannot deliver your objectives is simply opting to fail, and in seeking to limit your 'risk' (in the sense of the risk of a likely loss) you have actually massively increased it (in the sense of the risk of not being able to pay your future liabilities). Needless to say, Finance World has yet another mathematical technique, VaR (Value at Risk) which appears to validate such a misguided approach, at least if you believe in all the usual nonsense about normal distribution, the past being a good guide to future, periodic returns being a valid measure, and so on.

Something very similar is to be found in an apparent blindspot as to *sunk costs*. These are costs which have already been incurred on a project or investment. Since they have been incurred in the past they are by definition a fact. They have already occurred, and what has already occurred may not been changed. It is therefore logical, when analysing whether to continue with the project or investment, to ignore them completely. In assessing the attractiveness of the project, what matters are the cashflows which may be assumed to occur in the future. What has happened in the past is irrelevant. Yet whenever such a situation is encountered in practice, the mood of the meeting will invariably be 'but we've spent X on this already, so it would be crazy to stop now'. Perhaps more surprisingly, even after the concept of sunk costs has been laboriously explained, most prove intractable in their views.

Perhaps the problem of sunk costs is so acute because it plays to a number of psychological factors rather than just one. First there is loss aversion. To stop a project now would mean crystallising the sunk costs as a loss today, whereas continuing might offer at least the chance to postpone the day of reckoning.

Second, there is groupthink. If the project was originally the outcome of a decision collectively made by the same group or people, they will be snatching at any reason to continue with it (confirmation bias). There is also a separate but related cognitive bias called *irrational escalation*, which pushes us towards increasing our exposure to an under-performing investment even where there is clear evidence that the original decision may have been faulty.

Third, there is the apparent inability of the human mind fully to comprehend the effects of time, a failure to see us as being perched at a particular point in the time-stream (today) looking forwards into the future.

Money illusion

The tendency of most investors is to ignore the effect of inflation in their planning processes. If pressed on the matter, most will claim that they do it because future rates of inflation are so difficult to estimate. In reality, a more likely explanation is that to do so would expose the fact that many investment managers, particularly those in and around government bonds, fail even to match inflation, particularly after tax and fees. The problem is even more acute than it may seem, since the traditional measure of inflation – Retail Price Index (RPI) – is not a good proxy for the actual exposure to inflation of some groups of investors, most notably the clients of private banks and family offices, for whom the real rate may be more than double that indicated by RPI. Even RPI has itself been downgraded by government to Consumer Price Index (CPI). CPI ignores the cost of housing, presumably on the basis that housing is an optional luxury item, and that we could all choose, if we wanted, to take our family and go and live under a neighbourhood railway arch. A simple way of remembering these acronyms, by the way, might be the Real Price of Inflation and Civil Servant Pretend Inflation.

There is more to this than numerical convenience however. There is in fact a very real cognitive bias called *money illusion* that makes it very difficult to see money in anything other than nominal terms. The writer can call on considerable personal experience in asserting that it seems extremely difficult for some people to see a $10 bill to be received in the future as anything other than a $10 bill. The reluctance of the human brain to acknowledge the effect of inflation is closely related to the difficulty which we seem to experience in distinguishing between present value and future value.

Overconfidence effect

We seem to find it difficult correctly to assess levels of probability on any sort of instinctive basis. In particular, once we have taken a decision, we over-estimate the likelihood of a successful outcome. To give but one example, in a programme of research carried out in America subjects were asked to spell difficult words and then asked to rate the probability of their answer being correct. When subjects believed their answer to be correct, most answered '99 per cent', whereas in fact only about 40 per cent proved to be so.

This is probably related to a memory bias called *choice supportive* bias which causes us actually to remember things that we decided to do as having been more attractive, enjoyable, or successful than things we decided not to do, regardless of the true outcomes of either. There is an unconscious urge to validate our decisions, as we have already seen in things like confirmation bias, and to believe that the outcomes of our chosen actions are less prone to uncertainty than those which we have rejected.

Unfortunately, the techniques of Finance World, with their emphasis on scientific certainty, and talk of 95 per cent confidence intervals, play straight into this tendency. We fear uncertainty, therefore we want to believe that the indicated range of outcomes towards which we are working are indeed the ones which will prevail. Anything which will reinforce this belief, such as the mean variance analysis offered by Finance World, will be welcomed, and this may be one reason why criticism of the validity of these techniques is so unwelcome. Finance World, just like any religion ('dogmatic thinking'), appeals to deep emotional needs, and it is this which makes its inhabitants so ready to accept the apparent reassurance of the phoney science which it offers.

There are many other cognitive biases which we do have space here to consider. One of the most shocking, exploited cynically and mercilessly by politicians, is *availability cascade*, which causes us to accept as true something which is not, but is repeated often enough as a statement. Perhaps this too has something to do with people's readiness to believe that the volatility of past returns is the same thing as risk. It manifestly is not, but has been said to be so countless millions of times since 1952.

As already noted, there are many more biases out there. Yet hopefully even this brief sketch of the effects of just a few of them will be sufficient to show that the myth of the rational investor is hopelessly exploded. Investment data are the amalgamated result of investment decision making. Investment decision making is an example of human behaviour. Human behaviour is strongly influenced by emotion, and where emotion and logic vie for supremacy then logic will always be vanquished, or at best badly warped. This is true of human decision making generally and, as much research shows, true in particular when it comes to decisions made within the sphere of finance.

Again, it must be emphasised that this has nothing to do with intelligence versus stupidity. Intelligent people may well like to believe that their powers of logic are stronger than the average, yet they are just as likely to feel the powerful pull of emotions such as lust, jealousy, and grief as their less intelligent brethren.

Finance World sees investors as rational beings, who view financial data as expressing truth, just as if the data were demonstrating the observed outcomes of scientific experiments, perhaps showing the boiling point of a particular liquid. On this bed of 'truth' they erect scientific processes from which further 'truth' can be extracted by impeccable mathematical means. Because it is perceived as being true then the rational investor will accept it without question, and use it as a guide to their present decisions and future outcomes. Any elements of tiresome reality which threaten to intrude upon the process may be safely assumed away without affecting the validity of the calculated outcome.

Sadly for the high priests of Finance World, people are beginning to notice that the earth actually moves around the sun. In fact, probably not one single part of Finance World's approach is valid if examined in any detail. In particular, investors are not rational, as we have seen. Nor do financial data have any intrinsic truth in themselves. Data simply represent the outcomes of what von Mises calls human action, just as would be the case if the data set showed how many people were observed to turn left rather right within a particular period when stepping onto a railway platform.

Financial decisions have been shown to be highly influenced by emotional forces and in particular by cognitive biases which operate upon our mind without us even being aware that they exist, still less understanding what they do. These are hugely powerful because they appeal to deep-seated emotional drivers such as our fear of uncertainty, our need for affiliation with others, our need to validate our own decisions and beliefs and, most ironically of all, our desire to see ourselves as acting rationally.

In *The Political Brain: The role of emotion in deciding the fate of the nation*,[2] Drew Westen, a psychology professor at Amory University, explains that voters can easily detect contradictory statements when played speeches by politicians from parties that they do not support, but not when listening to those of their own party. He concludes that '60 per cent of the population are largely impervious to data'.

---

[2] Drew Westen *The Political Brain: The role of emotion in deciding the fate of the nation*, Public Affairs, New York 2008.

If we believe, with von Mises, that investment decisions are part of human action, and much more influenced by what Keynes called 'animal spirits' than by logic, and that emotion will always trump reason, then the logical extension of this argument is to say that in fact just about all financial theory is irrelevant. If what we are really studying is human behaviour, then does it really add to our understanding slavishly to measure the results of that behaviour and attempt to extrapolate from it into the future using dodgy statistical analysis? If we really want to know how an investor might act in the future (even if such 'knowledge' is possible) then is it not more meaningful to try to understand not what an investor does, but why?

Of course this puts forwards the most dangerous heresy yet so far as Finance World is concerned: finance might actually not be about numbers at all.

One may not wish to go quite as far as that. However the basic principle must hold true: if you want to understand finance then it seems more sensible to start with psychology rather than mathematics.

So this non-mathematical aspect is clearly crucial to any attempt at a proper understanding of finance. So crucial that we will endeavour to conduct the experiment of now examining many of the same themes we have already raised in this chapter from a rather different viewpoint. The word 'viewpoint' is apposite, because what we now need to consider is the very important difference between an objective and a subjective perspective on financial matters. Let us begin by reminding ourselves of the background.

Chapter 15

Personality, behaviour, and decision making

It is popularly believed that the left hand side of the brain controls functions such as logic while our emotions and imagination are governed by the right hand side. Unhappily for those who compile 'are you left brain or right brain?' quizzes, there is in fact little scientific support for such a view. The functions of the brain are much more complex than that, so complex in fact that even now they are not fully understood.

While this simplistic view will not hold, there is nonetheless a valid and useful principle to which it points. When we make decisions we attempt to do so rationally, at least when some business or financial issues are at stake. Making an investment or requesting a loan would be two good examples. We attempt to use logic, a technique first recognised by the ancient Greeks and now taught as a formal subject within philosophy courses. It was essentially logic which Alan Turing used to drive the world's first programmable computer during the Second World War, and which remains the basis for programming languages today.

However while it is tempting to view the brain as a sort of computer, a powerful logic machine which we use to drive our decision processes, such a view would be misleading, or at least incomplete. Our brain is simply one organic component of a greater organic whole, namely an animal. For animal is what we are. Unlike computers we need to consume other organic matter to survive, just as we need to respire, excrete, reproduce, and in due course die. As animals we are subject to the power of our emotions, whether they be basic survival instincts such as hunger and caution, or more complex feelings such as greed, fear, lust, and jealousy. In addition, as humans we are capable of imagination. Ironically it is this, along with the power of conceptual thought, which some believe separates us from other animals and led to us becoming the dominant species on the planet.

Ironically because imagination and conceptual thought are very different things, and symbolise exactly the sort of dichotomy which the left brain/right brain school of thought are seeking to express. This is often heard expressed as the difference between 'thinking' and 'feeling', the theory being that people in whom 'thinking' is dominant will approach tasks and decisions differently from those who are 'feelers'. The former will try consciously to use logic (reason, conceptual thought) while the latter will be driven more by intuition (emotion, imagination). If you have ever taken a psychometric test as part of a job application process then it is this basic balance that the test (or rather, those who create it and interpret its output) claim to be able to detect.

In fact even this is a simplification. The idea of different forces driving human behaviour was advanced by Carl Jung in 1921[1] and there are four, not two: thinking, feeling, sensation, and intuition. Thinking and feeling affect how we form judgements and make decisions, while sensation and intuition affect how the raw material for those judgements and decisions is created within us by means of perception. In addition, he posited that personality types sit on a continuum between introversion and extraversion, which raises yet another level of complexity since the four drivers may end up being felt and employed differently by someone who is heavily extrovert compared to someone who is heavily introvert.

Five factor psychological analysis

In *Intelligent Investing*,[2] while noting the binary play of thinking and feeling (logic and emotion) as forming the basic tug-of-war

---

[1] Carl G. Jung *Psychological Types*, Routledge, London 1992.

[2] Guy Fraser-Sampson *Intelligent Investing*, Palgrave Macmillan, Basingstoke 2013.

which results in investment decisions, I suggested adopting the concept of a five factor personality type map, the five factors being openness, conscientiousness, extraversion, agreeableness, and neuroticism, and the map itself being a five-pointed star. The following five paragraphs reproduce the description which I gave of each.

Openness does not mean openness in the sense of being quick to recount and explain one's actions, nor even of being approachable (though both these qualities will tend to be present), but rather openness to new experiences. These new experiences will include emotional states and acts of imagination. People who score highly on openness are likely to be creative and imaginative. They are likely to have the ability to present ideas as images, rather than dry textual descriptions. They are likely to juggle many different ideas at the same time, and to make apparently random mental connections between them. Perhaps in consequence, they will frequently hold unusual, even seemingly eccentric views.

Conscientiousness brings a need for order and an attention to detail. A neat desk-top, always arranged in exactly the same way, is a tell-tale sign here, as is a tendency to take detailed, methodical notes. This personality trait will induce a desire for planning and a mistrust of either improvisation or conceptual speculation. Those who score highly on conscientiousness are likely to fear uncertainty much more than those who are towards the openness point of the star, and thus to over-value certainty in consequence.

Extraversion and its opposite twin, introversion, are based around the need for, and level of comfort with, human interaction, together with the tendency towards either spontaneous (extraversion) or considered (introversion) action. A person at the extreme end of the extravert scale will want not only to be part of a group, but the focal point of it, while their introvert shadow self will be standing on the sidelines, or even off doing something by themself. Extraverts make good talkers, whereas introverts make good listeners. Extraverts make good salesmen, while introverts make good analysts, particularly if they also score highly on conscientiousness.

Agreeableness has a wider meaning than in everyday use. It encompasses a desire to make people happy, and to value doing so. A genuine feeling for the greater good of mankind in general. A subjection of self-interest to the interests of the group. While these may sound like admirable qualities, they do in fact have their negative aspects from an organisational point of view. Those who score highly on agreeableness tend to be very non-confrontational and over-ready to compromise their position. In approaching any issue, their overriding concern is often simply to reach a consensual outcome, almost regardless of what it is. In the investment strategy process, whenever any hitherto clear issue starts blurring around the edges you can be sure that some strongly agreeable personality types are at work.

Those who are neurotic are not, as many seem to believe, delusional. 'Psychotic' would be a more accurate description of such a state since, though it has a more precise psychological term, it usually implies some loss of contact with reality (assuming for a moment that any such thing as 'reality' actually exists). Neuroticism is rather the tendency to experience negative thoughts and states of mind. Those who score highly on this trait are more likely to experience depressive or melancholic spells, and these are also more likely to be prolonged. They will have a tendency to see problems as insuperable barriers to progress, rather than challenges to be overcome. They are nature's worriers, the Woody Allens of the world of investment. When they also score highly on conscientiousness and introversion, such characters can prove almost impossible to deal with, and are best exiled to run a branch office in the north of Sweden, where they may feel particularly at home during the winter months.

It is not necessary for our purposes to consider exactly how various positions on the five-pointed star may affect specific investment decisions. It is the point of this chapter simply to advance two propositions. First, different personality types may well approach the same decision-making scenario in different ways. Second, and as a related point, financial decisions are always driven at least in part by emotion, and in many cases overwhelmingly so. You may find these truths to be self-evident, as Jefferson had the Declaration of Independence assert, but if so then you are in direct disagreement with Finance World, whose inhabitants believe in the concept of the rational investor.

By definition, all rational investors must be the same, or at least operate in the same way when making decisions. Equally by definition, rational investors are not at all influenced by emotion. Yet how realistic is this assumption that financial decision making is carried out by rational investors, superior beings who can separate out their emotions and lock them safely away while they decide what level of gearing (borrowing) a business should take on, or whether to buy or sell a particular asset at a particular price? Remember, Finance World relies on the rational investor to form its population. If there is in fact no such thing as the rational investor then the streets of Finance World will empty and it will become a ghost town. Perhaps it will even fade from view, as people recognise that it was never anything more than a figment of their collective imagination, a film set rather than a town.

For it to be anything more than this, it must effectively be some sort of collective consciousness such as a gestalt. It must be an environment where lots of identical human beings, all thinking in exactly the same way, and all entirely immune to the effects of emotion, will come to exactly the same conclusion at exactly the same time, and act accordingly. For if all investors are rational then all investors must be the same, at least in any way which is material to financial decision making. Just as Finance World believes in one right answer, so there must be one right type of investor to arrive at it (mathematically, of course).

Finance World denies individuality and embraces the collective. In a way, this approach has a certain warped logic to it. Remember that Finance World believes only in an objective view of the world, and to admit individuality would be to invite consideration of a subjective perspective, to allow, for example, assets to be weighed against the particular needs of individual investors, rather than being rated mathematically against some model claiming universal validity.

The idea of a collective also suppresses original thought. For original thought to arise, there must be one person who is brave enough to be the first to express it, an unlikely eventuality if everyone realises that, like Gallileo contemplating the flames of his own destruction, they are likely to face being derided and ostracised as they slink in embarrassed fashion down the streets of Finance World.

Further, a collective view negates the power of perception. It seems likely that no two individuals view the same object or event in the same way; small differences in the way our senses work, and in the yardsticks against which we rate sensory experience, almost guarantee this. That is before we even begin to consider the impact of emotion on perception, the theme of Chapter 16. Thus if we believe, like Kant and Schopenhauer, that perception renders impossible any true knowledge of the noumenal world, then Finance World, with its utter certainty that it is possible to 'know' every important quality of an object such as an asset, cannot function.

Yet we have already seen that any attempt at understanding things such as risk positively requires us to adopt a subjective view and to accept, as Schopenhauer would doubtless have advised, a phenomenal view. We must accept that even if an asset has one true nature it is impossible for us to 'know' it, since any view of the object will be filtered through the perceptions of each individual observer and, as we will see, those perceptions may in turn be distorted by the individual's emotions, and these in turn will be influenced by the individual's desires and circumstances.

In fact, we can only attempt to find meaning in the nature of the relationship between the investor (observer) and the asset (object), just as Schopenhauer said, not in the nature of the object itself, not least because we can never 'know' this. As we saw in an earlier chapter, this points the way towards a real understanding of the nature of financial risk.

Finally, a collective view negates the possibility of emotion acting upon financial decision making; hence the concept of the rational investor. However not only is this view necessarily artificial, but it is also invalid within itself.

The first part of this proposition is self-evident and has already been touched upon. We are animals and are driven largely by emotions, no matter how well we may think that we keep these under control when it comes to financial decision making. In fact we fail dismally, as we will shortly explore.

The second may be less so, but its inherent self-contradiction lies in the implicit assumption that emotions can only be experienced individually, whereas we know this is not true. Why do financial markets suddenly leap upwards or plunge downwards? This happens because of collective fits of greed or fear. If it were otherwise then for every investor who thought the market suddenly over-valued, and sold, there would be another one who thought him or her deluded, and bought. After all, whatever we may think of 'value', it seems unlikely that in the absence of some specific external event a whole stock market should suddenly collectively be 'worth' considerably more or less than the day before, unless we simply equate 'worth' with market price.

It seems that there is an innate need within us to do the same as other people are doing around us. We have probably all seen the video clips of staged experiments in which everyone in an elevator suddenly turns ninety degrees in the same direction leaving one poor sap looking confused and uncomfortable until he too turns in compliance with – what? Some sort of herd instinct perhaps.

Every investor should read *Extraordinary Popular Delusions and the Madness of Crowds* by Charles Mackay, published as long ago as 1841, and usually referred to by just the last four words of its title. In the first part of the book he looks at financial bubbles, such as the Dutch tulip bulb craze, and the South Sea Bubble. He also mentions the Mississippi Company bubble in France caused by the same John Law whom we met earlier. The latter was a particularly extreme form of mass greed, during which high-born ladies are reputed to have haunted the streets around Law's house and offered the use of their bodies in return for an opportunity to 'stag' a new share issue. Incidentally, this episode also featured Europe's second experiment with paper money, a sad story which ended just as badly as had the Swedish one which preceded it.

Clearly investors did not read *The Madness of Crowds* however, or if they did then they failed to profit from its lessons, for shortly after the book's publication came the beginnings of the great railway company share bubble of Victorian Britain, a fact duly noted by Mackay in later editions.

Similarly, every business school student knows about groupthink, the tendency of discussion of a particular project to focus more and more rigidly within ever tighter parameters, with issues which may contradict the agreed view being either excluded from the conversation or explained away, a behavioural trait which we will explore in more detail in Chapter 16. It is for this reason that some investment organisations specifically ask someone to play the role of devil's advocate, or request someone who has not previously been involved with the process to conduct a full review before a final decision is taken.

So if, as it seems clear must be the case, emotion can operate equally well at the level of the group as at the level of the individual, then how is it possible to exclude its effects from any collective of investors? The whole idea of the rational investor is a non-starter.

In any event, how valid is a collective view of finance? If we accept Mises's view of financial activity as a catallaxy, simply the amalgam of an almost infinite number of individual transactions, and financial data as simply a record of the collective outcome of all these individual examples of human action, then surely it is logical to seek meaning for financial activity at the level of the individual? Finance World's view only stands up to scrutiny if the world is composed entirely of these fabled rational investors who all act in the same way and in response to the same sort of analysis of financial data. Yet what if investors are largely emotional rather than rational and, rather than acting upon data, they actually create data in the first place?

What if financial data, rather than being (after analysis and calculation) drivers of day to day investor behaviour are simply a record of it, rather like an old group photograph of a day at the beach now yellowing in a drawer, and of no value to anyone except as a sentimental record of a bygone family outing? It is faintly possible that people may determine their future actions by looking at old photographs of how other people behaved in the past, but it hardly seems likely.

Is it not much more probable that they might base their decisions on their own individual perspective of their own current circumstances, and their own perspective of the immediate future? Yes, these things may well be influenced by the views and conduct of others (the chatter perhaps of financial television in the background), but ultimately they operate at the level of individual human action, and it is accordingly at this level that it seems logical to begin any search for their 'meaning', if indeed meaning there may be.

Imagine, for example, a bull in a field. Let us accept for the sake of argument that this is indeed a true statement of a noumenal situation. There is indeed something which possesses all the qualities of a bull, and it is indeed standing in a field. However imagine now this same bull being viewed by four different observers, each from a different side of the field.

Not only will their physical perception be different (one will see the head, one the rump, and the others the two sides), but so might their emotional perception or reaction. Suppose that one of our observers is a vet, one a farmer, one a butcher, and the other a coward. The vet will see the bull as a potential patient, and will wonder about his state of health. The farmer will see the bull as a potential father of many calves with which to enrich the herd, and will wonder about his abilities as a stud animal. The butcher will see the bull as a source of meat for the shop, and will be mentally dividing it up into different cuts. The coward will be fearful of the animal as a potential aggressor, and will be worrying about whether he is properly secured and how much a barrier the fence might prove to be in the case of a determined charge.

We can best understand this by thinking again about perspective, in the sense of a viewpoint. A narrative which is told objectively is expressed in the third person. We are told what is happening to each character all viewed from the same external viewpoint. Collectively the characters are 'they' or 'them', while individually they are 'he' or 'she'. A narrative which is told subjectively is in fact 'narrated' in the true sense, that is, by a narrator. It is told in the first person, the narrator being 'I'.

Such a distinction raises many important issues. In the first place, an objective view is devoid of emotional or perceptual distortion. Hence the other meaning of the word 'objective'. It purports to state the world as it is, or to present a problem purely in terms of its factual background and the issues raised. Note the 'purports' however. The best propaganda works by being presented as an objective version of events, yet in reality being subtly slanted.

Even if one leaves aside the introduction of implied values and prejudices, it is possible to slant the meaning by verbal means. For example, Kahneman and Tversky pointed out that adding a stated cause to a stated fact or event makes people more likely to believe it, blinding themselves to the fact that even if the causative statement were true, there may also have been other causes. Noam Chomsky showed that changing the order of certain words can change the emphasis, and thus our perception, of what is being conveyed. Certain types of this technique are called foregrounding. For example, if we are told about a fat, blonde woman we tend to remember the fatness, while if we are told of a blonde, fat woman we tend to remember the blondeness.

With a subjective viewpoint we know that what is being told is being filtered by a mix of the perceptions, values, emotions, and existing knowledge of the narrator. Lawrence Durrell makes use of this in *The Alexandria Quartet*,[3] the first three books of which feature the same story being narrated from the viewpoint of three different participating characters. Yet even so this point is frequently overlooked. In part this seems to be because of what literary critics call the suspension of disbelief, an instinctive desire to be swept along by a story and enjoy it for itself. Hence the power of narrative, a point well

[3] Lawrence Durrell *The Alexandria Quartet*, Faber & Faber, London 1962.

known to every skilled presenter. Tell someone some facts, and they register briefly and ineffectually in the memory of the audience. Present them in a story, and not only will memory recall be significantly better, but the listeners will be more inclined to accept the facts as true. This probably plays to another human instinct which is to look at apparently related facts and try to weave them into a story, a tendency sometimes referred to as *narrative fallacy*.

When applied to finance, there are also clear and fundamental differences between an objective and a subjective approach, some of which we have already discussed. An objective view looks only at the asset, from the point of view of a notional rational investor. It sees the risk of the asset as being an intrinsic quality of the asset, sitting within it, and thus by definition the same for everybody. A subjective view looks at an asset from the point of view of every individual investor, and sees the risk of the asset as being a function of the relationship between the asset and the individual investor. Since the particular circumstances of each individual investor will be different, and thus what they need the asset to do for them will likewise be different, the risk can and will vary from one investor to another. A bond may be a very low risk asset to a short-term investor who may need urgent and unpredictable access to cash, but a very high-risk asset to a long-term investor in search of significant capital uplift.

We have already seen that this view of risk is greatly to be preferred. It sees any asset not as a *ding an sich* but as a tool, and recognises that its perceived value to any investor will depend upon what tasks an investor may feel required to accomplish, and how likely the tool is to assist in this process. If an investor wishes to slice some bread, then a bread knife should be viewed as a good thing to have, and a chainsaw as a useless and potentially dangerous one. However should the investor wish to cut down a tree, the position would be reversed. In reality the situation is usually much more complex than this, with an investor having to take into account a number of different objectives, some mutually inconsistent, and choose a number of different assets and asset types with which best to address these. So perhaps a better analogy might be with a golfer trying to decide exactly which clubs to put into a golf bag. In part the choice will be determined by the nature of the course to be played, and in part by the qualities of the golfer.

Of course a subjective view rules out a mathematical approach, at least one as simplistic as the volatility as risk view. If risk is actually a function of the relationship between the asset and an individual investor, then any numerical approach would have to involve constructing an incredibly complex model of the various issues operating upon an investor and the weighting to be ascribed to each different factor. Such a model would almost certainly be impossible to construct, and in any event many of the weightings could only be chosen on a subjective basis, thus rendering the whole approach void from an objective point of view anyway. It is presumably for this reason that the subjective approach has been so resolutely ignored by Finance World. If you believe that something is 'true' then there can only be one truth and it must necessarily be viewed objectively.

In fact the difference between an objective and a subjective view of the world adds not just to our understanding of risk, but also to our understanding of finance as a whole, or at least how we should approach it. As we saw in an earlier chapter, the existing way of teaching and studying finance is invalid, since it treats it as (1) a science (in the true sense) and (2) a branch of mathematics, and neither of these beliefs hold true when subjected to any sort of analysis. There is accordingly a clear need for a whole new approach to the study of finance, which for the sake of argument let us call New Finance.

Exactly what form New Finance might take we will examine in the closing chapter, but let us first turn our attention to reflecting a little more on the concepts of time and value.

Chapter 16

The angel of history

We have already identified time as one of the pillars of finance, or at least the medium within which the other three – return, risk, and value – must function. Perhaps this is the best view; time operates upon the other three, making them possible or relevant in the first place and also affecting their eventual outcomes.

It is clear that time must give relevance to risk, for if all outcomes occurred spontaneously rather than at some stage in the future, conditioned by all sorts of unpredictable behaviour and externalities, then there would be no uncertainty of outcome.

Similarly, time gives relevance to return, both within the traditional view of finance and otherwise. Within Finance World, returns for fixed income instruments (bonds) are expressed as compound returns over time, though that they are calculated and presented on this basis is not well understood. The returns of other asset types, most notably quoted equities, are stated in neat little slices, with each slice representing a period of time. We have already seen this view to be faulty, and it is a topic to which we will return, but let us note for the moment that even so it is impossible to make sense of such a return measure except within the context of passing time.

It may seem strange to say that time gives relevance to things such as value and yet it is so. For the main value of an asset to an investor is as a means of matching a future liability. Remember that an asset is a future cash inflow, while a liability is a future cash outflow. Other than as a cash substitute, and even then only in the case of a truly liquid asset, it has no value today which can be defined other than by reference to time (the future, in this case). Actually even this is a rather simplistic analysis, since 'today' is itself a point in time, and probably too clumsy a one given that we live in a world of instantaneous electronic trading. The current second might actually be a more appropriate expression, or even a philosophical instant, an idea we will explore further.

Yet we seem as human beings to have very little true temporal awareness. Conditioned by our understandably egocentric focus on the span of our own human life, we see ourselves as moving sedately through time, passing through the different ages of Man as we do so. Since we know that there is a hard stop at the end, at which point we literally fall into oblivion, but not when it will occur this arouses a natural uneasiness about the future, and a fear of uncertain future outcomes generally. This in turn leads to things like hyperbolic discounting, and favouring the present over the future, including a strong desire to cling to liquidity and short-term assets even though we may have long-term liabilities.

In fact it may be more helpful to think of ourselves as occupying a fixed spot, and time flowing towards us, through us, and continuing to stream away behind us. This helps to understand compound returns and the time value of money, with a future value moving steadily towards us to become a present value, and needing to be discounted for fewer and fewer periods the closer it approaches. If the first perspective of time is that of a passenger on a bus, watching it move steadily forwards along its route, the second is that of a man waiting at a bus stop, who sees the bus approaching and then, if he does not hail it – perhaps because it is not the bus he is waiting for – stopping briefly beside him before receding into the distance.

Perhaps the most compelling image of this was the angel of history, advanced by Walter Benjamin, a philosopher of the Frankfurt School who tragically committed suicide while attempting unsuccessfully to escape the advancing Nazis from France into Spain in 1940. A Jew, he chose to kill himself rather than face repatriation to Germany. The angel is a reference to a painting by Klee. Benjamin says in Part IX of *On the Concept of History* that he is one:

> who looks as though he were about to distance himself from something which he is staring at. His eyes are opened wide, his mouth stands open and his wings are outstretched. The Angel of History must look just so. His face is turned towards the past. Where *we* see the appearance of a chain of events, *he* sees one single catastrophe, which unceasingly piles rubble on top of rubble and hurls it before his feet. He would like to pause for a moment so fair, to awaken the dead and to piece together what has been smashed. But a storm is blowing from Paradise, it has caught itself up in his wings and is so strong that the Angel can no longer close them. The storm drives him irresistibly into the future, to which his back is turned, while the rubble-heap before him grows sky-high. That which we call progress, is *this* storm.[1]

Benjamin was actually working on this document while on the run in France, and it was subsequently rescued and transported to America by Hannah Arendt, who managed herself successfully to escape through Spain and was so struck by the image that she later referred to it in her own work. She actually subtly alters the image, by presenting the angel as having its hands covering its face so that it does not have to look at what a mess mankind has made of the world.

This is actually a pretty good description of the way in which an investor should see the world. We are travelling through time facing backwards, and thus unable to see what may be about to happen. We have a brief moment of present clarity as something appears on the platform at our feet, but no sooner have we had a chance to glimpse it than it starts to disappear again. Perhaps the best we can hope for is to sense certain sounds or smells or emotions which accompany or precede something's appearance and hope that as part of some hidden pattern the same thing will appear again in similar circumstances.

---

[1] Walter Benjamin *On the Concept of History*, Create Space Publishing, London 2009.

Finance World of course takes a different view, noting how many of each thing appear, and at what intervals, and then assuming, nay predicting, that similar patterns will inevitably occur in the future regardless of whatever external factors may be operating to cause the various appearances.

The angel of history offers a valuable image for the effect of time. People have a sense of moving through their own individual human lives, but usually only in the context of discrete periods elapsing, perhaps marvelling that a child has grown another year older with apparent speed, or looking at one's diary to note that another week has passed. But time does not really operate like that. Instead, it is flowing slowly but steadily towards us and past us, and if we are to attempt any understanding of finance then we need to take into account the way in which time actually operates on the pillars of finance, rather than the neat way in which Finance World would prefer us to look at it because it is convenient for their volatility as risk dogma.

Periodic return data can be calculated tidily as averages and standard deviations, and correlations can be measured across return generated by different asset types over the same series of periods. Nobody would deny that this is useful, although to pretend that standard deviation is a measure of risk is, as we have discussed at length, dangerously misleading. Things such as average periodic return, volatility, and correlation are all useful little dials to have on our dashboard. Yet they bring huge disadvantage too.

They blind us to the way time actually operates in practice. It does not come neatly packaged in bite-size periods like cans of soup in a supermarket, but in a solid and continuous stream, as if someone had turned on a pipeline of soup; a pipeline which cannot be turned off. For an investor to look at the market price of an asset on the 31 of December, see that it has gone up 3.1 per cent, enter the fact into a computer, and then sit back and wait to perform the process again in twelve months' time misses the point entirely. The only period which matters is the period over which the asset is held, which may rather inconveniently begin halfway through one year and end towards the end of another year, and its market price at any point during that period is irrelevant unless the investor actually chooses (or is forced) to sell it.

Apart from anything else, focussing on a periodic view of time makes it more difficult to understand the full implications of the time value of money. As we saw in Chapter 6, even a measure such as a geometric mean, which many believe fully reflects the time value of money, founders on its essential assumption that all periods in a series can and should be treated equally. This is of course a nonsense. Investors would rather experience an early gain and a subsequent loss rather than vice versa, and calculating an Internal Rate of Return (IRR) rather than a geometric mean shows why they are right to do so.

So here we have what seems to be a cognitive bias as yet unrecognised, to which we might perhaps give the name *periodic bias*, meaning a tendency to see time as a series of periods such as years or quarters rather than as a continuous temporal stream. As we have just seen, this may sound unimportant, yet is not. It chimes with Finance World's insistence that periodic measures are a valid way of looking at return, whereas in reality they are at best misleading, for all the reasons rehearsed fully in Chapter 7.

Periodic bias makes it difficult for anyone to challenge the supremacy of periodic return, and difficult for them fully to understand compound returns even when they do. Even experienced investment professionals can find a full comprehension of compound returns challenging, perhaps a result of the fact that IRRs and NPVs (Net Present Values) no longer have to be calculated manually as was the case in the days before spreadsheets. The idea that it really matters in which order cashflows occur seems to cause particular puzzlement.

Another problem with the traditional view of time as a series of periods rather than a continuous stream is that it tends toward an assumption that all we are usually dealing with is one outflow (when we buy an investment) and one inflow (when we sell it), although some asset types may of course also produce some income during the holding period, such as rent in the case of real estate or dividends in the case of equities.

However there are many types of investment vehicle, particularly those in what are typically called private markets, where investors' capital is called down as it is needed for making investments, sometimes over several years. Good examples would be private equity, venture capital, real estate, and infrastructure funds, particularly where operating within a limited partnership structure. Similarly, significant inflows will occur as investments are sold and the money returned to investors (limited partnership structures typically do not reinvest sale proceeds).

This is a good example of finance being operated upon by the time-stream, with inflows and outflows appearing unpredictably at the feet of the angel as it travels backwards. By the way, both the amount and the timing of these cashflows are completely uncertain, and it is no coincidence that funds of this nature, particularly private equity and venture capital, seem always to have been the target of much instinctive hostility among investors and advisers, surely a strong emotional response manifesting unreasonable fear of uncertainty.

So powerful is periodic bias that various very clever people have tried to find ways of creating some sort of weighted or blended periodic return measure for quoted equities which somehow reflect the timing of these private fund cashflows. Even if we leave to one side that the cashflows of these funds are not publicly reported, so that any such measure could not in any event be used as a valid comparator for any individual fund, the whole approach is topsy-turvy. Rather than using a made-up measure, which is not a valid indicator of private fund performance, why not use an unimpeachable one of public market performance, which is undeniably valid?

An IRR is a valid measure of the performance of any asset type. Indeed, for assets such as quoted equities, which produce dividend income, then it should reflect favourably upon their performance. Why then not use it? Using the same techniques as the data providers do for private equity funds, it is perfectly possible to prepare what are called vintage year returns[2] showing the IRR to date based on starting an investment programme at different times in the past, and assuming reinvestment of dividend or not as preferred.

Indeed, such an approach could be used validly to compare the performance of *any* asset or asset type against any other. Bonds of course already use this approach, though many do not properly realise this. Only quoted equities stand aloof behind the buttresses of Finance World, clinging to their volatility as risk Modern Portfolio Theory dogma. It is partly periodic bias which has made them much more difficult to dislodge.

In fact, we may understand even less about time than we think we do. Do we even properly comprehend the difference between the past, the present, and the future? What about the present, in particular? As soon as we start analysing it, it becomes clear that it may be a rather fuzzy term, as well as being used in different ways by different people. For an internet day trader, the present is probably thought of as the current trading day until the markets close. For a long only equity manager, whose performance is benchmarked annually, then it probably would be understood as the remainder of the calendar year, regardless of whether we were currently in January or December.

So the tendency may be to regard the present as whatever may seem a convenient and available period for any individual. William James suggests that to a listener all the notes in a bar of music seem to occupy the present, though he perhaps might have better expressed this as notes within a phrase rather than within a bar.[3] Other writers used the example of a single long musical note and mused upon exactly what part of the note's duration might be thought of as 'the present'.

This is a problem with which St Augustine had wrestled as long ago as the fifth century AD. He came to the conclusion

---

[2] Explained in my earlier book *Multi Asset Class Investment Strategy*, John Wiley & Sons, Chichester 2006.

[3] William James *The Principles of Psychology*, Dover Publications, New York 2000.

that only what was in the present had any existence since only in the present could we exercise direct perception. Thus for him there was the present of the past (memory), the present of the present (sight, but presumably embracing other sensory perception as well), and the present of the future (expectation). Hence for him the present had a very short duration, perhaps the shortest possible instant of perception, which would immediately become memory, the present perception of the immediate past.

So it seems that philosophy favours an alternative view to that suggested by periodic bias. In *The Metaphysic of Experience*,[4] published in 1898, Shadworth Hodgson wonders whether the present has any appreciable duration at all. If such a moment as 'the present' does exist, then for him it is a moment when 'perception and memory ... are indistinguishable from one another'.

William James would later talk about 'the specious present' in *Principles of Psychology*,[5] published two years later, though he gives credit for inventing the term to one 'E.R. Clay', which it seems may have been the pseudonym of Robert Kelly, who published a book on psychology in 1882. Quoting from that book,[6] James says:

> The relationship of experience to time has not been profoundly studied. Its objects are given as being of the present, but the part of time referred to by the datum[7] is a very different thing from the coterminous between the past and the future which philosophy denotes by the term Present. The present to which the datum refers is really part of the past – a recent past – delusively given as being

---

[4] Shadworth Hodgson *The Metaphysic of Experience*, Hardpress Publishing, London 2013.

[5] William James *The Principles of Psychology*, Dover Publications, New York 2000.

[6] Edmund R. Clay, but attributed to E. Robert Kelly, *The Alternative: A study in psychology*, Forgotten Books, London 2012.

[7] Since datum is the singular of data, the author is presumably referring to any single perceptual datapoint.

> a time that intervenes between the past and the future. Let it be named the specious present, and let the past, that is given as being the past, be named the obvious past. All the notes of a bar of a song seem to the listener to be contained in the present. All the changes of place of a meteor seem to the beholder to be contained in the present. At the instant of the termination of such series, no part of the time measured by them seems to be a past.[8]

It is unclear from James's own works whether he believes the present to have any duration at all, since some of his statements are contradictory, but he seems to tend towards the view that the present is that instant where the future is becoming the past so quickly that we are not conscious of the difference between the two. This seems a common sense approach. Whatever the case, the present can be no more than an instant, not the long, clear-cut periods so cosily imagined by Finance World.

Claude Monet, for example, said that his work was to capture an instant in each if his paintings, but that his task was impossible since fully to understand and express everything that an instant contained would take a lifetime. Perhaps this helps to explain why he painted the same few scenes so many times, often apparently employing multiple canvases and moving from one easel to another as the light changed.

Even our hitherto favoured approach of compound returns is not immune from such criticism. When calculating NPVs and IRRs it is customary to place cashflows at the end of periods such as years. One can shorten the length of the periods so as to ensure greater accuracy, but in reality it would be extremely unusual to use anything less than a quarter (three months). If the philosophers are to be believed, this might be about three months too long.

Of course, this is a silly objection. If you wish to calculate IRRs and NPVs then mathematically you have to use periods,

---

[8] William James *The Principles of Psychology*, Dover Publications, New York 2000.

and to use anything less than a quarter would usually be impractical, not least because more detailed data might not be available. Pointing out that we may have mis-imagined the present is not to suggest that techniques which work around calculating future values back to the present, such as IRR and NPV measures, are invalid. On the contrary, as we have already seen, they are undoubtedly the best and most powerful tools we have. It is rather to suggest that philosophy has a role to play in finance as well as psychology, that it strongly suggests that finance is an even more complex organism than we have suggested thus far, and that it is almost certainly not 'just about numbers' as Finance World would have us believe.

It also points up a fact which many might find disturbing. If the future is not next year but right now, unfolding around us from second to second, then we are actually subject to far more uncertainty then we realise. If we focus on what happens from one year to the next, or even one quarter to the next, then what happens from day to day seems largely irrelevant. It is this sort of day to day uncertainty which Value at Risk (VaR) addresses, albeit subject to all the false assumptions we have noted throughout the book. So, despite our irrational fear of uncertainty, perhaps we should be even more frightened of it than actually we are.

We worry about the future precisely because it is uncertain. Julius Caesar said that men worry more about what they cannot see than about what they can. Further, we seem to equate uncertainty with a lack of control, and we all have an instinctive fear of that state of affairs as well. So in turn we fear the future because we see it as representing uncertainty of outcome; a whole range of outcomes in fact, from which blind fate, not we, will select which ones are actually to occur.

A more logical approach would seem to be to embrace future uncertainty, since present certainty is but a fleeting moment anyway (and there are no such things as 'certain' outcomes, only highly probable ones), while trying to minimise so far as possible the impact of any foreseeable adverse consequences.

For with uncertainty comes opportunity, and risk taking, sensible risk taking that is, should be seen not as a failing in an investor, but as a desirable quality. 'Sensible' will of course need to be judged in each case relative to the individual investor's attempts to fulfil particular objectives. This point is lost on many investors, who persist in ignoring the blindingly obvious: in the absence of a risk free rate, let alone a risk free rate which can preserve the value of invested capital, then holding higher volatility assets, or private market assets, is forced upon them. It will be sensible, or rational, for them to hold what Finance World would regard as higher risk assets, and totally irrational to do otherwise. How can holding assets which are guaranteed to reduce the value of invested capital be a 'low risk' approach?

Hedging, sensible hedging, also makes sense. This is where you can try to limit the damage that may be done to your efforts to meet your objectives by possible adverse events. 'Sensible' here will be judged by what is both practical and cost-effective. Airlines, for example, understandably hedge the cost of aviation fuel, Starbucks hedge the price of coffee beans, and many businesses hedge their exposure to the US dollar. Sadly, the cost of any hedge increases dramatically once one moves much beyond the next few months, and non-US dollar investors are also badly disadvantaged in term of available hedging product.

Those who embrace uncertainty by actually starting and funding new businesses are surely among the most valuable of economic agents. In the US, annual venture capital investment is only about 0.2 per cent of GDP, whereas companies which either are or were venture backed contribute about 20 per cent of GDP.[9] In Europe, where risk-taking has rarely been genuinely encouraged, and often frowned upon and punished, this economic multiplier does not exist.

This is also an example of time operating upon value. If we accept that the value of any investment is the cashflows which accrue during the holding period, then venture capital is probably the most extreme example of this, with an exit sometimes not occurring until well after ten years from

[9] Numbers from National Venture Capital Association (NVCA).

the original funding round. If we really care about creating 'value' then we should be prepared to hold very long-term investments such as this (other examples might include forestry, agricultural land, and secondary infrastructure) – particularly if we are a long-term investor and are only allocating some part of our portfolio to such assets – but in fact this falls foul of what Keynes called the fetish of liquidity, with many investors eschewing such assets altogether.

As we have seen, 'value' is at best a nebulous term anyway, with confusion ironically being created by many of those to whom we look to bring clarity, such as accountants and regulators. For example, nobody really knows how to value a brand. How can we actually calculate the value to Coca-Cola Corporation of the Coca-Cola name? To do this we would have to know what sort of difference would be made to its earnings by not having the Coca-Cola or Coke names on its products, and this would clearly require us to venture into the realms of speculation.

So a sensible approach would be simply to put a statement in the accounts saying something like 'clearly the ability to use brand names such as "Coca-Cola" and "Coke" adds considerable value to the company, and this should be taken into account in any overall valuation exercise'. Instead, accountants put hard numbers on these 'values'. Again, the curse of the *Tractatus*[10] has struck. If something cannot be stated (calculated) then it is irrelevant. Brand value is deemed (correctly) to be relevant, therefore it must be calculated.

This is a huge issue. It is arguable that various companies which have been the subject of an IPO (initial public offering) have consisted *only* of brand value. Amazon, Google, and Facebook all spring to mind. Yet the fact that the market price of some of these has fluctuated wildly surely demonstrates all too clearly that there is no real consensus at all on what that value is, nor on how it should be calculated.

---

[10] Ludwig Wittgenstein *Tractatus Logico-Philosophicus*, Routledge, London 2001.

Again, Finance World is imposing a hard, objective view on something that is in reality fuzzy and subjective. It is requiring us to adopt a quantitative approach when a qualitative one would be more appropriate.

So what is wrong with Finance World is not just some of its most cherished doctrinal beliefs but its basic approach. We have already seen that we do not understand what finance is, so it should perhaps not be surprising that neither do we understand how to approach it as a field of study. In the same way, during the Reformation what was at stake were not just certain matters of doctrine but also the way in which religion might be practised.

Hopefully the time is at hand when we in the field of finance can experience a Reformation of our own, with tired, old, discredited dogma being abandoned, but also with discussion on how we might best approach the study of finance so as to gain new levels or understanding. In the final chapters we will examine how this might unfold.

Chapter 17

A new approach

Hopefully by now we can all agree that the current approach to learning about finance is not in fact appropriate, as it is based upon a view of the subject which is fundamentally flawed. It therefore becomes necessary to consider what form a better approach might take. What might New Finance look like compared to the volatility as risk world of Modern Portfolio Theory?

As has happened throughout the book, there may be instances of repetition in what follows. This is because finance is a complex organism with many different parts, all of which operate upon each other. It can be helpful to separate out specific issues for discussion, as this chapter does, but since many of the same issues will arise in each case then it is difficult to avoid duplication, and tedious to have to keep saying 'as we have already seen ...'.

Keeping a grip on reality

It may first be helpful to look at one of the main drivers of the need for a new approach. It is apparent that a gap has opened up between many of the world's finance academics and some of the world's investors. When theory does not work in practice, people start to ask questions, though still not enough people, and not the right sort of questions.

What is required, then, is something which takes what actually happens in practice in the world of investment as the starting point and seeks to extrapolate principles and guidelines from that, rather than carving out some theories and then sending out the killer robots to blast reality into the right shape to fit them. We need to understand how and why people actually behave in making investment decisions, rather than being required to assume that they will behave in a certain way, regardless of whether they actually do or not.

Assumptions have a part to play when we are conceptualising, provided that we recognise them for what they are, and that we handle them with care. Yet when they are inconsistent with observed outcomes only a fool would persist with them, particularly as the only argument for doing so (not that one is ever sought or advanced) is that to abandon them would render invalid a theory which relies upon them for support. A fool or a madman, perhaps. Locke describes a madman as one who builds a system of impeccable logic on a mistaken premise.

Such foolishness not only misses the point about assumptions (that they must yield to observed reality), but is a travesty of academic discipline. If you want to set up rules which are universal in their scope, then you must be prepared to spend your whole time trying to disprove them, and to abandon them in favour of something potentially better when you succeed. Finance World's persistent failure to live up to this obligation not only debases finance as an academic calling but forfeits any claim to finance being any sort of science, properly so called.

Where it may be the case, as it usually will in finance, that once subjected to this process a rule will fail, we need to recognise that it is a mark of intellectual strength, not weakness, to acknowledge that perhaps all that it is possible to advance is a guideline, based on what we hope will generally happen most of the time, rather than a hard predictive rule.

That this has not happened speaks to two things. The first is that those who enter upon any serious study of finance seem ready to accept the requirement that they should think what they are told to think, rather than questioning things for themselves. They are the academic equivalent of recruits on the parade ground, being drilled endlessly and noisily into a state of numbed obedience.

The second is that they seem to feel a desperate need to believe that finance is a science, and in particular a branch of mathematics. It is almost as if they feel that if this were not to be the case then their labours would have no meaning. The idea that finance may be at best a pseudo-science, a social science like psychology or sociology, appears repugnant and unacceptable. As Aldous Huxley said of scientists in general, anything which they cannot calculate has no relevance for them.

They mistake a desire for knowledge for a desire for certainty. Ironically, of course, many have pointed out over the ages that true knowledge must include an acknowledgement that there is still much that we do not know, and may never know. Knowledge is incompatible with certainty.

Miss this point, as Finance World does, and you head off down a very dangerous false path which leads to you having to turn everything you believe into religious dogma, and to require not just yourself but everyone else in the world to believe it, on pain of the Inquisition.

So our starting position must be that certainty is impossible, and that if we do want to set up rules which we hope will be both universal and predictive then we must be prepared to abandon them when they prove not to be so.

Since, if experience to date is anything to go by, this would be a frequent occurrence, it may be more sensible to seek to advance not hard and fast rules but broad guidelines, which we recognise in advance will not always hold true but which may nonetheless prove useful in practice.

These guidelines must be firmly grounded in the day to day activity of what actually happens in the real world of investment. Only in this way can we avoid the present mismatch between theory and practice.

Multi-disciplinary approach

Another point worth making while we consider our overall methodology is that it seems from what has been discussed in the book already that areas such as philosophy and psychology can produce valuable new insights when applied to finance. Others might include linguistics, economics, and history. So a multi-disciplinary approach seems indicated.

This would run counter to what happens at present, where the prevailing opinion seems to be that finance is far too complicated for non-financial folk to understand. This tends to become a self-fulfilling prophecy, with finance lectures being larded with letters of the Greek alphabet, financial jargon, and mathematical formulae.

So opening finance up to people from other disciplines would render a valuable service in making it accessible to all, not just those with a mathematical background. The problem with the current approach is that concepts get taken for granted instead of being questioned and explained. The fact that nobody thinks to ask the obvious question 'what is risk?' is a good example.

When we develop the theme that finance is largely a matter of human behaviour, as we will later, then the need for a multi-disciplinary approach becomes even more obvious. You cannot expect a mathematician to understand psychology any more than you can expect a psychologist to understand mathematics.

The role of data

Since we are speaking of philosophy, this may be a convenient moment to refresh ourselves on the role of data in our quest for knowledge. Again, it is the failure of Finance World to think conceptually which has resulted in the question 'what is data?' never being posed. Doubtless its inhabitants would testily retort that the question is futile, since it is obvious what data is: quantitative record of financial outcomes.

Yet this is only part of the truth, and contains a questionable assumption. It is only partly true since financial outcomes are themselves caused by human decisions, many of them taken or acted upon by other market participants or even external parties (politicians, central bankers, etc.), and human decisions are an aspect of human behaviour. So financial data are really recording many individual human actions, as Mises said. It is true in the sense that a set of data faithfully records what certain people did, or caused to happen, at a certain time, but, contrary to the implied assumption, has no intrinsic truth in itself beyond that.

Since numbers appear solid and reassuring this fact is difficult for many to grasp, or even to be prepared to consider. It is a matter of stripping away successive layers of language and meaning in a search for deeper understanding. Perhaps an example may help.

Suppose that we were to measure the length of the Golden Gate Bridge in San Francisco. Assuming that we did so correctly then the resulting number would be 'true'. It would be stating a fact which could be ascertained to be true by repeated measuring of the bridge. Only if we got a different reading one day, and could rule out any possibility of experimental error, would we be able to reject the truth we previously accepted.

From this true fact, the length of the bridge, we could calculate other true facts, such as how long it would take a car to cross the bridge if travelling at a certain speed, or even how much fuel it would consume while doing so, given a certain rate of consumption. All these would be truth statements, allowing us to 'know' something, because we would be entitled to accept them as true unless and until the contrary was proved.

Financial data are not like this. These data record what certain people did at certain times, but unless some specific pattern of cause and effect can be established, and shown to be highly correlated with the recorded data pattern, then they tell us little that is useful, and certainly nothing which can be 'known'. For that, we would need to understand not what people did but why, and how likely they were to exhibit similar feelings and actions in the future.

Using numbers such as this to calculate the probability of likely future outcomes gives a comforting feeling of false certainty, but it is just that: false. How Finance World may be able to cope with life without this particular comfort blanket remains to be seen.

For the length of the Golden Gate Bridge will remain the same, unless somebody saws a piece off, or part of it collapses.

There is an acceptable level of certainty that if we measure it again next month or next year we will still arrive at the same number. Because of this level of certainty we can legitimately use it not just to calculate other things about the bridge itself but also more generally, perhaps comparing it with the length of other bridges in different places.

Financial data however are in a constant state of flux. It is unlikely that any active financial market has ever closed at exactly the same level it did at the end of the previous day. Further, the data change not just in themselves but also as to how you calculate them. Take a look at the Bloomberg page of any stock and you will see different numbers for the volatility of the same stock, all depending on the number of days over which you wish to measure it.

Even if we can establish the sort of correlation referred to here, this proves nothing; correlation is not causation. There may be an undetected variable at work (trading volumes for example) or unpredictable externalities (a profit warning, or a failure in the trading systems). The truth is stark and, for Finance World, unwelcome. Not only does financial data have only a very limited capacity for truth within itself, it is impossible to calculate anything from it that may be any more true. Von Mises and Keynes got it right; it is not possible to predict future outcomes, even ranges of future outcomes, by applying quantitative models to historical financial data.

This is not to say that quantitative techniques have no role to play in finance; of course they do. Yet they produce indicative material, not determined outcomes. Each such technique represents a dial on the dashboard, but they are only meaningful if they are viewed in combination with each other, and filtered through the personal expertise, feelings, and circumstances of an investor.

One dial might tell a driver how fast the car is travelling, but the question of how fast the car can safely travel is one which must be left to the subjective judgement of the driver, and will depend on such non-quantifiable factors as the road and weather conditions, visibility, how many other cars are using the road, and a self-assessment of the driver's skills.

This is particularly true of volatility. To manage an investment portfolio having regard only to volatility would be as inadvisable as to drive a car looking only at the fuel gauge.

If we properly appreciate the true nature of financial data then it becomes obvious that finance cannot possibly be 'just about numbers', but sadly there will be many who still fail to grasp this, or refuse even to consider it as a possibility. We should therefore move on to be more specific about how we should address the limitations of mathematical technique within New Finance.

Taking off the blindfold

Seeing things through the eyes of someone who can only think in mathematical terms is not so much like wearing blinkers as like wearing a blindfold. You think you understand everything, and yet there is so much that you do not even see.

If you *do* see financial data as carrying some intrinsic inner truth then the urge to 'understand' it by imposing order upon it in such a way that it can be packaged neatly into meaningful rules and categories is overwhelming. If you carry this desire to its ultimate conclusion, it even offers the exhilarating possibility of being able to predict the future, or at least being able to predict the range within which future outcomes will occur.

All of this rests upon sound mathematical logic, but there are various problems with such an approach which are not always well appreciated by those who practice it. For a start, there is gambler's fallacy. Just because we know (or think we know) the odds of a particular outcome occurring, it does not allow us to predict any individual outcome. Just because I know it is unlikely that zero will come up twice in succession on the roulette wheel does not mean that it will not happen (I know because I was there, and I only bet on it the first time). Ask any number of people to predict how often four will come up if you roll a normal six sided die six times, and many of them will answer 'once' without even thinking about it.

Then there are situations where a mathematically correct calculation can create a result which is absurd in practice. Let us take by way of example the Capital Asset Pricing Model (CAPM), which we have not examined in any great detail thus far, but which forms an important part of Modern Portfolio Theory.

CAPM calculates the beta of any stock (company share). The beta measures how widely the return of that stock will fluctuate (whether for good or bad) relative to the return of the whole market, or, in the jargon, 'relative to the market portfolio of which it forms part'. It does this by using something called co-variance, which basically does exactly what has just been described. A stock which fluctuates more than the whole market will have a beta greater than one, and one which fluctuates less which have a beta of less than one.

A stock with a beta of precisely one will perform in exactly the same way as the market as a whole. For this reason, the return of the market is often referred to as beta, even though CAPM uses the same term to denote the riskiness (in terms of range of uncertainty) of a single stock. This seems perfectly natural and straightforward to mathematicians, but confuses the hell out of everybody else.

Don't worry if you do not understand the maths. Let us take a possible example and see what happens. Suppose that you are an Australian investor and have a nicely diversified portfolio of about thirty different stocks (as recommended by Modern Portfolio Theory) in roughly equal proportions. One of them is a mining stock called Poseidon, which is trading at 80 cents. One day Poseidon announces a major nickel discovery, nickel at this time being in very high demand. The price of the stock climbs rapidly, reaching a peak of $280.

At this point, had you sat back and done nothing to your portfolio but rub your hands greedily, Poseidon would have risen from 3.33 per cent of your portfolio and would now represent over 90 per cent of it. Think what would have happened had we calculated the beta of Poseidon before and after this dramatic chain of events.

Since we would be calculating the extent to which Poseidon behaved differently from something else, and given that

Poseidon would now represent a greater part of that 'something else' than it had before, then logically the degree of difference must now be less. In other words, the calculated beta now would be less than it was before.

So Finance World would be telling us that, at least so far as this particular view of 'risk' was concerned, Poseidon would now be a less risky stock than it was before. Yet would any sane investor regard holding over 90 per cent of their capital in one stock as lower risk than holding just 3.33 per cent? Of course not.

The problem here is twofold. First, any mathematical process must of necessity look only at what it is calculating, and ignore extraneous circumstances. Second, as already noted, Finance World is capable of looking at the world only objectively, and thus views the risk of an asset, in this case stock in Poseidon, as sitting within that asset and being the same for every investor. Since it does not recognise that the 'risk' of an asset (whatever risk may be) is a function of the relationship between that asset and each individual investor, the particular circumstances of any individual investor are seen as irrelevant.

At least with CAPM the basic concept is valid, in that you are comparing the performance of one thing with another, larger thing of which it forms part. If we turn our attention to the Sharpe Ratio then even this does not hold true.

By way of reminder, the Sharpe Ratio claims to measure the 'risk adjusted' return of any asset. Of course even this falls apart if you do not accept the simplistic 'volatility as risk' belief of Finance World, but let that go. The real problem lies not with the concept of risk but with how the Sharpe Ratio goes about measuring it.

It does this by trying to strip away from the return of the asset that level of return which could have been earned without taking any risk whatsoever (the 'risk free rate'). This leaves what is called the 'excess return', that layer of return which can only be achieved at the expense of taking some level of risk. This excess return is then stated relative to its own standard deviation. So far so good, at least mathematically.

If you are thinking that this all seems rather too easy, it is because it is. It is executed like a conjuring trick. While your attention is drawn to one thing, calculating the excess return and its standard deviation, you are distracted and do not notice that trick has been played with something else, namely the risk free return.

Remember that Finance World sees the risk of any asset other than a bond or debt-like instrument as the volatility of its historical returns. Hence the calculation of the standard deviation, the classic measurement of volatility. So if you are running the Sharpe Ratio calculation on a stock, which is of course an equity, you would need to use as your comparator a stock which exhibits zero volatility. Except of course that there is no such thing, which means that you cannot use the Sharpe Ratio; it's a nice idea, but impractical.

Finance World however brushes aside this trifling objection and, as will presumably by now come as no surprise, simply substitutes something which it can calculate for something which it cannot, regardless of what this does to the validity of the process.

So rather than a zero volatility equity instrument (which does not exist) they use a risk free government bond. Yet this is risk free only when using the word 'risk' in a completely different way to that in which they have already decreed that it should be used in the case of equities. Instead of volatility of historical returns, this is risk in the sense of default risk. Of course, even this is now suspect, since given the level of indebtedness of many leading governments there is no such thing as a bond with no default risk, but again let that go.

So what Finance World is hoping to get away with from this sleight of hand is that it can compare a given level of one type of risk (volatility) with a different level (zero) of a totally different type of risk (default). It is comparing apples with oranges.

The deception is even more cynical than it might appear at first sight. For if Finance World was to be intellectually honest (unlikely, I know) then it would have to compare the volatility of the equity against the volatility of the bond and, far from being 'risk free' in this respect, bond yields have actually exhibited significant volatility over the years. So Finance World's approach to 'risk adjustment' is not just dishonest, but hopelessly muddled and impractical.

If we were tasked with creating some mathematical tools which might actually be of use to investors then we would need to look, as Finance World does not, at what investors are actually trying to achieve in practice. As we have seen, were they not brainwashed into obsessing about volatility and liquidity they would instead focus on identifying and achieving their objectives, and chief among these would be at least to match a given target rate of return over time after taking into account the effects of inflation and taxation. To do otherwise would be like specifying that a new car had to be black and petrol driven, rather than worrying if it could transport the number of people in our household and whether it could fit in our garage.

We would therefore deduct from the observed return not the return of some mythical 'risk free' asset, but the projected rates of inflation and tax so as to arrive at a true 'excess return', the extent to which it could be hoped to exceed our target return. Incidentally, were we to undertake such a task then the excess return of government bonds would in fact be heavily negative, and their true nature revealed. Rather than being 'risk free', they are so high risk ('risk' in the true sense of the chance of not achieving your objectives) that no return-seeking investor can possibly afford to hold them. To continue with our motoring analogy, having bonds in your portfolio is like driving a car with the handbrake on.

This also points up just how ridiculous is the assumption supporting many of the tools of Finance World that we can safely ignore the effects of taxation, or in some cases that we can assume that everyone pays tax at the same rate. It is not even the case that inflation (also often simply left out of account) is the same for everyone. Recent studies show that high net worth individuals suffer much higher levels of inflation that those suggested by CPI (Consumer Prices Index); over twice as much in fact. Different socio-economic groups buy different things. Bodyguards, yachts, and private jets do not feature in the average supermarket shopping trolley.

Towards New Finance

This chapter has really been about how, drawing on the discussion of points raised earlier, we should *not* approach New Finance.

It seems clear that finance is not 'just about numbers', so we need to find a way of exploring it which is not mathematical, or at least not strictly mathematical. We also need to bear in mind that the validity of any mathematical output based on the input of financial data is highly suspect, since that data has no essential validity in itself other than as a record of human behavioural outcomes. Even something seemingly solid and truth-like such as a base rate set by a central bank is simply a record of a human decision, acted upon in this case by political considerations.

Because we cannot rely purely on quantitative techniques then we need to be ready to consider and discuss concepts, emotions, and behaviour, as well as the wider environment within which financial activity takes place. Clearly this requires input from other disciplines not hitherto traditionally associated with the study of finance. In this book so far, for example, we have made use of examples and techniques drawn from the fields of economics, physics, astronomy, history, philosophy, psychology, linguistics, literature, and art, not to mention the noble game of bridge (which, if made compulsory for all who studied finance, would greatly enhance their understanding of risk and return).

Such work will need to take place within a very different intellectual framework than that which we employ today. One of the most important changes, a switch from an objective to a subjective approach, we will reserve for Chapter 18.

Another should be touched upon here, though, since it derives directly from the abandonment of the search for mathematical answers, or at least a proper recognition of their possible shortcomings. To abandon that search is to acknowledge that true certainty about anything, let alone something as complex and unpredictable as finance, is impossible and that, when offered, is almost certainly illusory. Quantitative output can suggest a range of likely financial outcomes but it cannot actually *predict* anything in the same way that, say, chemistry can predict what will happen when two hydrogen atoms attach themselves to one oxygen atom.

It follows that the rules of finance cannot be 'rules' in the same sense as those which govern chemistry or physics. As we have seen earlier, they are neither universal nor predictive. Hence they are not falsifiable and consequently, according to Popper, finance is not a science. Instead of seeking comforting but phoney certainty, our job is to derive guidelines, amid intelligent discussion of how these might operate in different circumstances and environments.

In other words, in order even to be able to begin our progress we need to acknowledge something which will be the deepest anathema to the high priests of Finance World. We need to abandon our quest for the one right answer, for no such thing exists, at least not in finance.

Chapter 18

What will New Finance look like?

We mentioned the great Impressionist Claude Monet earlier. It is not widely known that as a young man he joined the French colonial cavalry. However he became very ill after the first couple of years whereupon his aunt, who had looked after him since the death of his mother while he was in his teens, managed to extricate him from the army and arranged for him to study with the art teacher Charles Gleyre.

Gleyre was famous as a great craftsman. For him a painting had to be exquisitely rendered, a perfect representation of reality. Even today, his paintings look remarkably like colour photographs. For those students who studied with him who would go on to become known as Impressionists (Monet, Bazille, Sisley, and Renoir) there was no such 'reality'. When Gleyre complained that their drawings of the same model in the same position were all different, they pointed out that this was inevitable as none of them would perceive the same scene in the same way. A rupture soon followed, with the young men leaving his studio and going off to paint on their own.

A break was perhaps inevitable since their views of the world were irreconcilable. For Gleyre, there was such a thing as objective reality and he would painstakingly capture it, working sometimes for several years on the same painting. Monet, by contrast, pursued exactly the opposite approach, painting multiple canvasses of the same scene at the same time. Gleyre was trying to capture the eternal, while for Monet there was only the moment. Gleyre believed in objective truth, while for Monet subjective perception was everything that mattered. Gleyre believed he could convey the noumenal world, while Monet knew we were stuck with the phenomenal.

The move to New Finance requires a similar shift of perspective. Just as Gleyre believed that there was an essential truth which sat within a scene and could be depicted, Finance World believes that qualities such as risk attach to an asset and can be calculated. In each case that depiction or calculation must of necessity be the same for everyone, irrespective of their own circumstances. New Finance must take the Impressionist approach instead.

Like Kant, we must believe that even if there is such a thing as objective reality, it can never be 'known'. However like Schopenhauer, we should also believe that the interaction between object and observer does not cloud any attempt to define reality, but actually expresses it and gives it meaning, at least for that individual. So, qualities such as risk are not intrinsic to the object but are some sort of function of the relationship between the object (asset) and any individual observer (investor). Thus not only is it possible for this to be different from one individual to another, it is inevitable and essential.

There is a further parallel to be drawn here. The traditionalist painters such as Gleyre, so beloved by the establishment, tried to convey what something was, what its essential essence might be. In layman's terms they painted something as it looked. The Impressionists tried to convey not only what impact the scene had upon their own feelings, but also what made it happen, for example the impact of wind on trees, or of current or waves within water. So with finance: Finance World looks at what happens, and from those observations seeks to deduce connections and causality. New Finance needs to look at how and why things happen, and from that analysis advance suggestions as to what may happen in consequence.

Similarly with externalities: in the traditional approach the scene was cast in stone so far as the execution of the painting was concerned. If the sun went behind a cloud, or day gave way to evening, the painter continued to depict the original scene as though nothing had happened. The Impressionists tried to reproduce each changing state of the scene. If Finance

World were inhabited by painters, they would surely simply make an assumption that the sun never went behind a cloud and require us all to accept it.

Subjectivity, which is of course what we have just been discussing, goes hand in glove with a qualitative approach. If we are going to sit within a particular observer looking outwards then what we see will be filtered not just by their perceptions but also by their mind-set; a farmer will not see a bull in the same way as a bull-fighter. Part and parcel of this will be qualitative judgement, and we must also be aware that different tilts can be imposed on which qualitative factors to apply. The farmer will rate the bull on his known and likely performance as a stud, while the toreador will be considering what sort of fight the animal will put up when released into the ring.

If we are to reject numbers as showing the way, at least to any complete understanding of finance, then a qualitative approach is all that is left to us, and a qualitative approach must necessarily be subjective in nature, conditioned by the practical circumstances of an investor, as well as their personality and mind-set. These will in turn be operated upon by things like the length and nature of their expertise, their cultural and social upbringing, the belief system within which they operate, and how they view their available options.

In order even to make sense of these qualitative responses it is vital that we should all understand exactly what is being conveyed. Thus jargon should in general be avoided, since it will hamper the ability of someone from a non-financial background to participate in the process, and words should be used only in their clear, everyday meaning. Thus linguistic engagement is an essential prerequisite, and a question such as 'what do you mean by risk?' is not, as Markowitz seemed to believe, an irrelevant distraction, but a possible gateway to true understanding. Similarly 'what do you think?' is not a cop-out, but an attempt to anchor a subjective response.

Markowitz, as we have seen, attempted to short-cut this procedure by proceeding straight to step three rather than beginning at step one.

Step one: what do we mean by 'risk'?
Step two: is this something which can be calculated?
Step three: if so, how can we calculate it?

Of course, it is clear in practical terms why he did this. Had he started in the proper order, he would never have got beyond step one. Far from clear in intellectual terms, though. Why should a highly intelligent and well-educated person make such a fundamental blunder, ignoring something which was so obvious?

The answer is the *Tractatus*.[1] Whether Markowitz had actually read it or not is unimportant. The central tenet of logical positivism had already permeated the scientific thought process. As we have now noted many times, Huxley said that science ignores anything which it cannot calculate (or, in the language of the *Tractatus*, which cannot be 'stated'). Thus when Markowitz went looking for risk, he went looking for something which he could calculate. Positivism, remember, refuses to allow us to ask a question unless we know in advance that it can be answered in some 'if A, then B' manner. What positivists would regard as abstract conceptualising is banned.

This may seem a rather strange and dated approach. After all the *Tractatus* was published as long ago as 1921, and Wittgenstein more or less expressly renounced it with his *Philosophical Investigations*[2] published in1953 after his death. In this work he seems to be urging the application of ordinary everyday language in the solving of philosophical problems, arguing that trouble often comes from words being divorced from any proper context, describing this as the verbal equivalent of walking on ice. At the very least, this is inconsistent with the *Tractatus*, particularly with its famous last proposition.

Yet such a view, with 'calculated' being substituted for 'stated', continues to echo down the halls of Finance World.

---

[1] Ludwig Wittgenstein *Tractatus Logico-Philosophicus*, Routledge, London 2001.

[2] Ludwig Wittgenstein *Philosophical Investigations*, Wiley-Blackwell, Oxford 2009.

Any attempt at qualitative assessment is viewed with grave suspicion, any 'proper' work of financial research having to have several formulae on each page and be overwhelmingly quantitative, while any suggestion that an answer could validly be different for different people would be met with significant glances in the direction of the nearest security guard.

It is this view which must be overthrown and ejected from the building, for it has no place in New Finance's search for understanding. Even if a numerical approach is to have relevance, it can only be allowed to do its job once the ground has been cleared, including defining our language and terms of reference, and deciding in which areas it can properly be used, and those others in which we have to make use of something else.

So New Finance will embrace a subjective view. It will allow the validity of qualitative assessment as much as quantitative analysis. It will reject the idea that finance is 'just about numbers', and will welcome into its endeavours those from other disciplines, not least to help analyse and arrive at commonly accepted terminology, and explore the concepts and drivers which lie behind financial outcomes.

Behavioural issues

One of those concepts is undoubtedly human decision making, and its behavioural drivers will be a heady mix of emotion, environment, and cognitive biases.

Behavioural finance is of course studied already in business schools around the world, but it is usually treated as an elective module which can be taken by those too weak mathematically to study a 'real' financial subject, such as derivatives. The change which New Finance should seek to make is to bring it off the periphery of financial study and make it part of the very core activity.

Indeed, there is an argument that finance, far from being all about numbers, is actually all about human behaviour (human action, as von Mises said), and that accordingly if you want to understand finance you should really need to study *only* psychology. This is undoubtedly too extreme a view. Nobody could analyse different available investment options without a good grasp of numbers and calculation. However if one had a choice between the two, then probably psychology should get the nod, not least because of the lack of 'truth' contained within financial data which we have discussed extensively already.

Financial outcomes are produced by human decisions, and human decisions are part of, and conditioned by, human behaviour. It is clear that such behaviour is driven at least as much by emotion as by reason, and further that some human decisions are apparently taken even without the individual being aware of the reasons for doing so. How often does the simple question 'why did you do that?' evoke the response 'I don't really know'?

So any meaningful study of finance must consist in large part of the study of human behaviour and anybody who does not make some attempt to understand the latter is most unlikely ever to have any real understanding of the former. Therefore rather than obsessing about whether a student is likely to be able to pass heavily quantitative modules, business schools should actually be more concerned about their conceptual abilities, and whether they have any background in subjects such as psychology.

We considered briefly in Chapter 14 the very significant role played by cognitive biases. This is a subject which merits an entire book to itself, and one in which our understanding is in any event still unfolding, slowly but steadily. If they really do hold the key to beginning to comprehend investment decisions in more detail then it seems that here, at least initially, should lie one of the most important fields of endeavour within any finance faculty. In other words, it is behavioural rather than quantitative subjects which should make up the core modules of any finance degree course.

The importance of understanding risk and return

These two pillars are of fundamental importance. We cannot hope to acquire any real knowledge of finance unless we understand what they are, and how they operate. Unfortunately this is not the case. We do not properly understand the shortcomings of the way in which periodic return measures are prepared, nor the essential difference between these and compound return measures, such as Internal Rate of Return (IRR). Nor do we have any real understanding of risk, which is in truth a much more complex and varied factor than we suspect, and no more than some small part of which may be subjected to calculation (and even then, not in the way commonly adopted).

We have seen that a compound return measure such as IRR more closely approximates to the real life impact of an investment on an investor's portfolio and liabilities. It is based only on actual cashflows, and it takes full account of the time value of money. It is also a simple and effective measure to adjust for factors like inflation and taxation.

Where we advance mathematical techniques for consideration it would therefore seem sensible to choose ones which make use of IRRs rather than periodic return measures. A good example might be the use of vintage year returns, as already happens in the field of private equity funds. This will hopefully pose an enjoyable challenge to those mathematicians within the field of finance, since it will require a whole new approach to the sort of modelling currently applied to such things as portfolio theory.

A move to compound returns will also have two important practical advantages. First, it will enable for the first time valid comparisons to be made across different asset classes, something which is currently impossible (not that this stops people from trying!). Second, it forces the effects of inflation and taxation, hugely important issues in real life, into prominence, making it more difficult for them to be ignored in the planning and analysis process.

Risk, or at least the highly artificial view of it advanced by Finance World, represents the biggest single stumbling block to the advance of New Finance. Our only option here is to acknowledge from the outset that we have fundamentally misunderstood risk, and to seek out a whole new approach.

We should also acknowledge something which will not come easily to those who have been used to labouring in the fields of Finance World. We have sought out something which is capable of calculation, whereas risk is in reality too complex a matter to be reduced to formulae and statistical analysis. It remains possible that some aspects of risk may be susceptible to mathematical treatment, but not those aspects currently chosen, and not in the way in which they are presently addressed.

Ironically, it is many of the areas of risk which are not capable of calculation, as opposed to subjective qualitative assessment, which currently occupy the minds of investors. A few examples will suffice: regulatory risk, political risk, terrorism risk, reputational risk, and so on. Thus we must recognise that even if we can somehow get the numerical side of things right this can offer at best only a partial guide to investment decision making.

Pursuing our subjective perspective, we will seek out the meaning and relevance of risk having regard to the particular circumstances of individual investors, not just their target rate of return and investment time horizon (derived by reference to their liabilities), but their emotions, financial environment, and other factors which may in any way impact on their investment decision making.

In particular we should investigate the concept that those parts of material risk which are capable of being expressed numerically (though having due regard to the limitations of financial data discussed earlier) could most usefully be aimed at the possibility of any asset, or mix of assets, making it more likely that any individual investor might fail to achieve their investment objectives over time, namely to have at least enough purchasing power available to pay future liabilities as they fall due. This seems not just less intellectually objectionable, but also of much more practical relevance than the simplistic volatility as risk concept advocated by Finance World.

This would satisfy two practical requirements which seem at present to go unrecognised. First, that there should be some tangible connection between financial theory and investment practice. Second, that the 'one size fits all' nature of an approach which ignores the differing requirements and circumstances of individual investors is itself something which prevents financial theory from being applied as a practical guide to decision making.

Assumptions and reality

Since we are in search of financial theory which can actually be applied in practice, it is also important that any financial models which we do advance are capable of working in the real world. Where they are shown not to, we must attempt to find new ones which do. The present practice, as exemplified by the killer robots of Kriket, is instead to try to bring reality into line with the theory.

Rather than blasting deviant reality into compliance with laser guns however, Finance World does it with assumptions. These sanitise and bend reality, sometimes very substantially. Express assumptions are encountered in different models requiring us to believe things such as that all investors are rational, all markets are perfect, tax and borrowing costs can safely be ignored, and so on. Perhaps one of the most dangerous ones in recent years has been that the amount of debt within a company should make no difference to its perceived attractiveness.

Our approach must be more honest. Rather than requiring people to believe something because if they ceased to do so then some long-cherished dogma would fall to the ground under the weight of its own ridiculousness, let us kick the props away and stand back and watch it collapse. Any assumption that cannot be justified by real life experience must be rejected.

This will not prove an easy task for those who crave certainty, and the comfort of a rule-based system. For if we once subject financial theory to such rigour, then little of it will survive, at least as hard and fast rules. This is in fact precisely why the rules have survived for so long. Our fear of uncertainty makes us that much readier to accept their 'scientific' status, whereas ironically the approach which they allow (ignoring inconsistency with actual outcomes) is exactly the opposite.

Once we start from observed reality and seek to move towards theory, rather than vice versa, it becomes apparent that most of the time all that are possible are guidelines, not rules, and that we must necessarily accept that these are neither universal nor predictive.

Certainty

So we come back finally to certainty, that false god worshipped so avidly by so many in the financial community. As Markowitz said, investors treat variance of return as an undesirable thing, and he got that right, though he then over-leaped himself in thinking this must mean that uncertainty of outcome (as measured by variance of historical periodic return) was the same thing as risk, or that variance of past periodic returns was a good guide to the future, or even that periodic return is a good starting point in the first place.

For most investors, uncertainty of outcome is indeed an undesirable thing. This is if anything an under-statement. For most, uncertainty is not just something undesirable, but something to be feared. Because of this, we over-react in all sorts of ways, whether it be ignoring the long-term nature of our liabilities in seeking out liquid investments, or hyperbolic discounting, over-pricing the peril of the future.

Finance World has in part been so successful precisely because it plays to this fear. Investors and their advisers around the world have sought to limit the amount of 'risk' (volatility) in their portfolios because they wish to limit the negative impact of any unwelcome future outcomes. This feels instinctively the right, and indeed even the responsible, thing to do. Discussion of how this impacts the chance of an individual investor achieving their individual objectives never takes place.

In fact, the limiting of volatility seems to have become an objective in itself, rather than an exercise (assuming for a moment that one believes in Modern Portfolio Theory, if only because so many investors do) in finding the lowest possible level of volatility consistent with hitting the target rate of return. Too often the tail wags the dog, with an incorrect and artificial target rate being adopted because the level of volatility as risk indicated in attempting to achieve the real target rate required is deemed unacceptably 'high risk'. Nobody, of course, troubles to enquire how adopting an investment policy which seems guaranteed not to achieve your objectives could be 'low risk'.

It is in this sense that Bernstein said Markowitz had put a number on risk. Out there in the jungle, untamed and largely unknown, risk is the great bogeyman. Capture it, put it in a cage and study it, and it soon becomes much less terrifying. What Markowitz offered people was the opportunity to measure 'risk', and in doing so to believe that they might in some way be able to control it, or at least to predict the range within which future outcomes were likely to fall. No matter that in order to do so he had adopted a measure which was not risk, nor that it could not actually be used predictively as people imagined. What was important was the perception, and the perception, which persists to this day, was that Markowitz had gone into the jungle and tamed risk.

For the reality is truly terrifying and few are prepared to face up to it. Uncertainty is everywhere, and much greater than we allow ourselves to imagine. All we really know is a fleeting instant that is no sooner come than gone, and so quickly that even then we cannot really 'know' it since our attention has already moved on to the next piece of debris at the feet of the angel.

Nor is the past any good guide to predicting the future, as Tilly discovered at Breitenfeld. Making an assumption just because a certain pattern, or correlation, or range of outcomes occurred in the past is meaningless so far as the future is concerned. Even if all the constituent circumstances were exactly to recur at the same moment, the actual future outcome would be determined by human action, and human action is notoriously unpredictable. Uncertainty is total.

On the basis that it is logical to accept what we cannot change, would it not make more sense for investors to embrace uncertainty, rather than to sit around indulging in meaningless attempts to measure it ('meaningless' since it cannot be measured)? In other words, we need to drop the pretence that we can somehow control or even understand uncertainty. After all, anything which is uncertain is by definition unknowable.

This is not to say that we should cease our efforts to look into the future and wrestle with the implications of possible different outcomes, but this cannot be done by mathematical models. As illustrated by Asimov in his *Foundation* series, no matter how sound the science and clever the calculations, sooner or later a random element will intervene.

What investors should be doing, and how New Finance should be assisting them, is looking into the future having due regard to political, technological, environmental, social, and demographic factors and attempting to identify trends which may emerge. Obvious ones would include an ageing population and the growth of super-cities, for example. These would not be predictions, but informed guesstimates of possible future outcomes.

Once gained, these insights could be used to consider how the choice of current assets might be positioned either to take advantage of any opportunities offered, or to offer protection against any possible adverse consequences. Yet we can only engage in this sort of exercise once we have accepted that we are incapable of predicting the future and that uncertainty reigns supreme. To try to 'put a number on it', as Markowitz purported to do, misses the point. Uncertainty is uncertain, so at best any such exercise is nothing better than a gambler's fallacy.

Into the future

A gap has opened up between financial theory as taught to students and investment reality as experienced by practitioners.

In truth the gap has probably always been there and it is more accurate to say that a significant number of investors are now beginning to wake up to the fact.

In particular there is growing dissatisfaction with the volatility as risk approach, not least because it seems to over-simplify what is in reality a very complex concept. So complex, in fact, that any claim to 'knowledge' may actually be seen as troubling in itself. Such simplification also comes at a considerable price, namely the obligation to accept all sorts of supporting assumptions, both implicit and explicit, which rarely seem to hold true in reality, at least on any universal basis.

This inability to posit universal, predictive rules, and to treat them with the scientific rigour which they should merit, show us that finance is not really a 'science' at all, at least not as defined by Popper and various leading scientists. It is at best a pseudo-science, which term is not intended to be disparaging, but merely to describe a discipline such as psychology, where individual observations can be built up into suggested guidelines and statements of general principle of what is likely to happen in a large proportion of cases, but not into rules which are 'falsifiable'.

Indeed, using Popper's approach, finance would not even make it into this category, but would seem to fit better his description of dogmatism – a clinging to rules which have long since been discredited, but to which one is required to adhere anyway on pain of intellectual exclusion.

To those who wish to cling to the old way of doing things, any thought of a radical change of approach from the comfort of a rule-based objective system to a non-universal and subjective framework will seem threatening. Change always does. Yet for those who are prepared to embrace uncertainty and accept that there is much that we may never know, such change will be a liberating experience, enabling them to discuss any aspect of finance without the necessity, at least initially, of having to reduce everything to numbers and formulae.

So fundamental does the change need to be that we require a whole new starting point, for where Finance World went wrong was with the very first step it took. We need at the very least to define our terms, and at best to seek to understand the basic building blocks of finance and the environment within which it operates. In other words, we need to start with concepts, not numbers.

If you move from an understanding, or at least an appreciation, of the basic concepts and move from there towards a practical framework then there is a fighting chance that we will end up with some guidelines and basic principles which are consistent with day to day reality. There is no doubt that mathematics will play a part in that process, but a part not the whole, and the extent of that part and the way in which it may operate cannot be determined in advance.

So we circle back to the pillars of finance: return, risk, time, and value. Earlier we posed the hypothesis that just as time, space, and causation framed our view of physics, so did these our view of finance. In the light of what we have learned in the course of our journey thus far, it may be more accurate to say that everything that happens in finance is some sort of function of return, risk, and value but operating in the presence of both time and human behaviour. Such a view may seem simplistic, but it is not; this simple proposition is fundamental and offers a considerable improvement over the current approach. For example, it becomes obvious straightaway that finance cannot be just about numbers since we cannot calculate human behaviour, but only observe and record it.

It is appropriate that in the end we should find ourselves back with the pillars of finance, for it is worth reminding ourselves that they provide both the boundaries of our subject and the potential for a true understanding of it. Any time we find ourselves moving somewhere which forces an artificial view of any of them upon us, as of course Modern Portfolio Theory does, we should feel uncomfortable, for unless and until someone comes up with a better suggestion they are all we have.

GPSR Compliance

The European Union's (EU) General Product Safety Regulation (GPSR) is a set of rules that requires consumer products to be safe and our obligations to ensure this.

If you have any concerns about our products, you can contact us on ProductSafety@springernature.com

In case Publisher is established outside the EU, the EU authorized representative is:

Springer Nature Customer Service Center GmbH
Europaplatz 3
69115 Heidelberg, Germany

Batch number: 10726227

Printed by Printforce, the Netherlands